THE DIFFUSION OF LAW

This volume truly demonstrates the ubiquity of the need for comparison, especially in law, resulting from globalization. The authors effectively demolish any doubts over the merits of comparative scholarship. The range of jurisdictional and disciplinary perspectives is extraordinarily wide, but it promotes insight into the world-wide circulation of legal notions.

Francois Venter, North-West University, South Africa

This volume is full of engaging and superbly researched contributions on the diffusion of law. A must for anyone interested in comparative law, the book covers a wide range of important topics from a truly comparative perspective. It is a pleasure to read.

Heikki Pihlajamäki, University of Helsinki, Finland

This book is an important contribution to both legal theory and comparative law. It is full of original insights on the ways legal norms, ideas and concepts travel across the globe. In addition to its valuable theoretical input, it presents a fascinating panorama of world-wide examples for legal migration and transplants.

Nir Kedar, Sapir Academic College, Israel

Juris Diversitas

Rooted in comparative law, the *Juris Diversitas* series focuses on the interdisciplinary study of legal and normative mixtures and movements. Our interest is in comparison broadly conceived, extending beyond law narrowly understood to related fields. Titles might be geographical or temporal comparisons. They could focus on theory and methodology, substantive law, or legal cultures. They could investigate official or unofficial 'legalities', past and present and around the world. And, to effectively cross spatial, temporal, and normative boundaries, inter- and multi-disciplinary research is particularly welcome.

Forthcoming titles in the series:

The Practice of a Mixed Pluralistic Legal System
State and Non-State Orderings in South Africa
Christa Rautenbach
ISBN 978-1-4724-3682-5

Indigenous Rights in Scandinavia
Autonomous Sami Law
Edited by Christina Allard and Susann Funderud Skogvang
ISBN 978-1-4724-2541-6

For more information on this series, visit www.ashgate.com

The Diffusion of Law
The Movement of Laws and Norms Around the World

Edited by

SUE FARRAN
Northumbria Law School, UK

JAMES GALLEN
Dublin City University, Ireland

JENNIFER HENDRY
University of Leeds, UK

CHRISTA RAUTENBACH
North-West University, South Africa

ASHGATE

Published by
Ashgate Publishing Limited
Wey Court East
Union Road
Farnham
Surrey, GU9 7PT
England

Ashgate Publishing Company
110 Cherry Street
Suite 3-1
Burlington, VT 05401-3818
USA

www.ashgate.com

British Library Cataloguing in Publication Data
A catalogue record for this book is available from the British Library.

The Library of Congress has cataloged the printed edition as follows:
The diffusion of law : the movement of laws and norms around the world / by Sue Farran, James Gallen, Jennifer Hendry and Christa Rautenbach.
     pages cm. -- (Juris diversitas)
 Includes bibliographical references and index.
  ISBN 978-1-4724-6040-0 (hardback) -- ISBN 978-1-4724-6041-7 (ebook) -- ISBN 978-1-4724-6042-4 (epub) 1. Law--Mobility. 2. Law--Foreign influences. 3. Legal polycentricity. 4. Law and globalization. I. Farran, Susan, editor. II. Gallen, James, editor. III. Hendry, Jennifer, editor. IV. Rautenbach, Christa, editor.
  K590.5.D54 2015
  340.9--dc23

2014049084

ISBN 9781472460400 (hbk)
ISBN 9781472460417 (ebk – PDF)
ISBN 9781472460424 (ebk – ePUB)

Printed in the United Kingdom by Henry Ling Limited, at the Dorset Press, Dorchester, DT1 1HD

Contents

List of Figures and Tables

Figures

Tables

Notes on Contributors

Biagio Andò is Associate Professor of Comparative Law at the Dipartimento di Scienze Politiche e Sociali of the University of Catania. His main research areas are tort liability and mixed jurisdictions.

Among Biagio's most recent publications are: 'On the interpretation of law and legal gaps: A comparative overview of the delicate trade-off between legal rules and judicial creativity in Louisiana and Italy' (2014) 29 *TECLF* 1–23; 'Primavera arabe y relaciones conyugales en las tradiciones europea e islamicas: algunas notas' (2013) 19 *Revista de Derecho Constitucional Europeo*, 167–84; 'Judicial methodology and codification in Malta and Louisiana' (2012) *Cedam*; (with S. Donlan and D. Zammit). '"A happy union"? Malta's legal hybridity' (2012) 27 *TECLF* 165–208; 'The foundations of private law in a mixed jurisdiction: The case of Louisiana' (2012) 3 *DPCE*, 1351–88; and, 'Alla ricerca di un "contenuto minimo" del diritto all'istruzione del disabile fra giurisprudenza nazionale e corte EDU' (2012) *Comparazione e diritto civile* 1–16.

Alessio Bartolacelli holds a Doctor in Law (University of Modena e Reggio Emilia, 2004) and a PhD in Business Law (University of Brescia, 2008) and has been Research Assistant at the University of Trento since 2009, and a TRENTINO and Marie Curie Fellow since 2011.

Alessio's current research interests are: EEIG, corporate governance, voting rights, hybrid securities, exit rights, legal capital, private companies, start-up enterprises.

His recent publications include: *Il GEIE 'italiano' tra impresa e società* (Editoriale Scientifica, 2014); 'Nuove esperienze europee in tema di costituzione "semplificata" e "a basso costo" di società con responsabilità limitata' forthcoming in *Giurisprudenza Commerciale*; 'L'insostenibile leggerezza dell's.r.l.s. Nell'intricata "matassa" delle "nuove" s.r.l. ricercare un bandolo o tagliare il filo?' (2014) *Rivista ODC* 1–78; 'Società chiusa e capitale sociale minimo: tendenze europee' (2014) *I Giurisprudenza Commerciale* 519–51; '"Novissime" modifiche alla disciplina della s.r.l.s.: saggio minimo di diritto transitorio' (2013) 11/16 *Il Nuovo Diritto Delle Società* 7–30; 'Romanian EEIG (GEIE) implementation law: A draft' (2013) v(10) *EWIV-EEIG-GEIE-Ejournal* 23–9; and *La partecipazione non azionaria nella s.p.a. Gli strumenti finanziari partecipativi* (Giuffrè, 2012) – (*Quaderni Di Giurisprudenza Commerciale*).

Alessio would like to acknowledge that the chapter he has contributed is part of a research project he has been carrying out about the possibility of imagining European Economic Interest Groupings with limited responsible members. The research has been co-funded by the European Union and the Autonomous Province of Trento under the framework of the Marie Curie COFUND action, Programme TRENTINO and Project GEIE/GECT-TN.

Eoin Carolan holds an LLB (Dub), LLM (Cantab) and PhD (Dub), and is based at University College Dublin where he is Senior Lecturer in Law.

Eoin has particular research interests in the areas of constitutional and administrative law, media law, and law and psychology. His recent publications have included work on the Big Society (*Public Law*), developments in US privacy law (*Cambridge Law Journal*), and the future of press regulation (*The Irish Jurist*). He has recently completed work on an Irish Research Council-funded interdisciplinary project examining the legal regulation of online privacy from a behavioural perspective, the initial results of which will be published in the *Virginia Journal of Law and Technology*.

Rita Duca is Research Assistant in Law at the Department of European and Comparative Studies, Faculty of Political Science, University of Palermo, Italy. In 2011, she obtained her PhD in European and Comparative Law with a thesis on 'Multiculturalism in European Union: A Family Law perspective'. She carries out research on European Law, Comparative Law and Immigration Law whilst undertaking teaching duties at the Faculty of Political Science of Palermo. Rita has participated in many international conferences, including the Cambridge International Symposium on Economic Crime and she has also published in several international law reviews.

Sue Farran is Professor of Law at Northumbria University, UK, and Adjunct Professor at the University of the South Pacific. She has a long-standing interest in comparative law and legal pluralism, and much of her published research uses case studies from the island countries of the South Pacific region to focus on issues of human rights, legal pluralism, the challenges of development and sustainability, globalisation and legal colonialism. In particular she is interested in the interface between legal systems and normative frameworks within states and between states, and the relationship between national, regional and international players in shaping and developing legal responses to contemporary issues. Sue has contributed to two other collections in this series: 'Scotland: Is the tartan fading?' in *A Study of Mixed Legal Systems: Endangered, Entrenched or Blended* (Ashgate, 2014), for which she was also lead editor, and 'Pacific punch: Tropical flavours of mixedness in the Island Republic of Vanuatu' in Palmer, Mattar and Koppel (eds), *Mixed Legal Systems East and West* (Ashgate, 2015).

Thomas Favre-Bulle holds an MSc (EPFL, Switzerland) and BLaw (Paris 1 Panthéon-Sorbonne, France) and is a doctoral assistant and lecturer at the Swiss Federal Institute of Technology in Lausanne (EPFL), where he conducts doctoral research on Democracy in the Metropolis in collaboration with Stanford

University, and the support of the Swiss National Science Foundation. He investigates how people relate to metropolitan areas and how this affects their political and civic engagement.

James Gallen is a graduate and Scholar of Trinity College Dublin and a graduate of New York University School of Law. He is a former Transitional Justice Scholar at New York University and has served as an intern and fellow at the International Center for Transitional Justice in New York and Kathmandu. He is a lecturer in the School of Law and Government at DCU. James defended his PhD thesis in the School of Law at Trinity College Dublin in May 2012. His doctoral thesis examines the relationship between transitional justice, peace-building and economic development in international law. His research interests include human rights, international law and legal and political philosophy. His present research agenda concerns the implementation of policy coherence in international assistance to transitions and a transitional justice approach to child sex abuse in the Roman Catholic Church. James' recent selected publications include: (with Colin Smith, Trinity College Dublin), 'Cáin Adomhnáin and International Humanitarian Law' (2014) 16(1) *Journal of the History of International Law* 63–81 and 'Jus post bellum: An interpretive framework' in C. Stahn, J. Iverson and J. Easteryday (eds) *Jus Post Bellum: Mapping the Normative Foundations* (Oxford University Press, 2014) 58–79.

Jennifer Hendry is Lecturer in Jurisprudence at the University of Leeds, School of Law, prior to which she was a research fellow at the Tilburg Institute of Comparative and Transnational Law at Tilburg University. Jen has degrees from the University of Glasgow (LLB Hons, 2002), the University of Edinburgh (LLM, 2003) and the European University Institute (PhD, 2009). She has been a visiting fellow at the University of Sydney (2011) and the University of Arizona (2013), and is a principal investigator on a World Universities Network-funded interdisciplinary international research network focusing on 'Spaces of Indigenous Justice'. Her research interests are in the areas of social and legal theory and comparative socio-legal studies, specifically legal pluralism, legal culture, spatial justice and systems theory. Jen is a member of the senior editorial board of the *German Law Journal* and the executive of the UK Socio-Legal Studies Association (SLSA).

Recent selected publications include: 'Legal comparison and the im/possibility of legal translation' in S. Glanert (ed.), *Comparative Law: Engaging Translation* (Routledge, July 2014) and 'Legal pluralism and normative transfer' in G. Frankenberg (ed.), *Order Through Transfer: Studies in Comparative Constitutional Law* (Edward Elgar, July 2013).

Juliana Latifi obtained her PhD in 1997 at the State University of Tirana, Faculty of Law, in the field of Comparative Private Law (Heritage Law) and pursued post-doctoral studies at the Institute of Comparative Law at Robert Schuman University in Strasbourg during 2000–2002. Since 2013 she has held the scientific title of 'Prof. Asoc. Dr.'.

Juliana has taught Civil Law and Comparative Private Law since 1998 at the University of Tirana (Faculty of Law) and at present is teaching at the Tirana Business University while also working as a legal advisor in the Albanian parliament. Juliana also has extensive experience in the public administration of Albania as well as with international bodies operating in Albania and Kosovo in connection with the drafting of legal acts and the issuing of necessary legal recommendations for the approximation of Albania's and Kosovo's legislations with EU's *acquis*.

Juliana's research interests focus on the wealth of activity in the Albanian jurisprudence especially in the field of private law (property law, inheritance law, procedure civil law, commercial law, etc.) from a comparative approach with the European legislation

She is the author several books and articles including: *Civil Law (General Part)*; *Civil Law-Inheritance*; *Inheritance through a Will (A Comparative View)*; and *Inheritance Law of Kosovo*.

Elwira Macierzyńska-Franaszczyk holds a PhD, and is a member of the working group of the Codification Commission on Civil Law at the Polish Ministry of Justice. She is a lawyer specialising in Civil Law and Assistant Professor (Adiunkt) in the Civil Law Department at Kozminski University in Warsaw; she is also Research Assistant in the European Legal Study Institute at the Osnabrück University. She has contributed as researcher and coordinator of national and international legal research projects.

Elwira is the author of publications on the Europeanisation of private law, the law of succession, law of obligation, consumer law and personal interests. Her latest publications include a monograph based on comparative research *Odpowiedzialność za długi spadkowe* (Liability for Succession Debts, LexisNexis, 2014).

Pamela Martino has been Assistant Professor of Comparative Public Law at the University of Bari 'Aldo Moro' (Italy) since 2006. In 2013 she obtained the qualification of Associate Professor in Comparative Public Law.

Her research interests include: the role of second chambers in a comparative perspective, devolution and constitutional change in the UK, central–local realties in the States of the European Union, national security and most recently the judicial cross-fertilisation and the interaction between jurisdictions and pluralism.

She is the author of a book on the Second Chambers as well as several articles and book chapters in the field of Comparative Public Law (with particular attention to bicameralism and parliament, devolution in the UK, national security and the UK Supreme Court). Her recent publications include: '"Now it is our time to speak": i giudici supremi del Regno Unito e il dialogo rivelatore' in P. Martino (ed.), *I giudici di common law e la (cross)fertilization: i casi di Stati Uniti d'America, Canada, Unione Indiana e Regno Unito* (Maggioli, 2014) 83–117; P. Martino and A. Torre, 'La giurisprudenza della Corte suprema del Regno Unito nel biennio 2011–2012' (2013) 5 *Giurisprudenza costituzionale* 4141 ff. par. 3–9; and 'Il segreto di Stato in Canada: la cartina al tornasole della tenuta democratica dell'ordinamento' in E. Ceccherini (ed.), *A trent'anni dalla Patriation canadese. Riflessioni della dottrina italiana* (Genova University Press, 2013) 161–77, which was also published in A. Torre (ed.), *Costituzioni e sicurezza dello Stato* (Maggioli, 2013) 147–62.

Esin Örücü has been Professor Emerita of Comparative Law at the University of Glasgow since 2005 and Honorary Senior Research Fellow from 2008 to 2015. Esin is also Professor Emeritus of Comparative Law, Erasmus University Rotterdam; Visiting Professor of Turkish Family Law, Amsterdam Free University; Visiting Professor of Comparative Law, Okan University, Istanbul; and a titular member of the International Academy of Comparative Law. She was awarded an honorary doctorate from Upsala in 2009. Esin's research interests include: comparative law methodology; transmigration of laws; changing paradigms in the new world order; mixed jurisdictions; systems in transition, legal systems and legal cultures and convergence and divergence between legal systems and cultures; problems of the recipient systems in legal export/import, transpositions; core of rights; comparative jurisprudence; and Turkish law, culture and language.

Esin's recent publications include: 'The role of judicial creativity and equity in the development of Turkish law and its covert hybridity' (2014) 29 *Tulane European and Civil Law Forum* 217–34; with S. Farran and S.P. Donlan (eds), *A Study of Mixed Legal Systems: Endangered, Entrenched or Blended* (Ashgate, 2014); 'The gap between de iure and de facto of marriage in Turkey' in A. Singer and M. Lonton (eds), *Fornuft, kansla och rattens verklighet; Vanbok till Maarit Jantera-Jareborg* (Iustus Forlag, 2014) 75–94; 'Constructing a legal system without its history: The Turkish experience' in M. Breuer, A. Epiney, A. Haratsch, S. Schmahl and N. Weiss (ecs), *Der Staat im Recht: Festschrift für Eckart Klein zum 70. Geburtstag* (Duncker and Humblot, Berlin, 2013) 275–86; and 'A legal system based on translation: The Turkish experience' (2013) 6 *Journal of Civil Law Studies* 445–73 (also available at <http://digitalcommons.law.lsu.edu/jcls>).

Alessandra Pera is Aggregate Professor in the Department of European Studies and International Integration at the University of Palermo, Italy, where she teaches Comparative Law and European Private Law.

Alessandra is a lawyer with a PhD in European and Comparative Law and has over 10 years' research experience in comparative law, family law and social change and legal tools to protect weak individuals in modern societies. She is a member of the Scientific Board of the Italian Review *Diritto Civile e Comparato*. She was involved in a European project funded by the EU Commission in the programme Civil Justice in 2012, and has completed six national research projects and two international ones on diverse themes including: social inclusion, new forms of slavery, collective interests and consumer law and alternative dispute resolution systems.

Her recent publications include: 'Elderly caretaking: Badanti versus welfare policies – family needs have only private answers' in H. Fulchiron (a cura di), *Les solidarités entre générations* (Bruylant, 2013) 791–801; 'Modelli familiari. Limiti costituzionali ed interpretazione' in N.L.X. Baez-RL, N. da Sylva and G. Smorto (eds), *Le sfide dei diritti umani in America Latina ed in Europa* (Arancne Editrice, 2013) 81–101; 'Traduzione' in N.L.X. Baez-RL, N. da Sylva and G. Smorto (eds), *Os desafios dos Direitos Humanos Fundamentais na América Latina e na Europa* (Editora Unoesc, 2012); *nell'edizione italiana Le sfide dei diritti umani in America Latina ed in Europa* (Arancne Editrice, 2013); M. Nicolosi and A. Pera, 'Female work, family needs and equal opportunities. A comparative analysis among some EU legal systems' (2013) 5(2) *Sinossi internet di diritto del lavoro e della sicurezza sociale*, available at <www.temilavoro.it>; and *Il diritto di famiglia in Europa. Plurimi e simili o Plurimi e diversi*, vol. 1, *Collana del Dipartimento di Studi Europei e dell'Integrazione Internazionale dell'Università degli Studi di Palermo* (Giappichelli, 2012) 1–152.

Christa Rautenbach is Professor of Law at the Faculty of Law, North-West University, Potchefstroom, South Africa. B Iuris (*cum laude*), LLB (*cum laude*) LLM, LLD.

Christa has more than 30 years' experience as a legal scientist. She worked for the Department of Justice for 14 years as a prosecutor before she became an academic scholar at the Faculty of Law, North-West University (Potchefstroom) where she currently holds an appointment as Full Professor. She remains involved in private practice as an advocate of the High Court of South Africa. Christa is the treasurer of the Society of Law Teachers of Southern Africa, Scientist Ambassador of the Alexander von Humboldt-Foundation and also the chairperson of the North-Eastern Chapter of the Alexander von Humboldt-Association of South Africa. In addition she is a member of the Executive Committee of *Juris Diversitas*. She has published extensively on subjects dealing with legal pluralism, customary law, mixed jurisdictions, cultural diversity, comparative law and law of succession and also presented numerous papers on these subjects globally. She is co-editor and co-author of *Introduction to Legal Pluralism in South Africa* (LexisNexis, 2015) and *The Law of Succession in South Africa* (Oxford University Press, 2012, 2nd edn). Christa is also the editor of the internationally acclaimed electronic law journal, the *Potchefstroom Electronic Law Journal*, accessible at <http://www.nwu.ac.za/p-per/index.html> and serves on the editorial boards of the *Journal for Contemporary Roman-Dutch Law* and the *Journal of Comparative Law in Africa*.

Kateřina Ronovská graduated from the Faculty of Law, Masaryk University in Brno, in the Czech Republic, where she is currently employed as Associate Professor in the Department of Civil Law. She teaches Civil Law and is involved in the systematic study of law on foundation and association in the European context. Kateřina has also participated in a number of study stays abroad including at the Max Planck Institute for Comparative and International Private Law in Hamburg in 2011, at the Vrije Universtiteit Amsterdam in 2001 and at the Institute Suisse Droit Comparé, also in 2001.

Kateřina is actively involved in international projects of comparative law and the legislative process, mainly in connection with the reform of private law in the Czech Republic. She is a member of the Finance and Legislative Committee of the Government Council for non-governmental non-profit organisations and a member of the Expert Group of the Committee for the Application of New Civil Law Legislation.

She is the author of numerous publications and articles in professional journals for example: K. Ronovská, *Nové české nadační právo v evropském srovnání* (Wolters Kluwer, Praha, 2012).

Myra Williamson is Associate Professor of Law at Kuwait International Law School, Kuwait's first private university for law. Myra holds a BA in Political Studies and an LLB (First Class Honours) from the University of Otago, Dunedin, New Zealand. She also holds an LLM (First Class Honours) and a PhD from the University of Waikato School of Law, Hamilton, New Zealand. She teaches and writes mainly in the areas of comparative law, social theory and public international law although she also has an interest in human rights, intellectual property, constitutional law and both Islamic law and history. She is originally from New Zealand but has lived in Saudi Arabia, Syria and Kuwait, hence she is interested in all things associated with the Middle East.

Myra's recent publications include: 'The "responsibility to protect" and Syria: The international community's failure to prevent mass atrocity crimes (again)' (2014) 1(4) *Journal of the Kuwait International Law School*; 'The diffusion of Western legal concepts in the Kuwaiti legal system: A comparative legal analysis from an historic and contemporary perspective' (2013) 1(2) *Journal of the Kuwait International Law School*; 'Geographical indications, biodiversity and traditional knowledge: Obligations and opportunities for the Kingdom of Saudi Arabia' (2012) 26(1) *Arab Law Quarterly.*

Kurt Xerri (University Rovira I Virgili, Spain) graduated with an LLD from the University of Malta in 2013 and was admitted to the Maltese Bar in 2014. For the past two years he has been in charge of the Maltese response to the comparative European law survey on tenancy law coordinated by the European University Institute (Bremen) entitled 'TENLaw: Tenancy law and housing policy in multi-level Europe'. He also participates as the Maltese expert in the 'Pilot project – Promoting protection of the right to housing – Homelessness prevention in the context of evictions' managed by Human European Consultancy, FEANTSA and the National University of Ireland (Galway). He has recently submitted his Master of Arts (Law) dissertation to the University of Malta entitled 'Maltese

Tenancy Law: Tenants' perceptions and the prospects for revision' and is currently conducting further studies at the University Rovira I Virgili.

David Zammit LLD PhD (University of Malta) is currently Head of the Civil Law Department of the University of Malta Law Faculty. After graduating (LLD) from the University of Malta, he graduated with a PhD in Legal Anthropology from the University of Durham, UK in 1998. His PhD thesis focused on legal story-telling in Maltese civil litigation. He also pursued a Diploma di Perfezionamento in Tort law at the La Sapienza University of Rome in 1999. He is currently Senior Lecturer in Law and Anthropology at the University of Malta and, since 1996, the executive editor of the *Mediterranean Journal of Human Rights*. In 2006 he was awarded a Fulbright Research Scholarship to study clinical law teaching at the University of Villanova Law School.

His main fields of research include Tort Law, Legal Anthropology and Clinical Legal Education. His recent publications include co-editing the Malta chapter of V. Palmer's book: *Mixed Jurisdictions Worldwide* (Cambridge University Press, 2012); co-editing (with S. Donlan and B. Ando) '"A happy union?" Malta's legal hybridity' (2012) 27 *Tulane European & Civil Law Forum*; 'Maltese court delays and the ethnography of legal practice' (2012) 4(2) *Journal of Civil Law Studies*. In 2013 he published: 'Balancing between patronage and professionalism: An ethnographic account of lawyering in Malta' in Azzopardi, J., Formosa, S. and Willis, A. (eds), *Key Issues in Criminology Janus III; Consultative Assessment on the Integration of Third Country Nationals – Final (Malta) Report* available at <http://integration-iom.com/wp-content/uploads/2012/11/IOM-Report-DZ-Definitive-2.pdf> and Volume 17 (double issue) of the *Mediterranean Journal of Human Rights*. In 2014, he published with C. Grima, 'Medical liability and psychological damage in Maltese jurisprudence' in V. Ferrari, W. Tlokinski and D. Zammit (eds), *Responsabilità medica ed organizzazione sanitaria. Profili etico-giuridici e gestionali* (ARACNE, 2014). Apart from this, he has also co-edited, with G. Caruana Demajo and L. Quintano, the Malta chapter in H. Koziol and B.C. Steininger (eds), *European Tort Law Yearbook* (Walter De Gruyter GmbH & Co. of 2012 and 2013).

Chapter 1

Introduction

Sue Farran and Christa Rautenbach

The chapters collected here represent a wide range of legal systems, with contributions from established academics through to post-graduate and early career contributors. Each chapter is a reflection on particular aspects of a legal system or several legal systems and each provides a concrete example of the diffusion of laws and norms located against the wider academic context of diverse laws and legal systems (*juris diversitas*). While the aim of this introduction is not to revisit the existing literature on diffusion, much of which is referred to in the various contributions, it is perhaps worth drawing attention to the range of features which characterise diffusion and for which these chapters provide illustrative examples.

The diffusion of laws has been an important topic in comparative law and legal globalism discourses at least since the publication of Alan Watson's inspiring book on *Legal Transplants*.[1] He coined the term 'legal transplants' to indicate the moving of a legal rule or norm or a system of law from one country to another, and the notion of legal transplantation is based on diffusion of some form or another. Of course, most changes in the majority of legal systems are the result of transplantation. Although he did not use the expression 'diffusion of law' in the 1974 edition of his publication, it seeped into the afterword of the second edition, published in 1993,[2] where he contests the following comment of William M. Evan:[3]

> The concept of "legal transplant" has a naturalistic ring to it as though it occurs independent of any human agency. In point of fact, however, elites – legal and nonlegal – often act as "culture carriers" or intermediaries between societies

---

1 Watson, A. *Legal Transplants: An Approach to Comparative Law* (University Press of Virginia, 1974). W. Twining, 'Diffusion of law: A global perspective' (2004) 49 *Journal of Legal Pluralism* 1–45, 8–10 points out that there were other landmark studies on the diffusion of laws even before this date, albeit termed in other ways, such as the 'reception', 'importation', 'imposition', 'exports and imports', 'spread', 'circulation', 'expansion', 'transmigration', 'transposition' and 'transmobility of law', or as phenomena of other disciplines.

2 Watson, A. *Legal Transplants: An Approach to Comparative Law* (University of Georgia Press, 1993) 114.

3 Evans, W.M. *Social Structure and Law: Theoretical and Empirical Perspectives* (Sage Publications, 1990) 33–4. Watson (n2) 114, points out that Evan's viewpoint regarding his thesis is flawed – 'My whole point, of course, is precisely that legal change is brought about by human agency and is thus limited by the knowledge and culture of that agency'.

involved in a legal transplant. [...] Hence, it is a misnomer to describe and analyze the *diffusion of law* as if it were devoid of human agency. [Emphasis added]

Evan's equation of 'legal transplants' with the 'diffusion of law' is indeed one of the earliest examples where the existence and interconnectedness of the two concepts are indirectly acknowledged.

The expression 'diffusion of law' also appears in the well-known book of William Twining on *Globalisation and Legal Theory* published in 2000. He confesses that his view on the legal elites as the main receivers of law is only a moderated version of Watson's famous transplant thesis.[4] Since then Twining has published a number of scholarly works which focus specifically on the concept of 'diffusion of laws'. He has developed a model of reception based on 12 elements,[5] which also feature in some of the contributions included in this collection.

The lexical likeness between 'diffusion' and 'transplant' is quite obvious. The *Oxford English Dictionary* defines 'diffusion' in various ways including 'the action of spreading abroad' or 'the condition of being widely spread' of abstract things or knowledge.[6] Diffusion is thus either a process of spreading or a condition of being spread. The word 'transplant' is described in the same way as the process to 'convey or remove from one place to another' or 'to bring (people, a colony, etc.) from one country to settle in another'.

The lexical meaning of diffusion corresponds with Twining's idea of diffusion as something that 'is generally considered to take place when one legal order, system or tradition *influences* another in some significant way'.[7] A consideration of the '12 elements' of diffusion Twining isolates may conclude that the first is a broad concept in which there may be diverse sources of the reception of laws and legal norms, and where there may be a number of 'importers' and 'exporters' of these, acting either at the same time or sequentially over a period of time – Esin Örücü's four circles of diffusion illustrate this as does Juliana Latifi's exploration of the Albanian legal system. Secondly, diffusion may also take place across different kinds of legal orders and at different geographical levels, not just horizontally between municipal legal systems – Thomas Favre-Bulle's discussion of direct democracy engages with this. Thirdly, the routes along which laws and norms are diffused may be direct or indirect, and the 'traffic' of diffusion may pass both ways or be uni-directional – the contribution of Alessandra Pera on the diffusing/synthesising effect of the 'margin of appreciation' found in the European Convention of Human Rights and the jurisprudence of Strasbourg examines this, as does the contribution of Pamela Martino, which looks at the role and impact

---

4 Twining, W. *Globalisation and Legal Theory* (Cambridge University Press, 2000) 144.

5 Twining, W. 'Diffusion of law: A global perspective' (2004) 49 *Journal of Legal Pluralism* 17–34.

6 The Philological Society. *Oxford English Dictionary* (Clarendon Press, 1978).

7 Twining, 2004: 1–45, 14.

of the decisions of the Judicial Committee of the Privy Council, while (fourthly) the contribution by Rita Duca describes, how the movement of people from the non-West forces Western jurisdictions to adopt formal measures to provide protection to Islamic minorities. Fifthly, it is also the case that diffusion is not limited to the dissemination of legal rules and concepts only. These do not exist in a vacuum. So while one certainly does find the diffusion of these, for example of the English law of trust, as discussed by Kateřina Ronovská, or of the obligations of heirs and executors as considered by Elwira Macierzyńska-Franaszczyk, or of the private limited liability company as discussed by Alessio Bartolacelli, we are also reminded of this wider diffusion in the contributions by Eoin Carolan, David Zammit and Kurt Xerri. Many of the chapters here support Twining's sixth claim, that governments are not the only and may not be the main agents of diffusion. Indeed it is clear that in many cases governments react quite late in the day after the diffusion has already occurred. The seventh element has to do with the timing of diffusion. While a change of government or political structure may be a seminal moment for the rejection or acceptance of transplants and act as a trigger for a sudden diffusion or infusion of new laws and ideas – as illustrated in countries such as Poland, Albania, the Czech Republic and to some extent Turkey, all of which are considered here – often diffusion is a drawn out, sometimes insidious process, the impact of which may not be fully realised at the time. Biagio Andò's contribution on the civil code in Quebec and the consideration of diffusion in the Kuwaiti legal system by Myra Williamson illustrate this. Eighth, where there is diffusion this is never to a blank canvas. There is always an historical context, an existing legal, social and/or religious framework in which the past will continue to exist alongside the new introductions. This is well illustrated by the legal system of Turkey and also by that of Quebec. In ninth place, these diffusions are sometimes (but not always) closely linked to the influence of imperial powers under colonisation, or may be the product of a centralised force – the Privy Council and the European Court of Human Rights are examples that come to mind. Tenth, pragmatism may drive diffusion, as in the adoption of the Islamic concept of special guardianship in English law, discussed by Rita Duca, or the limited liability company considered by Alessio Bartolacelli. Indeed Alessio's contribution illustrates how an initial diffusion can then lead to other transformations within domestic law and may, through dispersal and modification, lead to the adoption of new concepts or models which have no clear national identity, such as the European Interest Group. Eleventh, many of the authors collected here also make the point that diffusion is not only the movement of ideas, laws, models and norms but a way in which new ingredients may be brought in and new ideas, laws and models made. For example, the diffusion of the trust into Czech law does not result in the replication of the original institution, as explained by Kateřina Ronovská, similarly rules on inheritance, contract and tort drawn from various continental systems in Albania, as explained by Julian Latifi, do not map exactly onto the originals. Diffusion can be good or bad – see the contribution by Eoin Carolan, or neutral in effect. Hence different terms are often used to describe this process, ranging from infusion – which seems to be benign, to seepage – which is less so. Lastly, diffusion might also be controversial. Indeed, the potential for diffusion to give rise to tensions is evident in the jurisprudence of the European Court of Human Rights with respect to the margin of appreciation in cases of abortion and assisted reproduction, considered by Alessandra Pera. The challenges of moving towards a European consensus on these controversial topics, which are closely linked to social, moral and religious views, are evident. How one measures the success or failure of diffusion is controversial and where there has been relatively recent diffusion, as in Albania, only time will tell. Much will depend on the tools used and the perspective adopted. Thomas Favre-Bulle offers an interesting methodology in his contribution. Myra Williamson's empirical work with students also offers a valuable insight into the extent to which diffusion in legal education and practice is perceived. Alessio Bartolacelli adopts a more business-focused model to examine the diffusion of commercial structures, while Eoin Carolan also scrutinises the market, but from a different perspective.

The study of the diffusion of laws and norms is not isolated from other genres of legal scholarship and clearly interacts with ideas drawn from comparative legal study. Indeed, the theme of the conference from which these chapters are drawn was 'Diffusion, an international, interdisciplinary conference on comparative law', and included considerations of hybridity and mixity in legal systems, debates about legal transplants, the harmonisation of laws and law reform; academic studies relating to plural legal systems, colonial and post-colonial legal development; and theories of the imposition and adoption of laws. As Biagio Andò (p. 147) points out '[w]ords such as "transplantation", "reception" and/ or "transposition" have become widespread terms in the scholarly debate, each underlying a different point of view on how the circulation of law may occur and has occurred throughout history'.

Nor can the diffusion of laws and norms easily be discussed in isolation from other disciplines. As Myra Williamson (p. 25) points out, 'The law is a social construct and it can never be studied with any meaning in isolation from the contributions made by those other branches of the humanities'. Elwira Macierzyńska-Franaszczyk (p. 169) takes up this point in her discussion of the diffusion of laws relating to succession when she states, 'The shape and function of such provisions are, however, designated by the political and economic priorities of national legislatures. These factors determine the character and specificity of the system [...]'. It is clear that history, social, economic and religious influences and political structures play a key role in determining the composition of legal systems. Indeed, it might be argued that diffusion is rather like the parable of the sower who scatters seed: some falls on stony ground and does not grow, while some falls on fertile ground and thrives. To this might be added the suggestion that some falls on ground which, while fertile, changes the nature of the crop which is produced.

Diffusion may itself be adopted as a vehicle or method of comparison. So, for example, in considering the diffusion of common law ideas and practices in Kuwait, Myra Williamson makes comparisons with New Zealand. Although at first glance these are two totally dissimilar legal systems, Williamson is able to consider them through the diffusion lens and highlights the role of the institution of the 'state' as being based on concepts derived from the common law found in New Zealand and in the Kuwait legal system, despite its absence from *Shari'a* sources.

The diffusion of one aspect of a legal system may also provide a pathway or opening for further diffusions. Alessio Bartolacelli argues that the uptake of the private limited liability company and its diffusion into other European forms may stimulate a revived interest in the European Economic Interest Groupings. Similarly the diffusion of laws and norms creates networks and shared legal approaches. For example, looking at succession law in Poland Elwira Macierzyńska-Franaszczyk finds a number of similarities across civil law systems.

These contributions also demonstrate through illustration that diffusion goes in many directions. Myra Williamson, for example, points out that the concept of the separation of powers is found in early Islamic law, as well as in the philosophy of Montesquieu, and that the rule of law might equally be said to originate in ancient Greece, as in Western legal thought or Islamic legal thought. Moreover, as is evident in a number of the contributions, diffusion may stem from and bring together laws and norms from a number of different systems. So, for example, in Kuwait one finds the diffusion of ideas and practices impacting on English legal education from continental and America systems, while in Albania and Turkey, it is clear that there have been many influences which are still reflected in the contemporary laws.

One of the challenges in editing a collection such as this has been in trying to decide how the contributions should be arranged within the collection. There is no obvious order. Diffusion has not been in one direction or predominantly from one source. Civil and common law systems have been influential, as has Islamic law and to a lesser extent customary law. The spread of ideas, models and norms cannot therefore be said to have originated from a single identifiable point. In the end, therefore, it was decided to adopt the sequence in which these papers were originally presented, making some adjustments for where they were presented at the same time or where they were not presented but were subsequently submitted for inclusion. The order may therefore be considered erratic, eccentric or eclectic, but then that is the nature of diffusion.

The collection starts with Esin Örücü's 'Infusion of the Diffused: Four Circles of Diffusion Infusing the Legal System of Turkey'. This is followed by an example of the domestication of Western legal ideas in the Near and Middle East: Myra Williamson's chapter on 'The Diffusion of Western Legal Concepts in Kuwait: Reflections on the State, the Legal System and Legal Education from Comparative and Historical Perspectives'. Diffusion and contamination in family law are considered by Rita Duca in 'Diffusion of Islamic Law in the UK: The Case of the "Special Guardianship"'. The theme of institutional, doctrinal and judicial vehicles of legal diffusion is considered by Pamela Martino in 'The Judicial Committee of the Privy Council: Common Law and its Local Variations in the Commonwealth'. Public policy and the internal diffusion of norms are addressed by David Zammit and Kurt Xerri in their contribution '"Lease, *Locazioni* and *Kera*": Merging Legal Concepts in Postcolonial Malta'. The role of diffusion in the business world and the diffusion of small business entities are considered by Alessio Bartolacelli in 'Legal Capital is Out – EEIG is Cool! How the Evaporation of Legal Capital in EU Private Companies might Provide a Revival Opportunity for EEIGs'. Thomas Favre-Bulle addresses the movement of constitutional doctrines in theory and practice in 'The Urban Diffusion of Local Direct Democracy between Switzerland and the United States'. Alessandra Pera engages with the theme of identity and transplant in Eastern and Western Europe in her chapter on 'The "Margin of Appreciation" in EHRC Case-law as a Boundary Line to Legal Transplants', while Biagio Andò's chapter 'The Feature of *Droit Commun* in the *Disposition Preliminaire* of the Civil Code of Quebec: A Clue to the Bijurality of the Legal System?' considers mixed jurisdiction on the move. Challenges to homogeneity are considered in Elwira Macierzyńska-Franaszczyk's 'Law in Changing Circumstances: Evolution of Liability for Succession Debts in Poland' and, staying in Eastern Europe to focus on legal transplants in recent codes, Juliana Latifi looks at the many examples of diffusion in her contribution on 'Albanian Civil Law and the Influence of Foreign Laws' and Kateřina Ronovská considers the '"Svěřenský fond" (Trust Fund): A Daring New Legal Transplant in Czech Law'. The collection concludes with a chapter by Eoin Carolan: 'Diffusing Bad Ideas: What the Migration of the Separation of Powers Means for Comparative Law'.

As illustrated by this collection, the use of the term 'diffusion' in law and other social sciences is very broad, as is its meaning. The authors in this collection reimagine the doctrines, discourses and meanings of 'diffusion' on a global scale. In doing so, they confront, integrate and transgress assumptions and methodologies. They confirm Twining's[8] contention that, 'in an era of globalisation, we need a broader and much more complex picture and a flexible methodology as a basis for studying processes of diffusion and their outcomes'.

Finally it is appropriate in this introduction to acknowledge and thank a number of people: the contributors themselves, who have patiently responded to editing queries and suggestions; our co-editors James Gallen and Jennifer Hendry, who have assisted with the editing work and the drafting of the publishing proposal; and the members of *Juris Diversitas*, who not only organised the conference in Lausanne, which was the initial springboard for this collection, but have also offered views on diffusion – with a special mention here to the president, Seán Donlan.

8   2004: 5.

Chapter 2

Infusion of the Diffused: Four Circles of Diffusion Infusing the Legal System of Turkey

Esin Örücü

Introduction

This contribution is both a theoretical and an empirical effort, attempting to elaborate on the concepts of diffusion and infusion, and to illustrate how they work together on and in a particular legal system. It deals with the story of diffusion and infusion as part of the story of the 'trans-frontier mobility of law'.[1] There are a number of approaches to 'trans-frontier mobility of law', which form some of the theories for analysis of such movements. These are in addition to classical concepts such as voluntary reception, imposition, imposed reception and the like. This introductory chapter first considers other possible theoretical foundations of analysis and then goes on to develop diffusion and wave theory to explain the spread of the laws, and infusion and transposition to explain the internationalisation of the laws that have been diffused. Further, it considers, with examples, the diffusion and infusion shaping a legal system into an eclectic and synthetic whole, in spite of the indigenous culture being different to those of the infusing models: the legal system of Turkey. I present rather than assess here the result: a synthetically constructed legal system with its diverse foreign sources that are still alive and used as 'source-laws' today: the Swiss diffusion for instance, that started in 1926 still continuing if we consider the new 2002 Civil Code, the 2011 Code of Obligations and partially the 2011 Commercial Code.

Possible Theoretical Foundations of Analysis

Pierre Guiseppe Monateri, suggested 'contamination' as the basis for understanding the world of legal systems, saying: 'the actual legal world is to be seen more as a world of "contaminations" than a world split up into different families'.[2] He claims

---

1   E. Örücü, 'A theoretical framework for transfrontier mobility of law' in R. Jagtenberg, E. Örücü and A. de Roo (eds), *Transfrontier Mobility of Law* (Kluwer International, 1995) 5.

2   P.G. Monateri, 'The "weak" law: Contaminations and legal cultures' in *Italian National Reports to the XVth International Congress of Comparative Law* (Giuffrè editore, 1998) 83 at 107.

that this idea is neither new nor linked to globalisation, since 'practically every system, even in antiquity has grown through "contaminations"',[3] the practice of borrowing having always been a normal path of development. In his view the 'widespread cross-diffusion of French and German patterns within civil law, and the overcoming of American models at the present, shape a similar legal landscape all across the world, with a wilderness of local variants'.[4] A comparative lawyer can detect cross-pollination, cross-fertilisation and 'horizontal transfers' between systems in all places and at all times.

Further, Monateri claims that a 'weak' legal tradition, in the sense of one being widely open to foreign 'cultural intruders', is formed by borrowings, and presents the process as evolutive. Strong proximate systems rather than distant ones, prestigious patterns rather than discredited ones contaminate the weaker system. This can even be regarded as an everyday occurrence.

'Contamination' indeed is one useful theoretical approach.[5] It is one of the more general paths of trans-frontier movement of the law. According to Olivier Moréteau, for instance, 'reception, migration, circulation, and the like describe the visible. Contamination refers to the less visible, since its effects may occur later on'. He states that contamination is not a concept generally used to indicate influences and cross influences but is a useful term 'to indicate the permeability of legal systems and the sometimes less visible influences they may have on one another', and reminds us that from an anthropological viewpoint, it is a very rich concept.[6]

'Derivation' is also of great significance in the historical development of many legal systems.[7] Mostly relevant for colonial relationships, it is yet another explanatory theory of legal development and especially of convergence of legal systems. As almost all legal systems are related historically and are derivatives of each other, the relationship between a legal system and its socio-cultural context does not stand in the way of its relationship with other legal systems or even with other socio-cultural contexts. Derivation however, implies a special relationship of parent and child. An inherent belief in 'dependency' forms the basis of this explanatory theory. Its use is rather limited; it is mostly Eurocentric and does not imply cross-fertilisation, confluence or overlap.

'Appropriation of common laws' has been offered by Patrick Glenn to form the basis of an explanation of legal development.[8] According to Glenn, although

---

3   Ibid.

4   Ibid.

5   O. Moréteau, 'The introduction to contamination' (2010) 3 *Journal of Civil Law Studies* 9–15 at 9. Compare this view with 'irritant' in view of the unforeseen results. See for this G. Teubner, 'Legal irritants: Good faith in British law' (1998) 61 *Modern Law Review* 11–32.

6   Moréteau (n5) 11.

7   Here we can also think of Alan Watson and his transplant theory. A. Watson, *Legal Transplants: An Approach to Comparative Law* (Scottish Academic Press, 1974).

8   P. Glenn, *On Common Laws* (Oxford University Press, 2005).

the English common law and the *ius commune* have been widely discussed within the context of Europe, the fact that there were many more common laws and that these common laws themselves were in dynamic relationship, has been neglected. Until the nineteenth century the numerous common laws of Europe – French, German, Spanish, Dutch and English – lived in constant interaction with the local particulars and with each other. As these common laws expanded both within and outside Europe, particular laws they met appropriated them. There was constant contact and intermingling. Common laws were the main instruments of 'conciliation' of laws, at a time when law was not seen as an exclusive product of the State. Even later, when legal nationalism burgeoned, this continued to be the case. This is another explanation of the trans-frontier mobility of law.

In linguistics, the theory of the 'family tree model' of language development reflects an evolutionary approach and is the one generally used to explain ramification.[9] This model (*stammbaum*) in linguistics was proposed by Augustus Schleicher in 1862.[10] It assumed that resemblances arose from common origin (understood in terms of parenthood), and languages closely similar and linked were thought to have separated or diverged from each other, with original divergence and further subsequent divergence. The underlying human reality was originally thought to be migration of peoples.[11] This theory can also be easily translated and applied to ramification of laws. Exclusive reliance on the 'tree-model' of development can only explain ramification and divergence. In response, the 'wave theory' was developed and is discussed below.

Diffusion and Wave Theory; Infusion and Transposition

Two theories I would like to highlight, enlarge upon and use in my attempt here, are diffusion in combination with the wave theory to show the spread, and infusion together with transposition to indicate the internalisation of the diffused.

The word 'diffusion' comes from Latin '*diffundere*' meaning to spread out, and in science is a theory used in fluids and has been defined as the process in which small particles released, or produced, in one part of a fluid spread out to form an even distribution throughout the whole volume of the fluid, or to pour out a liquid with wide dispersion or spread. It is synonymous with spreading, propagation and dispersal. Graham Thomson (1905–69) who studied the diffusion

---

9   See for an exposition and analysis of these theories, C. Renfrew, *Archeology and Language: The Puzzle of Indo-European Origins* (Jonathan Cape, 1987) especially 105, 244–8.

10   A. Schleicher, *Die Darwinsche Theorie und die Sprachwissenschaft* (Weimar, 1963). For the French edition: 'La Theorie de Darwin et la Science du Langage' in *Receuil de Travuax Originaux ou Traduit relatifs à l'Histoire Littérraire* 1 (Franck, 1968).

11   Renfrew (n9) 101–2.

of gasses, described this process (Graham's Law of Diffusion) and investigated the passage of dissolved substances through porous membranes coining the word *osmose* – an earlier form of osmosis.[12] An example is given in the *Oxford Reference Encyclopaedia*: 'a drop of ink added to a bucket of water will disperse and eventually colour all the water in the bucket, even if the water is not stirred'.[13] This needs to be elaborated upon as it also corresponds to my understanding of 'infusion' to be discussed further below.

The theory, originally used in physics, chemistry and biology, has been translated into social sciences and used in anthropology, sociology, economics and finance. It has been given a relevant and rather broad meaning.[14] William Twining for instance, believes that this theory rather than transplant theories should be taken up by comparatists to explain the phenomenon of how legal systems converge.[15] Twining advocates the use of social science sources and challenges what he calls the simplified notions of 'identifiable exporters and importers', 'export/import between countries', 'direct one way transfers', the classical beliefs related to 'objects' and 'agents' of receptions, 'parent systems and dependents'.[16] Instead, he advocates that a particular innovation, networks for and agents and channels of diffusion, and the adoption of the innovation, are processes that should be studied. Though diffusionism seems to have gone out of fashion in anthropology, this is not the case in sociology. In this approach, the spread of ideas is pitched against the concept of innovation. Twining talks of cross-level diffusion, as diffusion also implies interaction or 'inter-legality' born out of a spreading in space.[17] There is obviously a 'diffusion of innovations', but once the 'knock-on-effect' starts, very little remains of the original innovation, but there is probably further independent innovation. Diffusion is regarded as 'an informal spread', as a general and abstract term, 'embracing contagion, mimicry, social learning, organised dissemination' and other ways.[18] The diffusion theory as I see it, is in fact a glorified transplant theory, or better still, to be called 'trans-frontier mobility of law', put into social science terminology indicating the spread of ideas – a special type of communication.

---

12   See *Reference Encyclopedia* (Oxford University Press, 1998) 591.

13   Ibid. 420.

14   For instance, we can say broadly that democracy has diffused in the twentieth century through interdependent decision making, impact of powerful countries, emulating them and learning from their experience.

15   See W. Twining, 'Diffusion of law: A global perspective' (2004) 49 *Journal of Legal Pluralism* 1–45 and in (2006) 1: 2 *The Journal of Comparative Law* 237–60. Also W. Twining, 'Social science and diffusion of law' (2005) 32 *Journal of Law and Society* 203–40. Twining refers to the 'diffusion of law' research carried out by Everett Rogers (see E.M. Rogers, *Diffusion of Innovations* (Free Press, 1995 [1963]).

16   Twining (2006) (n15) 238–9.

17   Ibid. 249.

18   D. Strang and S. Soule, 'Diffusion in organisation and social movement' (1998) 24 *Annual Review of Sociology* 265 at 266.

Seemingly, the theory as such suffers from an 'export bias' as it looks at the innovator-exporter (diffuser), and therefore may lead to virtual convergence. It does not deal with 'infusion' that is, the importers' point of view, and therefore cannot measure genuine or actual convergence, which involves internalisation of the received.

As a scientific terminology, infusion is a steeping process, extracting chemical compounds or flavours from plant material in a solvent such as water, oil or alcohol by allowing the material to remain suspended in the solvent over time. More specifically, it is the process of pouring water over a substance, or seeping the substance in water, in order to impregnate the liquid with its properties or virtues. A herbal infusion is what comes to mind in ordinary life. Diffusion in law then would be the spread of laws from points of dispersal in waves and when the waves reach the shores of other legal systems then infusion must take place to impregnate the recipient legal system or systems, become internalised and fit the new environment.

If diffusion is envisaged as circles or waves spreading, then I suggest it should be considered together with the 'wave theory'. The 'wave theory' or 'wave hypotheses', which shows how changes spread like waves and disperse over a wide area, was introduced in the nineteenth century by another German linguist, Johannes Schmidt in 1872.[19] According to this hypothesis, different linguistic changes may spread like waves over a speech area and thus lead to convergence. A subsequent wave may also move to areas not covered by the earlier wave. Schmidt drew lines (isoglosses) on a map to separate places where there were language differences – one isogloss enclosing one area with a particular linguistic form (divergence). Successive waves create a network of isoglosses. If, however, 'one dialect gains a political or commercial predominance of some sort over adjacent dialects, those nearest to this central dialect may give up their own peculiarities and come in time to speak only that central dialect'.[20] Following various local divergences (the tree model indicated earlier), the subsequent groupings would then have come about by the operation of the wave model. In this hypothesis, two or more closely related languages may each have features in common with their own neighbours that they do not share with each other. The relationships are far more complicated than any which could be conveyed simply by means of a family tree, as the wave model caters both for convergence and divergence.

It must be remembered however, that similarities do not always arise from genetic relationships; neither does resemblance necessarily indicate common origin. There can be 'horizontal transfers' between adjacent systems. 'Horizontal transfer' can also explain why a borrowed concept or institution does not always exactly retain its original meaning. Areas nearest or adjacent to the initial change will change first and may even give up their own peculiarities. Subsequent

---

19   J. Schmidt, *Die Verwandtschaftsverhalnisse der indogermanischen Sprachen* (Böhlau, 1872).

20   Renfrew (n9) 105.

re-groupings may come about on the 'wave model'. Thus convergence can occur between concepts or systems originally very different.

The 'knock-on-effect', which can be regarded as the 'ripples' of the wave, can also be used to explain developments. As Renfrew says:

> It is, in fact, the resemblances between languages most distant from each other spatially which can least easily arise from the wave-like diffusion of an innovation, and are thus most likely to be the result, rather, of a relationship explicable in family tree terms.[21]

It is also the case that 'languages in different areas which were not themselves necessarily related, became Indo-Europeanised through the process of contact'.[22] Contact leads to convergence and convergence to uniformity. Thus, similarities can develop through time by the process of convergence through contact. Therefore, common parentage is not in issue since the ancestors could have been quite dissimilar but, through continuing contact, mutual influence and borrowing, the languages become significantly closer to each other, though never becoming identical. Thus waves cause diffusion and dispersals, occurring spontaneously through contact.[23]

If the term 'language' is replaced by 'law', one can see that this combined approach could also indicate a way forward for an understanding of how legal systems function, change and develop; converge or diverge, catering for our understanding of both.

As already indicated, contamination, derivation and diffusion are all variations on the theme of 'trans-frontier mobility of law', which shows that legal systems live in contact and interaction, and are interrelated. Systems may have common roots or may have heavily borrowed from each other or, through some historical accident, be derivatives from a parent system. However, when laws are moved and then 'transposed', that is, 'tuned' to create the 'fit', variations occur.[24] That is why I have used and defined the term 'transposition' thus:

> The term "transposition" is more apt in instances of massive change based on competing models, in that here the pitch is changed. In musical transposition, each note takes the same relative place in the scale of the new key as in the old,

---

21   Ibid. 111.

22   Ibid. 145.

23   A variant, 'wave of advance model', was also proposed to explain the random, unsystematic, slow, gradual and continuous convergence, as opposed to colonisation which also creates convergence, but through intentional and deliberate settlement. See A.J. Ammerman and L.L. Cavalli-Sforza, 'The wave of advance model for the spread of agriculture in Europe' in C. Renfrew and K.L. Cooke (eds), *Transformations, Mathematical Approaches to Cultural Change* (Academic Press, 1979) 275–94.

24   See E. Örücü, 'Law as transposition' (2002) 51 *International and Comparative Law Quarterly* 205.

the "transposition" being made to suit the particular instrument or the voice-range of the singer. So in law.[25]

In law then, each legal institution or rule introduced from one legal system (diffuser) to another (the recipient), is diffused into the system of the recipient, the transposition occurring to suit the particular socio-legal culture and needs of the recipient. Terminology used in classical statements of legal movements such as transplant, imposition and reception, have today been supplemented by a colourful vocabulary highlighting nuances in individual instances of this mobility such as grafting, implantation, re-potting, cross-fertilisation, imposed reception, solicited imposition, crypto-reception and inoculation.[26] We now also talk of cross-pollination, engulfment, emulation, infiltration, diffusion, infusion, digestion, salad bowl, melting pot and transposition.[27] New notions and bases for analysis are being developed such as collective colonisation, contaminants, legal irritants, layered-law, hyphenated-law and competition of legal systems. Images such as contamination, inoculation, irritation, diffusion, infusion, seepage, migration, circulation and infiltration are all appropriate in describing present day encounters, and the terms reception, imposed reception and concerted parallel development, the activities.

Although originally the term 'legal transplant'[28] has been the usual one applied to all these import and export activities, I believe that the term 'transposition', discussed earlier, is more appropriate as it also involves 'tuning', that is the process of 'fit', the most important element for the workings of a legal system. Legal developments of our day are best seen as instances of transposition. The 'tuning' to take place after transposition by appropriate actors of the recipient is the key to success: the diffused must be infused. In fact, there may be a number of transpositions, since no single model has to be used by any one recipient. Old models may be abandoned with 'optimistic normativism' while new legal models are looked for.[29] In such a case, a transplanted legal system not compatible with the culture in the receiving country, without the appropriate transposition and tuning, will create only a virtual reality.[30] In answer to the question, 'how do legal ideas,

---

25   Ibid. 207.

26   See, Watson (n7) 53 ff at 30.

27   See, Örücü (n24) 205–36.

28   Monateri claims that the term 'legal transplant' utilised by Watson for 'scholarly purposes' is today taken over by 'purposive practical lawyers' involved in projects of 'exporting their own legal systems'. See, Monateri (n2) 83. Transplants have also been classified into four groups: direct-receptive, direct-unreceptive, indirect-receptive, indirect-unreceptive, the indication being that even 'transplant' from 'transplant', that is indirect transplant, rather than from 'origin', that is direct transplant, are possible.

29   See G. Ajani, 'La circulation de modèles juridiques dans le droit post-socialiste' (1994) 4 *Revue Internationale de Droit Compare* 1087–105.

30   J.M. Smits 'Systems mixing and in transition: Import and export of legal models: The Dutch experience' in E.E. Hondius (ed.), *Nederlands Reports to the Fifteenth International Congress of Comparative Law* (Intersentia Rechtswetenschappen, 1998) 55.

institutions and structures find their way from one location to another?' it has been wisely put that 'laws do not have wings'.[31] This alone highlights the importance of those who move the law and help in its diffusion and infusion, and internalisation, that is, 'tuning'. Countries that adapt transplanted law can have more effective legality by further developing their formal sources and building effective legal systems with effective economic development. This receptivity can be enhanced by making significant adaptation in the foreign formal legal order to fit the pre-existing formal or informal legal orders. Additionally, the diffusion of innovation will create new developments through infusion and the knock-on-effect.

In historical terms, most tuning was carried out externally by imposers or exporters of law, that is, by diffusers. This cannot produce a very sensitive kind of tuning, since it cannot consider the new pitch in its entirety, as the tuner is not an active player of the new instrument. It is internal tuning that is required, and for that, the tuners are usually the domestic judges. However, for successful[32] transposition and then infusion, tuning is necessary at all levels, including legal education.

Below I trace Turkish courts as they cope with the tuning and transpose the received legal system, helping in the infusion of the diffused. Diffusion does not tell us anything of the outcome but only of the process. The outcome depends on the success of infusion of the diffused, and 'transposition' which talks of the process of 'tuning' and 'fit'.

The Four Circles of Diffusion Infusing the Turkish Legal System

The case I want to present as a supreme example of circles of diffusion, reaching the shores of a legal system, and being infused into it, is not the result of a people migrating from one land to another and taking their laws with them thus leading to a diffusion of laws. Neither is it a case of diffusion consequent to a colonial imposition or a transfer of sovereignties between two colonial powers, since the Ottoman Empire and its heir, the Turkish Republic, were never colonies. This diffusion is the result of the will and efforts of domestic renovators. In the case of the French administrative law this started with the elite of the Ottoman Empire, though under pressure, and in the others, the elite of the Turkish Republic. Between 1926 and 1930 the Civil Code, the Commercial Code and the Criminal Code were received into the legal system from Switzerland, Germany and Italy respectively. More borrowings followed, displacing all that was there before, Islamic law among others. The formation of the legal system relied entirely on reception and translation. Here we see four circles of diffusion, emanating from

---

31   F. Schauer, 'The politics and incentives of legal transplantations', Law and Development Paper No.2, CID Working Paper No. 44, April 2000, Center for International Development at Harvard University (2000), available at <http://www.cid.harvard.edu/cidwp/044.htm> accessed 30 May 2013.

32   Success has never been satisfactorily defined though.

France, Switzerland, Germany and Italy, arriving in Turkey mainly in the form of Codes and infusing the Turkish legal system and society.[33] The circles of diffusion did not reach Turkey in ripples or gradually, but flooded the legal system as major waves, foreign laws and doctrine being translated to allow the diffusion and the ensuing infusion to take place. When discussing 'legal transplants' it was referred to as the most extreme example by Alan Watson and other comparative law scholars.[34] Since the Turkish experience represents the passage of a legal system from one legal culture to another, historians and comparatists alike have hailed it as unique. Here, history was shifted. The switch in Turkey was to Roman law-based legal systems and its legal system can be classified as belonging to the Germanic sub-group of civil law countries.[35]

Viewed from the vantage point of the models, the Turkish experience is an excellent example of diffusion. Viewed from the internal point of view, it is an excellent example of voluntary receptions. In either case, it is an example of infusion of the Turkish legal system and society by four foreign laws and the accompanying doctrine. We can also regard this experience as the confluence or meeting and overlapping of four circles or waves of diffusion in one locale: Turkey. The infusion is near completion after nearly 90 years, as the 'fit' to the local values has also taken place in the meantime.

The Ottoman Empire was an Islamic state between 1299 and 1839, and a mixed legal system with considerable French influence from 1839 until the fall of the Empire in 1920. Following the collapse of the Ottoman Empire and the founding of the Republic in 1923, Turkey went through a process of total and global modernisation, Westernisation, secularisation, democratisation and constitutionalism with efforts of reform resting solely on imports from the major continental jurisdictions both as to form and content.

In the hope of joining the European Union and in order to fulfil the requirements of the European Union *acquis communautaire*, rapid law reform is carried out in

---

33 Note that diffusion from these four legal systems have reached and are still reaching the shores of many other legal systems worldwide though impositions, imposed receptions and voluntary receptions.

34 See for example, K. Zweigert and H. Kötz, *An Introduction to Comparative Law* (3rd edn. trans. T. Weir, Clarendon Press, 1998). As recently as 2000 Alan Watson cited the Turkish example to support his views. See A. Watson, *Legal Transplants and European Private Law*, Ius Commune Lectures on European Private Law: 2 (2000). William Twining also considers this example in Twining (n15) (2005) at 223–8.

35 Z.D. Tarman, 'Turkey' in J.M. Smits (ed.), *Elgar Encyclopedia of Comparative Law*, 2nd edn (Edward Elgar, 2012) 940–46 at 940. Although, I have also analysed elsewhere the present legal system as a 'covert mix'. See, E. Örücü, 'Turkey's synthetic legal system and her indigenous socio-culture(s) in a "covert" mix' in E. Örücü (ed.), *Mixed Legal Systems at New Frontiers* (Wildy, Simmonds and Hill, 2010) 150–203, and at the WSMJJ conference in Malta in 2012: 'Turkey's synthetic civilian tradition in a "covert" mix with Islam as tradition: A new hybridity?' in V. Palmer (ed.), *Mixed Legal Systems: East and West* (Ashgate, 2015).

the same manner even today. In fact, the inroads made by *acquis communautaire* into the Turkish legal system can also be regarded, though at a stretch, as the fifth circle of diffusion. These current 'receptions' in Turkey vis-à-vis European Union law are examples of weak 'imposed receptions', the qualifier 'weak' being attached to this analysis since the element of choice is still there.[36] Some other new waves, the result of globalisation, should also be mentioned here. A number of the new Turkish laws have been modelled on international treaties, UNCITRAL model laws or EU legislation, such as those on intellectual property, law for the protection of patent rights, law for the protection of trademarks, the law on international arbitration, on protection of competition, on protection of consumers, law on access to information and the law on electronic communications.

Since 1923, the Turkish Republic is a modern, Western, laic and civilian democracy. Even today law is principally regarded in instrumental terms. When the ideological and technological decision was made in 1924 to move outside the framework of the endogenous system of laws rather than to integrate and modernise the existing system, and to use the tool of reception as the sole method of law reform, a commission of 26 members was set the task of translating first the Swiss Civil Code from its French version. Subsequently, a number of special committees translated most of the important commentaries on various branches of law into Turkish. During 1926 Turkish legal experts produced three entirely new codes, and there were more to follow. The main aim of this 'purposive use of law' – a prime example of 'social engineering through law' – was to demolish the foundations of the old legal system by creating completely new laws, and to regulate the relationships of the people according to what was thought these relationships ought to be.

From its very inception, the Turkish legal system tried to transform the social, political, ideological, religious and economic systems it encountered. What instigated the legal evolution was a strong aspiration to become Western and contemporary. Turkey became 'European by law'[37] and the locale where different circles of diffusion met. By receiving, adapting and mixing laws from various foreign Western sources with very different historical antecedents and melting them down in the Turkish legal pot, through 'imposed receptions', voluntary 'receptions', 'imitations', 'adaptations' and 'adjustments', an 'eclectic', 'synthetic' and 'hyphenated' legal system was created.[38] The successful infusion of the diffused was extremely important here.

The various source-codes were selected from what were seen to be 'the best' in their field for various reasons. The choice was driven at times by the perceived

---

36   See E. Örücü 'Turkey facing the European Union – Old and new harmonies' (2000) 25 *European Law Review* 57.

37   The clause is borrowed from the title of Hernnfeld's book. See, H. Hernnfeld, *European by Law* (Bertelsmann Foundation, 1992).

38   See for further analysis E. Örücü, 'A synthetic and hyphenated legal systems: The Turkish experience' (2006) 1:2 *The Journal of Comparative Law* 27–47.

'prestige' of the model, and at other times by 'efficiency', sometimes by 'chance', or 'historical accident'. The civil law, the law of obligations and civil procedure were borrowed from Switzerland, commercial law, maritime law and criminal procedure from Germany, criminal law from Italy and administrative law from France; all translated, adapted and adjusted to interlock and solve the social and legal problems of Turkey. Four circles of diffusion were infusing the Turkish legal system.

In addition, the *Yargıtay* (The Court of Last Instance, Court of Cassation) was enabled to make adjustments to the law by the flexible rules present in the 1926 Civil Code articles 1 to 4, which correspond *verbatim* to articles 1 to 4 of the Swiss Civil Code. These are rules on justice and equity, judge's discretion, objective good faith and the abuse of rights. For the development of the Turkish law and legal system, the most important articles are 1 and 4, providing tools for the judge and helping further the infusion of the diffused:

> The law must be applied in all cases that come within the letter and the spirit of its provisions. If no relevant provision can be found in the statute, the judge must decide in accordance with the customary law and, in its absence, in accordance with the rule which he would lay down, were he the legislator. In so doing, he must be guided by accepted legal doctrine and case law. (Article 1)

> In those cases where the law gives the judge discretion and where he has to decide according to the circumstances or just causes, he must decide in justice and equity. (Article 4)

When Turkish courts look for new ways of dealing with emerging problems and difficult cases, where matters of principle are to be settled, Turkish legal scholars and the higher courts scrutinise the reception models, the so-called 'source-laws' (*kaynak kanunlar*). Thus the term 'hyphenated legal system' becomes appropriate in depicting this legal system as, for instance, at times reference is made to *İsviçre-Türk Hukuku* (Swiss-Turkish Law) to be seen below. Although interpretation tends to introduce subjective and cultural tonalities and values, foreign law always provides inspiration and stimulus. Transposition is continuous.

It is worth remembering that Turkish academics who transposed the foreign sources into Turkish law and undertook the 'fitting' of models to the Turkish situation and the 'tuning' of them, had most of their training in universities in the countries from where the receptions came. Language training and translations were extensive. In addition, in the early years of the Republic, Swiss, Austrian and German academics, given sanctuary in Turkey before the Second World War, contributed to the new legal system, greatly helping the imported system to take root and the infusion of the diffused. This was the consequence of a historical accident. The presence of such German and Austrian professors in Turkey fuelled the spread of legal ideas in support of the received. In time, many of their Turkish assistant lecturers themselves became professors and so helped further the infusion of the diffused and the internalisation of law. Professor Schwartz, who was one of the most influential and important of the foreign professors teaching in the İstanbul and Ankara University Law Faculties in the years following the receptions, and whose works are among the reference books still in use, is frequently relied upon for support in relation to the application of the Civil Code. He was definitely instrumental in the infusion of this Swiss diffusion. Professor Hirsch on the other hand is significant in the infusion of the diffusion of German commercial law.

The waves from the four circles of diffusion lap the shores of the Turkish legal system even today. As will be observed below, the relationship with the 'source-laws' are still being strengthened, so contributing to and maintaining the 'hyphenated' nature of the legal system, in spite of developing differences of interpretation due to context.[39]

The First Circle of Diffusion: French Law

The French circle of diffusion should be dealt with as the first circle because its waves started to spread into the Ottoman Empire following the 1839 Reformation (*Tanzimat*) movement before the Republic was born. By the 1860s, the bases of the main administrative institutions of today, such as the *Conseil d'Etat* and provincial and local administration were laid down following the French models.[40] Indeed, Bernard Lewis says: 'In February 1867 the French government, supported by England and Austria, presented a note to the Porte urging a more active policy of reform, and setting forth detailed suggestions. The Sultan was violently opposed to the idea, but gave way to the pressure of events'.[41] The year 1868 is generally regarded as the date when the *Conseil d'Etat* was established in the Ottoman Empire. Total adoption of French institutions can be seen, in addition to the *Conseil d'Etat*, in the Court of Accounts, in the Tribunal of Conflicts, in some financial organisations and the system of autonomous provincial administration, though they all vary from the models, being transposed and infused. These institutions may all be regarded as the result of imposed reception.

It must also be noted that the waves from this circle of diffusion were wider and brought in more than administrative law. Between 1850 and 1881 several Ottoman Codes were based on the French models: The 1850 Commercial Code based on the 1897 French Code, the 1856 Criminal Law Decree influenced by the French Code (but within the *Sheri'a* (Sharia) framework), the 1864 Maritime Code based

---

39   Over the years, a Turkish Civil law, a Turkish commercial law, and a Turkish Civil Procedure and other laws have developed, slowly diverging from 'the source-laws' and completing the infusion. A new history is being formed. However, even today, the higher courts make use of the models when reaching decisions, though never basing a decision solely on 'the source-laws', which are seen as aids to further modernisation.

40   See E. Örücü, '*Conseil d'Etat*: The French layer of Turkish administrative law' (2000) 49 *International and Comparative Law Quarterly*, 679–700.

41   B. Lewis, *The Emergence of Modern Turkey* (2nd edn. Oxford, 1968) 121.

on the 1808 French model (with additional influence of the Belgian and Prussian models), the 1879 Code of Criminal and 1880 Code of Civil Procedures, both based on French Codes. Thus French laws constituted the most significant circle of diffusion, which turned the Ottoman legal system into a mixed legal system in the second half of the nineteenth century, a mix between civilian and Islamic laws.

This first wave of receptions following the Ottoman Westernisation movement was indeed the result of voluntary domestic effort for economic and commercial purposes in order to harmonise with the national laws of Western powers. Nevertheless, the political pressures of the super powers of the nineteenth century for the purposes of protecting their own nationals living in the territories of or trading with the Ottoman Empire were largely behind the borrowings. The diffusion of this first circle was thus consequent to foreign driving forces behind the domestic elite.

Today the source French administrative law and the decisions of the French *Conseil d'Etat* are integral parts of administrative law scholarship and teaching in Turkish Law Faculties. Young administrative law academics are expected to know or to learn French, if they aim to be good and creative researchers. From time to time *Danıştay* (the Turkish *Conseil d'Etat*) decisions also make reference to French doctrine and very occasionally to French cases, though the frequency of these references has decreased, and over the years a strong local administrative law scholarship has developed, completing the infusion by the Turkish legal actors of the diffused French laws.

The Second Circle of Diffusion: Swiss Law

To reshape private law, the legislator of the Republic chose Swiss law. The 1907 Swiss Civil Code (in force in 1912) and the 1911 Swiss (Neuchatel) Code of Obligations (in force in 1912) were translated from their French versions with some alterations and modifications.[42] In 1927 the Swiss circle of diffusion spread beyond the Civil Code into the Code of Civil Procedure and in 1929 to the Code of Bankruptcy (Swiss Federal Code on Enforcement and Bankruptcy).

The infusion of the diffused Swiss Code has had an exceptional impact even on Family Law. Thus this circle of diffusion is to be regarded as the most exceptional, significant and far-reaching one, though not the first circle of diffusion to reach the shores of the legal system, as seen above. In the early years following the receptions, Turkish private law was referred to as '*İsviçre-Türk Hukuku*' (Swiss-Turkish law). There are still references to Swiss-Turkish law, thus indicating that the 'hyphenated' legal system is still in existence even nearly 90 years after the first waves of diffusion. Obviously the ties are not as strong today as they were, but especially in times of developing principles, changing general policy or introducing far-reaching change into Turkish law, and notably in 'unification

---

42   These alterations were mainly due to factors such as the different forms of the two states, cantonal laws, family law matters being different and social grounds.

of precedents',[43] the judiciary use such references either for justification or for comfort. Such references are frequent also in the usage of articles 1, 2 and 4 of the Civil Code. In addition, reference to 'the source-law' is often made in dissenting opinions in support of views for opposing majority decisions. In doctrinal works the references have always been there. Both the legal doctrine and the judges refer frequently to the works of scholars such as von Tuhr, Merz, Andrew Schwartz, Karl Lorenz, Hedemann, Egger, Escher and legislation such as the ZGB and the BGB.

For instance, in developing the principle of 'adapting contractual terms to changing circumstances' in private law contracts, reference to Swiss-Turkish law is frequent. Faced with extreme inflation and economic difficulties in the 1990s, the *Yargıtay* held the view that judges should have the power to intervene in contractual relationships and apply *clausula rebus sic stantibus* to private law contracts, or the '*imprévision*' theory, normally used for administrative contracts.

One of the most interesting of these cases deals with '*force majeure*', the 'collapse of the foundation of contract', 'the intervention of the judge into the contract', and 'adapting the contract to changing circumstances' in 'real property sales contracts by instalments' with payments to be made in foreign currency. In this case,[44] the *Yargıtay* indicated that *pacta sunt servanda* is limited by other principles of private law, the most important arising when the equilibrium of interests is distorted by supervening events. The *Yargıtay* stated that an insistence on performance may lead to a violation of article 2/2 of the Code (bad faith) and that, as an exceptional and secondary possibility, the judge can use his powers arising from article 1/1, and create rules for the facts before him to fill the gaps. The *Yargıtay* referred to a Swiss Federal Court decision, pointing out that this principle could also apply to contracts that would have future results and contracts that do not terminate by performance. Here justification was sought from the Federal Court of 'the source-law' when articles 1, 2 and 4 of the Civil Code were put into action and developments in the principle of adaptation were suggested.[45]

In a law-suit related to a contract of sale, the *Yargıtay*, after indicating that the applicable provision, article 2 of the Turkish Code of Civil Procedure is based on the Neuchatel Code, stipulated that: 'Though we should look at our own provisions, in our interpretation of our laws we cannot give up looking at the original texts, the source-laws'.[46] This maxim was already established by a 'unification of precedents' in 1945. The court went on to say that even though the parties may have agreed on the price of the real property, the court should determine its value independently, and article 2 must be understood in the manner enacted in the 'source-law'.

---

43   This type of decisions of the *Yargıtay* is binding on all lower courts.

44   95/145; 95/3339; 6.4.1995; 21 *Yargıtay Kararları Dergisi* 1995, 911. Turkish cases have been translated by the author.

45   The Federal Court accepted the doctrine of 'adaptation' on 4.5.1952 at 916.

46   2006/14–692; 2006/702; 8.11.2006, (2006) 32 *Yargıtay Kararları Dergisi*, 1902–1907.

In another unification of precedents, this time in a very different area, that of natural paternity, illegitimacy and inheritance rights, the *Yargıtay* unified the decisions of various of its chambers to the effect that when a natural child's paternity is determined by a court decision, that child becomes an illegitimate child and can inherit from the father according to the amended article 443 of the then Civil Code.[47] The *Yargıtay* looked specifically to the developments that have taken place in Switzerland as 'the source-law', 'the jurisdiction from where we took our Civil Code',[48] and pointed to the reforms there in 1976, stating that the two types of suits for paternity have been abolished and that no difference now exists between children who are acknowledged and those whose paternity has been determined by court decision. The *Yargıtay* then held that this was the path to be followed, and that Turkish law should be evaluated in keeping with contemporary and comparative developments.

There is also reliance on 'the source-law' where dissenting opinions seek support in opposing the majority decisions. In a case revolving around whether the invalidation of the inheritance rights of a father could have an impact on the rights of his heir,[49] the dissenting opinion discussed Swiss law, although the decision itself did not. The same was the case when possession leading to ownership was the issue and the discussion revolved around when the 20-year period needed for the duration of such possession, started.[50]

Turkish doctrine and jurisprudence also avail themselves of the Swiss doctrine and practice when interpreting several provisions and filling legal gaps such as in one case where, in the unification of precedents, the *Yargıtay* said: 'Regarding interpretation of our laws, though in principle we take into account our own texts, we cannot refrain from examining their origins'.[51]

'Family home' is a novel concept introduced into Turkish law by the 2002 Civil Code. In order to be able to rely on good faith, the third parties must establish the consent of the non-owner spouse to the sale of such property, even though the non-owner spouse may not have asked for the entry of this fact into the land register (article 169). The *Yargıtay* referred to the reasoning of article 169 to show that it was adopted from article 193 of the Swiss Civil Code, which introduced an exception to the general rule by curtailing the freedom of the owner spouse to dispose of his/her property. Nevertheless the concept of the general understanding and protection of 'good faith' was deemed to be pivotal to the case, and the decision was reached to protect the third party. On this issue there was one rather long dissenting opinion, this time claiming that though Turkish law was differently arranged compared to the Swiss law on this point, it was still the case that the Swiss doctrine and

---

47 96/1; 97/1; 22.2.1997; 23 *Yargıtay Kararları Dergisi* 1997, 853.

48 *ZGB*. Articles 252, 261. Ibid. 856.

49 96/2–888; 97/306; 9.4.1997; 23 *Yargıtay Kararları Dergisi* 1997, 1687.

50 2007/1; 2007/1; 19.1.2007, (2007) 33 *Yargıtay Kararları Dergisi*, 613–25.

51 See E. Özsunay, *Medeni Hukuka Giriş (Introduction to Civil Law)* (5th edn, Istanbul, 1986) 218.

jurisprudence, as well as Turkish doctrine, and more important, the wording of the Turkish Civil Code, necessitate the protection of the non-owner spouse.[52]

The Third Circle of Diffusion: Italian Law

The waves from the Italian criminal law reached the shores of Turkey and diffused into the Turkish legal system, and the 1889 Italian Criminal Code was translated into Turkish, though with amendments, indicating an original infusion. In the area of criminal law and criminal procedure, there are references even today to 'the source-laws', the Italian Criminal Code and German Code of Criminal Procedure, though, as would be expected, in these areas there are fewer references to 'the source-laws'. Here culture and context justify variations. These references are mostly in dissenting opinions rather than in the decisions themselves and are resorted to in order to challenge mistaken interpretation of the then 1926 Turkish Criminal Code and the 1929 Code of Criminal Procedure. Mistakes in translation at the time of reception are pointed out and the *Yargıtay* is called upon to search for the true meanings in the original versions.

For instance, in a case concerning 'murder to facilitate the committing of another crime', the dissenting opinion claimed that the term 'crime' in articles 135, 150 and 163 of the Code of Criminal Procedure was a mistaken translation of the term 'act' in 'the source-law', the term 'action' used in article 257 was the correct translation.[53] The dissenting judge said, 'as can be seen, as a result of giving wrong meanings to terms and concepts, the Turkish practice has become divorced from the laws of the legal systems that inspired it'.[54]

In a case[55] related to causing bodily harm to, and the maltreatment of, members of the family, again the dissenting judge referred to mistakes in translation and interpretation. He criticised the established view of the *Yargıtay* that regards the term 'a number of persons' as more than three, and 'a few persons' as three. According to him these variations do not exist in the Italian 'source-law', where the term '*plu persone*' is used to indicate more than two persons. The dissenting judge said:

> While the law was being interpreted, "the-source law" should have been consulted. It should not have been forgotten that the Turkish Criminal Code is the outcome of a reception and translation. Therefore, it is necessary to correct mistakes in translation by "corrective interpretation". The only acceptable departure from "the source-laws" is where the legislature has shown reasons for this departure in debate in Parliament. Therefore, whenever necessary the Italian Code and reasoning must be used.[56]

---

52   2006/2–591; 2006/624; 4.10.2006, (2006) 32 *Yargıtay Kararları Dergisi* 1889–1901.
53   97/1–76; 97/114; 13.5.1997; 23 *Yargıtay Kararları Dergisi* 1997, 1608 at 1615.
54   Ibid. at 1616.
55   96/8022; 96/9095; 3.12.1996; 23 *Yargıtay Kararları Dergisi* 1997, 617.
56   Ibid. at 620.

In 2005, the Turkish Criminal Code was amended and this new Code is also influenced by German law. This leads us into the fourth circle of diffusion.

The Fourth Circle of Diffusion: German Law

German law was a significant contributor to the development of the Turkish legal system. Its diffusion took place most prominently in the area of commercial law. Not only does the German Commercial Code form the basis of the Turkish one of 1926, but the 2011 Turkish Commercial Code derives most of its amendments from the German Code.[57] German diffusion can also be observed in Procedures, both civil and criminal, as seen above. In addition, after the setting up of the Constitutional Court (the *Anayasa Mahkemesi*) in Turkey in 1963, both the structure and the decisions of the German Constitutional Court served as models. As earlier indicated, the new 2005 Criminal Code is also heavily influenced by the German Criminal Code and doctrine.

As an illustration of its infusion into Commercial law, we can point to a case, in which sections 3 and 21 of the Commercial Code were applied, where the *Yargıtay* had to determine what a commercial act was and whether delictual activities could be considered commercial acts in relation to insurance policies.[58] According to the *Yargıtay*, in Turkish, German and Swiss laws, this delictual act should be regulated by the Commercial Code or be regarded as a commercial act both in view of the victim and the perpetrator in order to consider the possibility of drawback interest for delictual acts.[59] There was also some discussion in the dissenting opinions of German 'source-law' and doctrine on this issue.

In another case[60] dealing with letters of guarantee, bills of lading and 'clear on board', and the resolution of the question as to whether the carrier is free of liability when the sender enters wrong information on the bill of lading, the *Yargıtay* first indicated that the topic had been widely discussed in international law, and then referred to letters of guarantee (clear on board) in the French and the German Commercial Codes, showing that there is no agreement on the point.

Concluding Remarks

Laws of European origin, themselves the product of centuries long inter-receptions, diffusions, displacements and translocations, had their full impact on Turkey in the past century; not in ripples but in waves creating a tsunami both in legal and social terms. The four circles of diffusion blended when they reached Turkey and this blend gave Turkish law its civilian laic character: the Turkish legal system; this

---

57   Some other of the provisions derive from Swiss law and even English law.
58   94/2242; 94/7490; 10.11.1994; 21 *Yargıtay Kararları Dergisi* 1995, 425.
59   Ibid. 428.
60   93/565; 94/3295; 21.4.1994; 20 *Yargıtay Kararları Dergisi* 1994, 1782.

locale, became a delta. Diffusion was realised through translation; the Turkish elite and the translators enabled the spreading of the waves into the Turkish legal and social soil. Infusion was to follow with the work of German, Austrian and French professors, their academic translators and, later on, the courts. The law developed after 1930 in Turkey is the continuation of the trend that started between 1926 and 1930.

In the last decade, law in Turkey has been in transition. Developments such as the new 2002 Civil Code, the 2005 Criminal Code, 2005 Code of Criminal Procedure, 2007 Law on Private International Law and International Civil Procedure, 2011 Code of Civil Procedure, 2011 Code of Obligations and the 2011 Commercial Code, with the aim of further integration with Western Europe and the European Union, can be regarded as related to this steady line of development with further new waves of diffusion from Western Europe spreading even further, enlarging the delta. The desire now is to connect further to trans-national history.

The initial official programme was geared to eliminate any kind of personal choice regarded as undesirable by the formal legal system and a strong effort was made to achieve infusion. The major receptions took place while the legal system was in the process of evolving and incomplete. Thus no significant obstacles or barriers existed in the way of the incoming waves. The legal tradition was certainly 'weak' and open to foreign legal and cultural intrusion.[61] The dissolved substances (law in this case) continued passing through the porous membranes (of the Turkish legal system) by osmosis.[62] In fact, some of the existing institutions of the Republic were themselves objects of earlier diffusion and infusion, such as French laws. Nevertheless, as there was no direct social contact between the models and the recipient, the culture of the masses, though changed, remained on the whole unrelated to the models in spite of domestic efforts to change the people. Because of this factor, though there was no 'limited diffusion', the most important aspect of this extreme case of diffusion must be the infusion of the diffused and transposition

We know that, 'borrowing and imitation is [...] of central importance to understanding the course of legal change', and 'the birth of a rule or institution is a rarer phenomenon than its imitation'.[63] Monateri goes even further and says that practically every system has grown from 'contaminations'.[64] Moreover the Turkish case provides additional evidence that there is not much that is original in law.

Thus, the Turkish experience can be presented as the story of four circles of diffusion infusing the Turkish legal system and Turkey as the locale where different circles of diffusion meet and their waves overlap and intermingle.

---

61   See Monateri (n2) 85.

62   See (n12).

63   Sacco says that 'between two totally different systems, an overall reception is easier than wide-ranging imitation of particular rules and institutions'. The Turkish case vindicates this view. See R. Sacco 'Legal formants: A dynamic approach to comparative law' (Instalment ii of ii) (1991) 39 *American Journal of Comparative Law* 343 at 400, and 394, 397.

64   Monateri (n2) 107.

Chapter 3

The Diffusion of Western Legal Concepts in Kuwait: Reflections on the State, the Legal System and Legal Education from Comparative and Historical Perspectives

Myra Williamson

Introduction

This chapter examines the diffusion of Western legal concepts in Kuwait. Before embarking on this project, a few introductory remarks are proffered regarding the chapter's purpose and perspective.

First, it adopts a *prima facie* comparative law approach but it is interdisciplinary to the extent that law is always (necessarily) interdisciplinary. The borders between the study of law, politics, history, economics, geography, language, sociology, psychology, religion, philosophy, anthropology and virtually any other area of study in the humanities, are always somewhat blurred. The more one learns about the law and different legal systems, the fuzzier those borders become. That is a good thing. The law is a social construct and it can never be studied with any meaning in isolation from the contributions made by those other branches of the humanities.

Second, this is not a pure 'comparative law' text in the sense of comprehensively and systematically comparing two or more legal systems. A few tentative comparisons are drawn between Kuwait and New Zealand without artificially extending this comparison beyond what it can stand but this chapter does not purport to provide a comprehensive comparative analysis of the New Zealand and Kuwaiti legal systems. The purpose is to explore the diffusion of Western legal concepts in Kuwait in three specific areas.

Third, the final form of this chapter was influenced by the theme of the conference for which it was originally researched and written.[1] The author was originally motivated to focus on the concept of 'diffusion' as that term is understood

1   The conference which provided the impetus for writing this chapter was the inaugural conference of Juris Diversitas organised in conjunction with the Swiss Institute of Comparative Law. The theme of the conference was: 'Diffusion: An International, Interdisciplinary Conference on Comparative Law' and the conference was held in Lausanne, Switzerland, 3–5 June 2013. A slightly different version of this text was published in the

in comparative law. With teaching and/or research experience in areas as diverse as public international law, jurisprudence, comparative law, constitutional law, company law, terrorism and international law, law and societies and legal terminology in English, one often notices connections and relationships between subject areas. In all these areas of teaching and research one may unconsciously undertake comparative legal analysis without calling it by that name. The overlaps that exist between discrete subjects of law study and comparative law have been described and discussed in the literature.[2] However, the author does not purport to be an expert in the field of comparative law thus the conclusions offered here will no doubt benefit from further research.

The fourth and final introductory comment is a self-admonishment: there are several dangers in utilising comparative law methodology, many of which were identified by the famous legal comparativist, Alan Watson, in his intriguing book, *Legal Transplants*.[3] Watson wrote a chapter called 'The Perils of Comparative Law' which contains several warnings for budding legal comparativists including his statement that 'comparative law is superficial' – a peril that is usually compounded with simply getting the foreign law wrong. Watson intoned that '[e]rror of law is probably more common in Comparative Law than in any other branch of legal study'.[4] Watson's 'third peril' of comparative law methodology is that 'comparative law can scarcely be systematic'.[5] These warnings apply to the current inquiry: in selecting a few concepts for discussion, this chapter is far from a systematic and comprehensive analysis but hopefully it will provide some food for thought.

Definitions: 'Diffusion' of 'Western Legal Concepts'

It is appropriate to briefly clarify two terms used in the title of this chapter. There is a body of *diffusion* research in various areas of the humanities. As noted by Carolan:

> Diffusion research combines scholarship in areas such as sociology, anthropology, psychology, marketing and communication studies *to examine the process by which ideas and innovations spread*.[6] (Emphasis added)

Kuwait International Law School Journal (June 2013) 1: 2 and the publishers have kindly given permission for a later version to be published here.

2   For example, see M. Reimann, 'Comparative law and neighbouring disciplines' in M. Bussani and U. Mattei (eds), *The Cambridge Companion to Comparative Law* (Oxford University Press, 2012) 18–34.

3   A. Watson, *Legal Transplants – An Approach to Comparative Law* (2nd edn, University of Georgia Press, 1993) 10–15.

4   Ibid. 11.

5   Ibid.

6   E. Carolan, 'Diffusing bad ideas: What the migration of the separation of powers means for comparative constitutionalism and constitutional transplants' (1 July 2010) Hart

This chapter adopts Carolan's interpretation of diffusion: research that looks at the process by which legal ideas and legal innovations have spread. 'Diffusion' is a concept that is gaining ground in comparative law circles and it is appearing frequently as a focus point for discussion.[7] That is not to say that it is a new term but it has, arguably, been more associated with the hard sciences and the social sciences generally rather than law in particular.[8] As for the phrase 'Western legal concepts', this is a little trickier to define. The phrase could be the subject of a chapter in and of itself. Here, it is used in a fairly loose way to refer to legal concepts that could be traced to Ancient Greece or Rome, but are likely to be traceable to more recent developments in either Europe or the United States. 'The West' is a term that is used (overused) frequently, supposedly without any need for definition or clarification. Perhaps it has lost its exact meaning over time although it seems to refer to anything belonging to Western Europe and any of the countries that trace their origins to that region, which share common values, traditions and religion. This chapter will touch on selected concepts such as the notion of the sovereign state, the separation of powers, the rule of law and common law and civil law legal traditions, which are all usually accepted as Western legal concepts. However, it is noted that arguments could be raised against such a classification. To round out this point, the author agrees with the view, expressed more elegantly by Glenn, that '[t]he "West", as it is usually described, contains some of the "East". The French expression "mixité" thus best describes the common condition of humanity'.[9]

Diffusion: 'The West', Kuwait and New Zealand

An analysis of the diffusion of Western legal concepts in the Kuwaiti legal system ought to begin with some background information regarding the Kuwaiti legal system. However, whilst researching Kuwaiti legal history, the author began to notice some unexpected parallels with New Zealand legal history. New Zealand has a common law legal system and was formerly a colony of Great Britain. The exact date on which New Zealand gained its full independence from Great Britain is not a simple matter to ascertain. Perhaps it could be said to have occurred in 1947 when the New Zealand Parliament adopted the Statute of Westminster Adoption Act, giving it full legislative powers. That date is not conclusive, however, as

---

Legal Workshop, 2010 available at <http://papers.ssrn.com/sol3/papers.cfm?abstract_id=2203680> accessed on 1 June 2013.

7   For example, see the title of the Juris Diversitas conference (n2). See also a conference entitled 'From diffusion of practice to practices of diffusion: Workshop on the circulation of ideas, procedures and regulations in culture, law and economy' held in Poland in May 2014.

8   For an interesting discussion of the gap between social science writing on diffusion and legal literature on transplantation, and the implications for legal diffusion, see W. Twining, 'Social science and diffusion of law' (2005) 32 *Journal of Law and Society* 203–40.

9   H.P. Glenn, *Legal Traditions of the World* (4th edn, Oxford University Press, 2010) 39.

the constitutional changes that were needed to completely separate New Zealand from Great Britain occurred slowly and in stages over many years. As all students of comparative law seem destined to repeat, there are both similarities and differences between New Zealand's path to independence and Kuwait's. It is noted at the outset that Kuwait is a mainly civil law legal system, which was a former British protectorate – it gained independence in 1961. At the risk of falling into one of Watson's other 'perils' (choosing systems for study which have no proper relationship, thereby leading to conclusions which are lacking in significance),[10] there are some Western legal concepts, familiar to a New Zealand observer, which are visible in the Kuwaiti legal system and worthy of discussion.

Three main areas are discussed below: the concept of the 'state', the classification of Kuwait's legal system and legal education in Kuwait. They are discussed in a particular order, moving from broad observations towards more narrowly focused ones. The objective is to identify Western legal and/or political concepts and determine to what extent the Kuwait legal system is influenced by the diffusion, dissemination, transmission and movement of those so-called Western concepts.[11]

Diffusion of the Concept of 'the State'

Kuwait, officially known as 'The State of Kuwait' or (in Arabic) *'Dawlat al Kuwayt'*, is a small state in the Middle East that has a 222-kilometre land border with the Kingdom of Saudi Arabia to the south, and a 242-kilometre land border with Iraq to the north.[12] On its eastern coast it is bordered by the waters of the Persian Gulf. As for its government, Kuwait is sometimes described as a 'nominal constitutional monarchy'[13] or as a 'constitutional emirate'.[14] Kuwait has some democratic features: Article 6 of the Kuwait Constitution states that 'the system of government in Kuwait shall be democratic'. Whilst it is often lauded as the most democratic of the Gulf States it is arguably not a 'democracy' in the sense in which that term is usually defined in the literature since it does not satisfy all the generally accepted criteria.[15] The question of whether Kuwait is or is not a

---

10   Ibid.

11   Assuming, of course, that we can call these 'Western' concepts. That is taken for granted here, but see discussion above.

12   International Business Law Publications, *Kuwait Business Law Handbook – Volume 1 Strategic Information and Basic Laws* (International Business Publications, 2012).

13   Ibid. 12.

14   Central Intelligence Agency, *World FactBook – Kuwait* available at <https://www.cia.gov/library/publications/the-world-factbook/geos/ku.html> accessed on 1 June 2013.

15   A democracy could be said to possess four minimum characteristics: 1) free, fair and competitive elections; 2) full adult suffrage; 3) basic civil liberties, including freedom of speech, press and association; and 4) the absence of non-elected authorities such as militaries, monarchies and non-elected bodies that limit the governing power of elected officials: see R.A. Dahl, *Polarchy: Participation and Opposition* (Yale University Press,

genuine democracy could be discussed here (is democracy a 'Western legal concept' anyway?) but it entails a wider discussion, which is beyond the scope of the current chapter. Kuwait gained independence from Great Britain on 19 June 1961 in an amicable split. The Constitution of the State of Kuwait was approved and promulgated on 11 November 1962. Article 1 of the Constitution states that, 'Kuwait is an Arab State, independent and fully sovereign'. Article 2 states that 'The religion of the State is Islam and the Islamic *Shari'a* shall be a main source of legislation'. Kuwait is a Muslim country with a Sunni/Shi'a split usually estimated at approximately 70/30 respectively. It is noted that Islamic *Shari'a* is a main source of legislation in Kuwait but it is not the *only* or even the *main* source of legislation. The debate around that particular wording in Article 2 is interesting and is discussed elsewhere [16] Yet hidden amongst these mainly straightforward and fairly well known facts about Kuwait lies the first point to be raised in this chapter: the very existence of the 'State of Kuwait' as a sovereign and independent *state* is evidence of a profound diffusion of Western political and legal concepts.

It is contended that in Islam there is no concept of a nation state. Various writers have explored whether the concept of a 'state' existed in the traditional Islamic sources (the *Qur'an* and *Sunnah*) and the consensus seems to be that Islam did not provide for 'states' in so far as that concept is understood today.[17] Islam was not a political movement – it did not seek to create political or legal entities.[18] At the time that the *Qur'an* was revealed, there were no 'states' in existence and, as an aside, the concept of a state did not exist in pre-Islamic Arabia either.[19] Kuwait has a long archaeological record that pre-dates Islam. The earliest traces of civilisation in what is modern-day Kuwait, can be traced back to the second

---

1971). It would be interesting to assess Kuwait against each of those four criteria in turn. Currently, Kuwait does not satisfy 3) and 4) in the author's opinion. Other writers have also treated Kuwait as a non-democracy. For example, see J. Goldenziel, 'Veiled political questions: Islamic dress, constitutionalism and the ascendance of courts' (2013) 61 *American Journal of Comparative Law* 1, in which she discusses judicial independence in non-democracies. Goldenziel categorises Kuwait as a 'hybrid' in so far as it has both democratic and authoritarian features. A discussion of the meaning of 'democracy' and Kuwait's satisfaction of democratic criteria is beyond the scope of the present chapter.

16   For example, see M. al-Moqatei, 'Introducing Islamic law in the Arab Gulf States' (1989) 4 *Arab Law Quarterly* 138, for a discussion of this provision.

17   For example, see A.A. Engineer, 'Asia-Pacific Human Rights Information Center' (1999) 16 *FOCUS* wherein he notes that: 'A thorough examination of the scripture and Hadith literature shows that there is no such concept of Islamic state' available online at <http://www.hurights.or.jp/archives/focus/section2/1999/06/the-concept-of-islamic-state.html> accessed 30 May 2013.

18   Ibid.: 'the *Qur'an* lays more emphasis on values, ethics and morality than on any political doctrines. It is *Din* (religion) which matters more than governance. Allah says in the *Qur'an* that *al-yauma akmaltu lakum dinakum* (I have perfected your *Din* today, 5:3). Thus what the *Qur'an* gives us is a perfect *Din*, not a perfect political system'.

19   Ibid.: 'the pre-Islamic Arab society had not known any state structure'.

millennium BCE with the colonisation of the island of Failaka (or Icarus) by the Mesopotamians and then later by the Greeks. It came under the Islamic caliphate during Arab expansions throughout the Arabian Peninsula. It seems fairly well accepted that the area was permanently settled by the Bani Khalid tribe around the seventeenth century.[20]

It is also fairly well-accepted that the 'sovereign state' is a Westphalian creation, dating back to the signing of the Peace of Westpahlia in 1648. Glenn notes that nationality and statehood 'appear historically as creations of the western enlightenment'.[21] The notion of the state has become an enduring concept of international law and politics that now permeates and dominates the global community. The modern State of Kuwait, as with all other Muslim-majority nations, has completely embraced the Westphalian notion of the sovereign state and (almost) all that that entails. Space does not permit a detailed analysis here of the concept of the 'Islamic state'; that substantial topic has been explored elsewhere.[22] The point made here is a simple one: it is interesting that a modern 'State of Kuwait'[23] has evolved and exists today, given that the land, which is now modern Kuwait, was once occupied by nomadic, tribal, people who fished for pearls and seaweed, and herded camels without any notion of statehood. The people of the land that later became the State of Kuwait had no interest in the concept of states, with their related requirements of borders, passports, citizenship, immigration, policing and the like. They moved freely around the land of the Arabian peninsula as members of the wider Muslim '*umma*'. Yet when one speaks to a young Kuwaiti law student today one observes that their understanding of the notion of a 'state' is integral to their self-identity and they consider that the concept of their state sits easily alongside their Islamic beliefs, of which they are equally and justifiably proud. They take Kuwait's statehood for granted.[24] Vehicles in Kuwait are occasionally seen emblazoned with stickers that loudly and proudly state that 'Kuwait is for Kuwaitis'[25] and it is clear that modern Kuwaitis identify closely with their *state* as it is currently defined, politically and geographically.

---

20   Oxford Business Group, *The Report Kuwait 2013* (Oxford Business Group, 2013).

21   Glenn (n9) 38.

22   For instance, see W. Hallaq, *The Impossible State: Islam, Politics and Modernity's Moral Predicament* (Columbia University Press, 2012).

23   The name of 'Kuwait' comes from a diminutive of an Arabic word that literally means 'fortress built near water'.

24   The meaning of a 'state' is clearly defined in international law, but arguably the definition is a Western-oriented definition focusing on the need to have a permanent population, a clearly defined territory, a government and the capacity to enter into relations with other states: see article 1 of the *Montevideo Convention on the Rights and Duties of States, League of Nations Treaty Series* vol. 165, 20–43.

25   This phrase was seen on a sign in the Kuwaiti Parliament. Member of Parliament Mohammed al-Juwaihel placed a sign on the podium in front of him reading (in Arabic) 'Kuwait is for Kuwaitis', which apparently was meant as a protest at other Members of Parliament who possess dual citizenship: see *Arab Times Online* (8 May 2013), available at

It has been taken as a given that Kuwaitis are part of a state and there is little pause for thought about the theoretical underpinnings of the origins of the concept of the 'state'.

The state of Kuwait is, according to Article 2 of the Constitution, based on Islamic values. This creates a strange juxtaposition of Islamic and Western political and legal concepts since, as noted above, Islam itself does not recognise the concept of 'states' – it recognises only a Muslim '*umma*'. An 'Islamic state', then, is practically a contradiction in terms. But this is not a conclusion that could be easily drawn from observing modern-day Kuwait. Take for example the English language newspapers in Kuwait: they frequently feature stories about how to best preserve Kuwait for Kuwaitis. Articles and opinion pieces abound in the English-language press on how to best reduce the number of foreigners residing here (the stated goal is to reduce foreigners by 100,000 per year), how to protect Kuwaiti nationality and why some 'stateless' or '*bidoon*' people may or may not be entitled to Kuwaiti citizenship. On top of that, for decades now, Kuwait has struggled with its neighbours over the exact location of its borders. When these facts are read with 'diffusion' in mind, it is clear that Kuwaitis have, as a society, completely embraced and internalised a Western political and legal paradigm – the sovereign and independent Westphalian nation state.

It is submitted here that the diffusion of Western laws and legal concepts has occurred on a large-scale and those Western constructs have been assimilated to such an extent that the present generation of Kuwaiti law students do not notice the origins of these laws and concepts as being Western at all. When this author taught a class on public international law, only one student was aware that the sovereign state dates to the Peace of Westphalia. There is a tendency to accept that what is, has always been. Thus, the first area of diffusion of Western legal concepts relates to the very nature of the state construct and the subtle yet undeniably successful diffusion of this Western concept in the Islamic society and Arab nation of Kuwait (and of course, in the wider Muslim world). The flow-on effects of adopting the sovereign state, such as nationality and citizenship, are also necessarily diffused and transmitted.

Before moving to the second main point of this chapter, it is worth noting that there are other areas related to the constitution of the sovereign state that could be explored in here if space permitted; two in particular spring to mind. Without going into much depth, these are separation of powers and the rule of law.

Separation of Powers

First, the concept of 'separation of powers', which is certainly evident in the Kuwaiti Constitution, is possibly a Western concept and capable of inclusion here.

<http://www.arabtimesonline.com/NewsDetails/tabid/96/smid/414/ArticleID/182995/reftab/36/Default.aspx> accessed 1 June 2013. Dual citizenship is forbidden in the State of Kuwait.

The ideas of the French aristocrat Montesquieu may be 'Western' but whether or not they were *first* thought of by Montesquieu is a topic worthy of further analysis. It could be argued that it was a Muslim leader who first practiced the separation of powers in government. The second Caliph of Islam, Umar ibn Al-Khattab (may Allah be pleased with him), is sometimes cited as the first ruler in the history of the world to separate the judiciary from the executive.[26] If that is the case then the 'separation of powers' would not be evidence of a diffusion of Western legal/political concepts to Kuwait but a diffusion of an Islamic concept to the West. That claim cannot be properly investigated here and is beyond the scope of this chapter. Suffice to say that the modern understanding of the 'separation of powers' does exist in modern Kuwait and is now enshrined in the Kuwaiti Constitution.

The Rule of Law

Secondly, there is a substantial body of literature on the diffusion of the concept of 'the rule of law', which is tempting to delve into here. The 'rule of law' has a deep historical lineage, possibly traceable to ancient Greece but certainly evident in, and usually referenced to, the English *Magna Carta/Charta* of 1215.[27] Thus, it may seem to qualify as a 'Western legal concept' but on the other hand it may also be disputed that 'the rule of law' is originally a Western concept. There is much scholarly writing on Islamic constitutionalism, which suggests that 'the rule of law' concept as understood in light of the *Magna Carta* was already practiced in the early years of Islam by the Prophet Muhammad (peace be upon him) and by the 'rightly-guided Caliphs'.[28] Notably, Islam (historically) never had cause to be troubled with rulers claiming to be divinely inspired, as in England. The Prophet Muhammad and the following four 'rightly-guided Caliphs' never claimed to hold their position because God had appointed them to rule. The Prophet Muhammad like the rulers who followed him, ruled in accordance with God's law not as God's representative on Earth. The 'rule of law', which is captured in the *Magna Carta*, was a reaction to the assertion of the 'divine right of kings' to rule, but the Islamic

---

26   The discussion as to whether the judiciary was a separate branch of government, and Umar ibn al-Khattab's role in separating the judiciary from the executive is discussed in A.U. Rehman, M. Ibrahim and I.A. Baker, 'The concept of independence of judiciary in Islam' (2013) 4(2) *International Journal of Business and Social Science* 67, 69 and elsewhere.

27   For a brief summary of the history of the rule of law see 'The legal history of the rule of law', available at <http://www.mansfieldfdn.org/backup/programs/program_pdfs/leghistory.pdf> accessed 23 July 2013. See also U. Mattei and D. Morpungo, 'Global law and plunder: The dark side of the rule of law' (2009) *Law and Globalization* Bocconi Law School Student-Edited Papers, available at <http://papers.ssrn.com/sol3/papers.cfm?abstract_id=1437530>.

28   For instance, see Aziza al-Hibri, 'Islamic constitutionalism and the concept of democracy' (1992) 24 (1) *Case Western Reserve Journal of International Law* 1.

caliphs never asserted that God had appointed them to rule. Instead, they sourced their authority from the people: the *bay'ah* or declaration of allegiance from the people was the factor that determined the leader.[29] Therefore, the 'rule of law' in Islam began from a different place to that of its counterpart in the West. These days, things are done somewhat differently. Although the *bay'ah* or declaration of allegiance is still theoretically taken, the constitution of Kuwait in common with its other Gulf neighbours, severely curtails who is eligible to be the leader. In Kuwait, only the male descendants of the late Mubarak al-Sabah are eligible to hold the title of Emir.[30] Another aspect of the 'rule of law' is that all people are equally bound by the law and no one is above the law. In the author's personal experience, that aspect of the rule of law does not effectively exist in Kuwait. For example, in a recent conversation with the customer services representative of the Al Shaya Group, which owns many of the malls in Kuwait, the author was told that although it is against the law to smoke in public places, such as malls, the management of the malls cannot stop some people from smoking because 'some government people believe that they are above the law'.[31] In light of the foregoing, it would be an interesting topic in its own right to discuss the extent to which the 'rule of law' is or is not a Western concept and, furthermore, the extent to which the rule of law exists in the modern State of Kuwait, given that the religion of the State is Islam and *Shari'a* is a main source of legislation.[32]

These two areas – the separation of powers and the rule of law – are not explored in this chapter since they require substantial research and more space than can be afforded here. Suffice to say that comparative constitutional law provides a fruitful opportunity to discuss the diffusion of 'Western legal concepts' in Kuwait, yet the logical starting point would have to be to first determine what *is* a 'Western' concept. The short discussion above shows that determining what counts as a 'Western' concept is, itself, a difficult question.

Diffusion of Western Legal Concepts within the Kuwaiti Legal System

The second main area of analysis in this chapter relates more directly to the Kuwaiti legal system. Kuwait has an interesting and complex legal history. Kuwait's legal system appears to be an amalgam of two legal systems. As mentioned above,

---

29   Ibid., especially at 11–12.

30   See Article 4 of the Kuwait Constitution 1962.

31   Conversation between the author and a representative of the Al-Shaya Group on 18 February 2014 in response to the author's complaint about excessive smoking in cafés and restaurants in the malls owned by that group. The words in quotation marks are the exact words spoken by the customer service representative. She freely admitted that people who worked for the government often did not respect the law and moreover did not believe that they had to adhere to the law.

32   See Article 2 of the Kuwait Constitution 1962. For a discussion of the negative aspects of the diffusion of the rule of law, see Mattei and De Morpurgo (n27).

Islamic *Shari'a* (or Islamic Law) is present in Kuwait and regulates personal status, that is, laws relating to marriage, divorce and inheritance. Sunni and Shi'a Muslims are each governed by the relevant Islamic Laws pertaining to their faith in personal areas. In all other areas, Egyptian/French-inspired codified law applies. However, it must be noted and understood that *Shari'a*'s influence is not limited to personal status laws alone. Kuwait boasts one of the largest and most diverse Islamic financial service industries in the world. Banking, investment, insurance and other financial services are influenced by Islamic laws, as are some tax laws.[33]

Although these two sources of law (Islamic *Shari'a* and Egyptian/French-inspired civil law) are both present in Kuwait, scholars classify Kuwait's legal systems differently. All comparative law scholars are familiar with the debates over classifications of legal systems. This area has historically been one of the mainstays of the discipline. Even if one finds that the topic of categorisation/taxonomies of legal families may be exhausted as an area of scholarly writing and is somewhat lacking in relevance for present-day challenges, nevertheless, it is still a good starting point to ask how a particular legal system has been classified. Vernon Valentine Palmer classifies Kuwait as a '[m]ixed system of civil law and Muslim law'[34] whereas the Central Intelligence Agency's World Factbook describes Kuwait as a 'mixed legal system consisting of English common law, French civil law and Islamic religious law'.[35] Another source classifies Kuwait as having Muslim law/civil law/customary law.[36] The discrepancy between these classifications might be explained by examining Kuwait's tangled legal history.

In 1899 Kuwait and Great Britain entered into the Anglo-Kuwaiti Treaty. This treaty promised the then ruler of Kuwait, Mubarak bin Sabah al-Sabah (and his successors) protection from outside aggression and non-interference in Kuwait's internal affairs. In return, the ruler of Kuwait was prohibited 'from establishing diplomatic relations with any other foreign power and from alienating any part of its territories to any other foreign state or foreign national without the prior consent of the British government'.[37]

---

33   For further information see the Oxford Business Group (n20).

34   V.V. Palmer, 'Mixed legal systems' in Bussani and Matei (eds), *The Cambridge Companion to Comparative Law* (Oxford University Press, 2012) at 381.

35   CIA World Factbook, Kuwait, last updated on 7 May 2013, available online at <https://www.cia.gov/library/publications/the-world-factbook/geos/ku.html> accessed 1 June 2013. Other sources that describe Kuwait with this mixture of three types of law include UNICEF: see the 2011 report on Kuwait entitled 'MENA gender equality profile Kuwait – Status of girls and women in the Middle East and North Africa' 1, available at <http://www.unicef.org/gender/files/Kuwait-Gender-Eqaulity-Profile-2011.pdf> accessed 1 June 2013.

36   JuriGlobe, University of Ottawa, Alphabetical Index of the 192 United Nations Member States and Corresponding Legal Systems, available at <http://www.juriglobe.ca/eng/syst-onu/index-alpha.php> accessed 14 October 2013.

37   A. Hijazi, 'Kuwait: Development from a semitribal, semicolonial society to democracy and sovereignty' (1964) 13 (4) *American Journal of Comparative Law* 428–9.

The relationship between Kuwait and Great Britain led, in 1925, to the establishment in Kuwait of the British Jurisdiction, which was separate from, but running side-by-side with, the National Jurisdiction. In effect, there were two completely separate legal systems operating in Kuwait until its independence from Great Britain in 1961. The National Jurisdiction (which applied to approximately 250,000 people) embraced all Kuwaiti citizens, nationals of independent Arab States, nationals of Iran and citizens of British-protected states in the Persian Gulf. According to Ahmed Hijaz , a Registrar of the British Court in Kuwait in 1954, the National Jurisdiction was semi-tribal except in personal status matters, which were (and still are) governed by Islamic Law.[38] Interestingly, under the National Jurisdiction there were no written laws, no procedure and no defined courts. Hijazi observed as follows:

> It is true that in theory the Majellah (the Ottoman Civil Code, based on Islamic Law) was the law of the land but in practice the law was the conscience of the official dispensing justice [...][39]

The British Jurisdiction (which applied to approximately 30,000 people) embraced all other persons in the State. These 'other persons' consisted mainly of British subjects, citizens of all nations of the British Commonwealth, mainly Indians and Pakistanis, citizens of the United States and a few Greeks, Germans and Italian citizens who came to Kuwait with the oil boom.[40] According to Hijazi:

> The British Jurisdiction was administered along English lines. The laws and procedure applied were based on English principles, and the courts functioned like an English court in England, the main difference being the absence of the jury system in Kuwait.[41]

There were apparently substantial differences between the British Jurisdiction and the National Jurisdiction, yet the two systems existed side-by-side for many years and raised many interesting questions (especially relating to conflict of laws), discussed elsewhere.[42] During the oil boom of the 1950s, the British Jurisdiction increased in importance and in the sheer number of cases to come before the British courts. Many expatriate Arabs and non-Arab foreigners were attracted to Kuwait with the development of the oil industry and they seemed to acknowledge the clear advantages of being under the British Jurisdiction rather than being 'left at the tender mercies of the arbitrary National Jurisdiction'.[43] But eventually, the British

---

38   Ibid. 429.
39   Ibid.
40   Ibid.
41   Ibid.
42   Ibid.
43   Ibid. 432.

Jurisdiction was a victim of its own success. It came under attack from various quarters, including the younger generation, the nationalists and the Islamic sheikhs who felt uneasy with the presence of the British Jurisdiction: a daily reminder of protection and semi-colonialism. The British government was under pressure to give up its jurisdiction but it did not wish to do so unless and until some sort of modern national legal system was set up in Kuwait with written laws, proper and prescribed procedures and a trained judiciary. That is where one of the most famous jurists of the time, the Egyptian Dr Abdel-Razzaq al-Sanhouri, came into the picture. Dr al-Sanhouri was one of the foremost drafters of the 1948 Egyptian Civil Code and he was commissioned by the Kuwaiti government to modernise and bring up-to-date Kuwait's legal system – which in the end meant transplanting an entire legal system. As an Egyptian he naturally turned to Egypt for inspiration. Within one year of Britain declaring, in 1959, that British Jurisdiction would be repealed and replaced as soon as an additional legal system was introduced, the Kuwaiti authorities had settled upon an entirely new and foreign legal system. As of 1 July 1961, by enactment of the British Parliament, all British courts operating in Kuwait were closed and all laws in force in those courts were repealed.

The new transplanted legal system was based heavily on the Egyptian system, which in turn was based on the French system. Thus Kuwait turned a sudden corner from having a National/Islamic/British Jurisdiction to a civil law/Islamic law system. But as Hijazi, writing in 1964, pointed out:

> [The new system] did not develop as a natural growth from either of the two systems previously in existence; it was borrowed from the outside and implanted in a very short time. This wholesale and hasty introduction of a new legal system with unfamiliar and rather complicated principles led, naturally, to a species of "indigestion" which resulted in hostility on the part of various sections of the community.[44]

Although those comments were written in 1964, the 'new system' seems to have been adopted by today's law students as the only system they have ever known and is rarely questioned. However, the 'indigestion' to which Hijazi refers may still be evident. Students routinely mention issues which rankle with them such as the extremely long periods of time it takes cases to move their way through the court system, the strong presence of foreign (mainly Egyptian) judges working in the Kuwaiti judiciary and the seemingly complex and lengthy codes which govern their entire civil law structure.

It is indisputable that Kuwait suffers in some areas from unnecessarily complicated, inflexible and sometimes outdated laws and procedures, not to mention frustrating bureaucracy. One might think that this reaction is natural, coming from a New Zealander. But this observation is not just personal bias: the International Bank for Reconstruction and Development/World Bank's *Doing*

---

44   Ibid.

Business 2013 global report comparing business regulations for domestic firms in 185 countries found that New Zealand is ranked number one in the world in terms of how easy it is to start a business. The 2013 *Doing Business* report shows that in New Zealand it is extremely easy to do business. For example, to start a company in New Zealand it takes one procedure, one day, it costs less than 1 per cent of income per capita and it requires no paid in minimum capital.[45] On the same measure, starting a company, Kuwait does not do so well,[46] being ranked 142 out of 185 countries. The difficulty of starting a company in Kuwait is evident not only in the *Doing Business* data but also in the anecdotal experiences of local business people.[47]

Looking more broadly than just starting a company, Kuwait ranks poorly across all of the *Doing Business* indicators when compared with the 184 other countries, except in two areas (protecting investors and taxes). The overall ranking for each country is generated by analysing the regulatory requirements in 10 areas, thus, a low ranking means that the regulatory framework makes it easy to do business and a high ranking means it is much harder to do business.[48]

Looking at the evidence, Kuwait is nowhere near as business-friendly as New Zealand.[49] The same could be said for the whole Middle East and North African region but Kuwait ranks surprisingly poorly against its Gulf Co-operation Council (GCC)-member neighbours.[50] Out of the six GCC member states, Kuwait ranks worst.[51] Out of the 50 states that are considered 'high income', Kuwait ranks a

---

45   *Doing Business 2013 – Smarter Regulations for Small and Medium Sized Businesses* 10th edn (World Bank/International Bank for Reconstruction and Development) at 59, available at <http://www.doingbusiness.org/~/media/GIAWB/Doingpercent20Business/ Documents/Annual-Reports/English/DB13-full-report.pdf> accessed 2 June 2013.

46   Ibid. 175, Country Tables 'Kuwait'.

47   For example, an American woman who wanted to start up a second-hand bookstore and café in Kuwait explained the difficulties and duration (six months) of dealing with Kuwait's bureaucracy in order to be granted permission: see *Arab Times Online* 'Starting Up Business in Kuwait a Nightmare', available at <http://www.arabtimesonline.com/ NewsDetails/tabid/96/smid/414/ArticleID/199621/reftab/36/t/Curiosity-can-foster-love-for-books/Default.aspx> accessed 13 October 2013.

48   The 10 areas that are surveyed in the *Doing Business* report (n45), with rankings for New Zealand and Kuwait in brackets are: Starting a business (NZ = 1; Kuwait = 82); Dealing with construction permits: (NZ = 6, Kuwait = 142); Getting electricity (NZ = 32, Kuwait = 55); Registering property (NZ = 2, Kuwait = 89); Getting credit (NZ = 4; Kuwait = 104); Protecting investors (NZ = 1, Kuwait = 32); Paying taxes (NZ = 21; Kuwait = 11); Trading across borders (NZ = 25; Kuwait = 113); Enforcing contracts (NZ = 17; Kuwait = 117); Resolving insolvency (NZ = 13; Kuwait = 92).

49   Kuwait's overall ranking is 82; New Zealand's overall ranking is 3.

50   The states in the Middle East and North Africa region rank between 22 and 171.

51   Saudi Arabia is the highest ranked GCC state in the *Doing Business* report with an ease of doing business ranking of 22; United Arab Emirates is 26; Qatar is 40; Bahrain is 42; Oman is 47 and the non-GCC Arab state of Tunisia also ranks above Kuwait with an index of 50.

lowly 45th out of 50. One might ask how much impact *the type of legal system* has on these core business performance indicators. Without wanting to delve too far into the realm of law and economics in which this author professes no expertise, it may be noted that in the area of economics and comparative law, research has been undertaken to determine whether there is a connection between economic growth in civil law as opposed to common law countries. Research has shown that 'legal systems that originated in the English common law have superior institutions for economic growth than those of French civil law'.[52] There are essentially two reasons: first, the common law provides more adequate institutions for financial markets and business transactions generally, which in turn fuels more economic growth. Secondly, civil law is based on an assumption of greater state intervention that is generally seen as being detrimental to economic growth and market efficiency. Although these conclusions are contestable, they do appear to be supported by evidence. The authors of the Oxford Business Group's 2013 report on Kuwait, a comprehensive analysis across all aspects of Kuwait's economy, mentions that 'restrictive legislation' is a key challenge in almost all areas that they survey. There is a substantial body of scholarship that suggests that there are clear and proven connections between the type of legal system and the legal origins of that legal system.[53] Many research papers suggest that common law legal systems are more effective for business than civil law legal systems. For example, a study of 49 different countries carried out in 1997 found that '[...] on all measures, common law countries provide companies with better access to equity finance than civil law countries, and particularly French civil law countries'.[54] Common law countries also have more listed companies per person than civil law countries, and far more Initial Public Offerings than civil law countries. That research also found that common law countries come out well ahead of civil law countries in the protection that they offer to shareholders. It concluded, *inter alia*, that French civil law countries have both the weakest investor protections and the least developed capital markets, especially when compared to other civil law countries.[55]

   It is interesting that Kuwait did not adopt the common law legal system of its 'coloniser' or 'protector' but it decided to transplant a legal system from Egypt. It is argued here that the Egyptian/French civil law legal transplant may have

---

52   N. Garoupa and T. Ginsburg, 'Economic analysis and comparative law' in Bussani and Mattei (n2) 67.

53   See, for example, the links at *Doing Business*: Research on Legal Origin, Institutions and Institutions, available at <http://www.doingbusiness.org/research/legal-origin-and-institutions> accessed 12 October 2013.

54   R. La Porta, F. Lopez-de-Silanes, A. Shleifer and R.W. Vishny, 'The legal environment, banks and long-run economic growth', National Bureau of Economic Research, Working Paper 5879, January 1997, available at <http://www.nber.org/papers/w5879.pdf> accessed 20 October 2013.

55   Ibid. Although Kuwait was not one of the French civil law countries, the study examined 21 French civil law countries including Egypt and France.

been a quick fix at the time, but it may not have been the best solution in the long run. Kuwait is currently hampered by an inefficient political and legislative environment which is slow to respond to business needs and difficult to navigate. It is not user friendly and is, in many areas, an obstacle to present and future progress.[56] Kuwait suffers from a public-sector dominated environment with 77 per cent of the population being employed by the government.[57] Despite Kuwait's undisputed wealth, its legislative framework is fraught with inefficiency, delay, deliberation and under-development. Although some changes have been made recently,[58] the entire legal system (business and beyond) seems to have inherited the genetic defects inherent in the French civil law legal family.

Could/should Kuwait have gone down a different path and could it/should it instead have adopted English common law? Could a different road have been travelled when it stood at the crossroads in 1961? Instead of opting for an entirely new Egyptian/French legal system, could the Kuwaiti authorities have continued with an English legal system and kept the British Jurisdiction? Could Kuwait have been a mixed Muslim law/common law legal system like, say, Singapore, Pakistan, Bangladesh and Sudan.[59] Or could Kuwait have been a mixed Muslim law/common law/customary law legal system like, say, Malaysia, Nigeria, Kenya, Brunei, Gambia and India?[60] Kuwait opted for French/Egyptian civil law over English common law and thus, according to the University of Ottawa's *JuriGlobe* classification, finds itself sharing legal system characteristics with states such as Djibouti, Eritriea, Indonesia, Jordan, Oman and Timor Leste.[61] What is interesting is to look at the various groupings of legal systems and see how they rank in terms of the ease of doing business. Out of the first group mentioned above, the mixed Muslim law/common law group, Singapore is ranked number one in the world in the 2013 *Doing Business* report (compare with Kuwait at 82). Singapore topped

---

56   For example in the area of international investment, which Kuwait is very keen to increase, the International Finance Corporation ranks Kuwait 119th out of 184 countries in terms of dealing with construction permits: see the Oxford Business Group (n45) 34.

57   Ibid. 37.

58   For example, on 29 November 2012 Kuwait officially received its new companies law after 50 years of waiting. Law No. 25 of 2012, the New Companies Law, was issued and its publication in the *Kuwait Official Gazette* marked the culmination of a long legislative process.

59   *JuriGlobe* (n36) classifies these four states as having mixed Muslim/common law legal systems: see 'Muslim law systems and mixed systems with a Muslim law tradition', available at <http://www.juriglobe.ca/eng/sys-juri/class-poli/droit-musulman.php> accessed 17 October 2013.

60   Ibid.

61   Ibid. These states are listed by *JuriGlobe* as mixed Muslim law/civil law/customary law systems. In the 2013 *Doing Business* report, the countries are ranked as follows: Djibouti = 171; Eritrea = 182; Indonesia = 128; Jordan = 106; Oman = 47; Timor-Leste = 169. See *Doing Business*, 'Economy Rankings', available at <http://www.doingbusiness.org/rankings> accessed on 17 October 2013.

the rankings in 2013 for the eighth consecutive year. The other three countries in the same group as Singapore, which also have Muslim/common law legal systems (Pakistan, Bangladesh and Sudan), do not rank well[62] but to be fair they are not high-income countries like Singapore and Kuwait so that may well impact on their overall business effectiveness.

The question of what 'might have been' for Kuwait becomes even more interesting when one focuses on the countries that have mixed Muslim/civil law legal systems.[63] Those countries are ranked very poorly in the 2013 *Doing Business* report.[64] With the exception of Tunisia, which is ranked at 50, all of the other countries with this type of legal system are in the bottom half of the *Doing Business* rankings, some at the very bottom. The *JuriGlobe* research suggests that there is one state that has a mixed Muslim law/customary law legal system, namely, the United Arab Emirates. The UAE is ranked at a respectable 26 in the *Doing Business* economy rankings.[65] One underlying message to come out of this data is that having Islamic law or customary law in a legal system's mix is *not* harmful to its chances of ranking well across a range of business indicators – it is the ingredient of *civil law* (especially *French* civil law) versus common law that seems to be the problem factor. When one looks at *JuriGlobe*'s various groupings of legal systems which have Muslim law in the mix, the only detrimental factor is the inclusion of civil law.

Whilst the World Bank's data and other scholars' research suggests that a French civil law origin is bad for business, the majority of Kuwaiti law students surveyed recently did not seem to think it was a poor choice. Asked whether Kuwait ought to have adopted British common law instead of Egyptian/French civil law, 60 per cent of students surveyed thought that the Egyptian/French choice was the right one.[66] This author has not come across any scholarly writing that openly advances the proposition that Kuwait made the wrong choice in 1961. Kuwaiti law students mainly seem to have accepted that their system is the way it is. Although they recognise that it has some defects, the majority do not think it is the wrong system,[67]

62　Pakistan = 107; Bangladesh = 127; Sudan = 143: ibid.

63　Ibid. The *JuriGlobe World Legal Systems* research lists the following countries as mixed Muslim law/civil law: Algeria, Comoros Islands, Egypt, Iran, Iraq, Lebanon, Libya, Mauritania, Morocco, Palestine, Syria and Tunisia.

64　Their overall rankings out of 185 are as follows: Algeria = 152; Comoros Islands = 156; Arab Republic of Egypt = 109; Iran = 145; Iraq = 165; Lebanon = 115; Libya = Mauritania = 167; Morocco = 97; Palestine = 135 (although it is ranked as 'West Bank and Gaza'); Syria = 144; Tunisia = 50: ibid.

65　Ibid.

66　In a survey of 45 Kuwaiti law students carried out by the author in October 2013, 27 out of 45 respondents (60 per cent) answered 'No' to the question: 'Should Kuwait have adopted British common law rather than French/Egyptian civil law in 1961?'

67　In the survey, students were asked: 'Do you think Kuwait has the "right" type of legal system for its needs?' In response, 25 out of 45 students answered, 'Yes'. Thus, 55 per cent thought that Kuwait has the right legal system.

nor do they think it should be changed.[68] They accept their legal system, although acknowledge that it is defective in some areas and in need of improvement. Despite those perceptions, the argument being advanced here is that the Kuwaiti authorities may have made an error of judgement by opting for a French civil law system in 1961. Perhaps it was more of a knee-jerk reaction to semi-colonialism and borne of a desire to end the colonial ties by ending the British Jurisdiction rather than by a desire to choose the most suitable legal system for the situation. The Egyptian jurist, Dr Sanhouri, could not be blamed for resorting to his own experience. Perhaps the Kuwaiti authorities were attracted by the comprehensive code-based approach of the civil law system, the idea that all laws are written down in one place, rather than opting for the uncodified and sometimes seemingly confusing (but more flexible) common law system. Perhaps it was just easier, since Egypt was a Muslim, Arabic-speaking country sharing more in common with Kuwait than the United Kingdom. In any case, the die was cast when Dr Sanhouri was engaged and the Kuwaiti government opted for an entirely new legal system, which, as Hijazi noted, did not develop naturally from either of the two previous systems.

Returning to the original point, about what type of legal system Kuwait possesses, it might be easier to understand the discrepancies between different categorisations when the historical context is understood: some studies classify Kuwait as a common law/Islamic law/civil law system and others choose to describe it as an Islamic law/civil law system. Kuwaiti law students are just as divided over what type of legal system they have. When surveyed, there was no clear consensus amongst 45 respondents, although there was a slight preference for classifying Kuwait as a mixed civil law/Islamic law system.[69] Students were asked to choose from a range of options and their responses varied widely. The different ways of classifying the Kuwaiti legal system by both scholars and students, professionals and amateurs, is perhaps telling of the subjective nature of making such categorisations. But it also speaks to the complexity of the legal system itself when it is so difficult to agree upon a classification and when even Kuwaiti law students cannot agree on what legal system they have.

---

68   In the survey, students were asked: 'Do you think Kuwait needs a different type of legal system?' In response, 27 students answered 'No', 16 students answered 'Yes' and one student answered 'Maybe' which was not a survey response option. Thus, 60 per cent believed that there was no need to change Kuwait's legal system.

69   In a survey of 45 students, seven students thought Kuwait has a civil law legal system, one thought it was common law, one thought it was Islamic law, one thought it was customary law, 11 thought it was mixed civil law/Islamic law, six thought it was mixed civil law/common law/Islamic law, eight thought it was mixed civil law/Islamic law/customary law, nine thought it was mixed civil law/Islamic law/common law/customary law and one student thought it was something else, which that student defined as mixed common law/ civil law. Thus, the most popular choice by students was civil law/Islamic law with 24 per cent choosing this option. Notably, there was no clear winner amongst the students as to what type of legal system they are studying.

As a postscript to the above analysis, it would be interesting to know what happened to the tribal-based customary laws that apparently existed under the National Jurisdiction. Once the 'modern' French/Egyptian civil law system was implanted in Kuwait, it may have stamped out the local and indigenous customary law. This question merits further investigation to discover whether there are still vestiges of traditional customary law present in Kuwait. Since Kuwait is still very much a tribal society, including the way that political allegiances are expressed, it would be interesting to know more about the tribal-based pre-colonial justice systems. The author is reminded of parallels with New Zealand's experiences in this regard. The indigenous Maori people, who lived in New Zealand for around 1,000 years before the British colonised it, had their own tribal customs, including tribal justice, and ways of regulating social conduct.[70] In New Zealand, indigenous legal customs were largely overridden and almost obliterated by the introduction of the British legal system, but they are nowadays re-emerging and there is an increasing interest in and knowledge of Maori customary law in New Zealand. The author has yet to come across writing on Kuwaiti customary law in English but this could well form the topic of a future text.

Before concluding this part of the chapter, a very brief reference might be made to the famous legal philosopher HLA Hart's comments in *The Concept of Law* when he discussed the meaning of 'law' and the challenges that 'primitive' societies pose. 'Are primitive legal systems law?' Hart asked, when discussing 'persistent questions' regarding the meaning of 'law'.[71] Do primitive legal systems qualify as law? Did Kuwait possess a fully-fledged customary legal system prior to the introduction of French/Egyptian civil law? And if so, are there still remnants of it today? These questions are flagged here as matters of interest that will hopefully be taken up at a later date.

Although it is clear that French/Egyptian civil law has overtaken British common law as an influence in Kuwait it is interesting to ponder what specific common law influences have remained. The author has asked comparative law students on various occasions whether they see any English common law influences in their present legal system and one of the points they raise is the modest use of *stare decisis* or precedent, the principle upon which common law legal systems are based. Some students have suggested that although precedent does not officially exist in Kuwait, and prior decisions do not bind the Kuwaiti courts, in practice judges usually do follow decisions of other courts. Lawyers

---

70   Although this is not strictly relevant to a comparative law text, the author notes that both Maori in New Zealand and some Kuwaitis have a similar social custom of greeting each other by touching noses. My students were intrigued when I shared this strange similarity with them. An anthropologist or sociologist might also draw comparisons between the traditional 'sword' dances of the Kuwaitis and the Maori war dance known as the '*haka*'. Both seem to have developed as pre-war and/or post-war dances but these days are used to celebrate special occasions.

71   H.L.A. Hart, *The Concept of Law* (2nd edn, Clarendon Press, 1994) 4.

have anecdotally mentioned to the author that in preparing cases for trial they try to find similar cases and use them successfully to influence the court's decision, just as common law lawyers would do. Although the author has tried to discover some hard evidence of this practice, no such data is available at present to substantiate this claim. If evidence can be found, this may arguably be proof that there is a surviving influence of the British Jurisdiction that once thrived in Kuwait.[72]

The Diffusion of Western Ideas in Kuwait's Legal Education

The third and final point to be pursued in relation to the diffusion of Western legal concepts in Kuwait concerns legal education. Kuwait has an interesting mix of civil and common law influences in the field of legal education. A brief catalogue of examples may be of interest (these comments are based on the author's limited personal experience teaching law in Kuwait for almost two years). First, the faculty of law in which the author is currently employed adopts American rather than British position descriptions, such as 'Assistant Professor' and 'Associate Professor' rather than 'Lecturer', 'Senior Lecturer' or 'Reader' which are more common in law schools modelled on the English model.[73] Second, there is a distinct American influence in the semesterisation of courses and the 'credit' system for organising courses in Kuwaiti legal education. Likewise the grading system and 'grade point average' utilised is American-influenced. However, there is a distinctly French/Continental/civil law influence in the division of both faculty and courses into 'public' and 'private' divisions. Staff is designated as 'professors of public law' or 'professors of private law' – a distinction that is largely foreign to law schools in common law jurisdictions such as the five that exist in New Zealand. The courses taught also reflect both civil law and common law influences but perhaps more the former than the latter. For example, the law degree at Kuwait International Law School includes courses such as 'the law of obligations' from the civil law tradition rather than the law of contract and the law of tort, which are the common law equivalents. The LLB degree in Kuwait is an undergraduate degree, as in the UK, unlike the US where the equivalent 'JD' can only be studied

---

72   I would like to admit that I am somewhat hampered in my research by my own lack of Arabic language ability. There is a growing body of scholarly literature on Kuwaiti law in the English language, which is readily accessible, but it mainly focuses on the Iraqi invasion of Kuwait in 1990, financial market analysis or issues around constitutionalism. I have found that there is a scarcity of academic writing, in English on Kuwait's legal system. This is a double-edged sword of course: whilst a lack of writing in an area can be frustrating, it also signals an area that may be ripe for exposition. Indeed, the bilingual law school in Kuwait where I currently teach will become a means by which more English-language legal analysis is developed and disseminated.

73   Kuwait International Law School (KILAW) in the suburb of Doha, in the State of Kuwait. The examples mentioned here are all drawn from KILAW. It is the first private law school in Kuwait. The other law school in Kuwait is a faculty within Kuwait University, a government university.

as a post-graduate degree. Judges in Kuwait are career judges – they must attend a 'judges training school' (the Judicial Institute) which is akin to the French system, unlike the common law countries where judges are not specifically trained or educated for that profession.

Aside from these rather obvious and perhaps superficial Western influences on Kuwaiti legal education there is one other point worth mentioning. When teaching students legal theory based on American concepts such as 'legal realism', it has been noted that it is sometimes difficult to persuade Kuwaiti law students of the relevance of legal theories that focus on the role of the judge. As anyone who has read anything about American Legal Realism will know, scholars such as Oliver Wendell Holmes and Jerome Frank place a great deal of emphasis on the role of the judge. When teaching this material for the first time in Kuwait it became apparent that the concerns of the common law legal thinker may not be the same as the civil law legal thinker. For instance, when Jerome Frank wrote about the judge deciding cases based on a 'hunch', a common law scholar might be interested to learn about what really influences a judge to make the decisions he/she makes. But a student of a civil law/Islamic law system appears to see the role of the judge in somewhat more 'black and white', formalistic terms. The author's experience in Kuwait is that law students do not generally see that the judge has or should have any personal influence on the outcome of the case. Students believe that the judge is there just to apply the rules and that he (in Kuwait it is always a 'he' because women are not yet permitted to sit as judges) has little personal input in the decision. When law students were asked, 'Do you think judges in Kuwait use their own personality and personal values when deciding cases?' 42 per cent said either 'not much' or 'not at all'. The emphasis seems to be squarely on the black and white letter of the law, and the judge is seen to be there merely to apply the laws and to come to the same decision as any other judge would reach.[74] Of course, this provides rich material for class discussions but these assumptions are widely and genuinely held. Likewise, when legal formalism and legal realism are explained, the latter being a reaction to the mainly discredited former, many students identify more with legal formalism than with legal realism. The oft-cited cliché that 'we are all realists now' might be slightly adjusted for legal education in Kuwait to something along the lines of 'we are not all realists yet'.[75] There is an apparently widely-held understanding and acceptance amongst law students that the judge is there to apply a formula and give the 'right' answer, uninfluenced by his personal biases or

---

74   In a survey of 45 Kuwaiti law students, they were asked the question, 'When you think about judges in Kuwait's legal system, how much flexibility do you think they have when deciding cases?' In response, only seven students (15.5 per cent) thought that they have 'a lot of flexibility'. The rest responded that judges have 'a little flexibility' (53.5 per cent), or 'not much flexibility' (26 per cent) or 'none' (4 per cent).

75   See M.S. Green, 'Legal realism as theory of law' (2005) 46 (6) *Williams and Mary Law Review* 1915–2000 at 1917, available at <http://papers.ssrn.com/sol3/papers.cfm?abstract_id=761007> accessed 1 June 2013.

prejudices, which probably do not exist anyway if he has been trained properly.[76] This reaction is interesting and one wonders whether the fact that a civil law legal system creates a more formalist approach to learning the law than a common law legal system could be the reason for these beliefs. If the legal system in place in a particular country acts as an all-pervading influence on society, then its effects on law students and lawyers must be visible since they are in closest connection to it. If the civil law, and indeed the Islamic/civil law mixed legal systems, can be said to be based on comprehensive codes, then this may influence the type of thinking that is engaged in by law students and it may become influential on how law students see themselves and other actors in the judicial system. As a law student, lawyer and then law academic from a common law legal system, the author has no trouble accepting that judges are greatly influenced by their background and experiences and that they may sometimes have to adapt their interpretation of the law to achieve justice in the circumstances. It is easy, perhaps even obvious, that judges will have personal biases and prejudices and that it is impossible, and perhaps not even desirable, to try to remove these completely from the judging process. Furthermore, the particular make-up of the bench will certainly have an outcome on the decisions the courts make.[77] Having read countless cases at law school, the author is aware that judges on the same bench often reach completely different but equally well-argued and compelling decisions. But the students being considered here, in Kuwait, are different in one key respect: they largely do not read case law in their legal education. They focus on the codes much more than the cases. Perhaps a civil law/Islamic law system creates different expectations about judges and the judging process than a common law system. Perhaps it creates an expectation that judges have very little room to manoeuvre and have little impact on the outcome of cases.[78] Again, further research would be needed to substantiate

---

76   The last note is a comment from a law student in Kuwait, who asserted that the legal realists (Jerome Frank in particular) were wrong in stating that judges are like everyone else, influenced by their own moral, economic, political and distinctly personal biases. One student asserted that if judges were properly trained, they would not have any of those biases because the judge's job is to apply the law without any bias or prejudice whatsoever.

77   In a Master's of Law class in Kuwait, the author once asked students whether the particular judges on the bench would have an influence on the decisions reached. The discussion was in the context of learning about the United States' Supreme Court. Somewhat surprisingly, the clear majority of students thought that the make-up of the bench would have no impact whatsoever on the outcome of the decisions the court reached.

78   In a survey of 45 Kuwaiti law students, the question was asked: 'Do you think judges in Kuwait use their own personality and values when deciding cases?' In response, only 4 per cent of students selected 'Yes, a lot'; 51 per cent selected 'A little bit'; 26.6 per cent selected 'Not much' and 13 per cent selected 'No, not at all'. That means 96 per cent of respondents did not believe that judges use their own personality and values much when judging cases. It would be interesting to conduct the same survey in a common law jurisdiction to compare the outcomes. It seems to this author to be a rather high proportion

this proposition and this is only offered as an insight based on personal experience of legal education in New Zealand and Kuwait.

Conclusion

This chapter has discussed the diffusion of Western legal concepts in Kuwait through the lens of the state, the legal system and legal education. There are many more areas that could be explored, such as the concept of 'insurance'. Insurance is not an Islamic concept, it is distinctly Western, yet it has been embraced and become embedded in Kuwait to the point that it is seldom questioned. This seems odd and, on a personal level, is somewhat challenging. To end this chapter on a personal note. As a law student I wrote my final year thesis on an area of insurance law (the disclosure of information by insurers to those taking out insurance). Insurance is an integral part of contract law, and business, in the Western world, but as a Muslim, I have never taken out insurance policies of any kind. In New Zealand, for example, I drive a car without car insurance, I own a house without house insurance, and I live without medical or life insurance. This is not because I do not understand the benefits of insurance but because my personal religious convictions do not permit me to enter into insurance contracts. But in Kuwait, I cannot own or even rent a car without taking out compulsory insurance and I cannot avail medical care without health insurance. Perhaps this is a classic example of a Western economic/ legal concept implanting itself into foreign soil and finding a fertile home, just like the other legal and political concepts discussed in this chapter. The diffusion of Western legal concepts has been occurring for many years and no doubt will continue into the future. But as Carolan argues, detrimental innovations are just as likely to diffuse as successful or beneficial measures.[79]

---

of students who do not see any injection of personal values and personality. This leads to the author's observation that these students tend to be more 'formalist' than 'realist' in their thinking about the judicial process. See also (n74).

79   See Carolan (n6).

Chapter 4

Diffusion of Islamic Law in the UK: The Case of the 'Special Guardianship'

Rita Duca

Introduction

The increase of migration fluxes has resulted in the consolidation of new ethnic minorities in Europe, where Western values and norms coexist, sometimes inconsistently, with the ones of minority communities, especially in the area of family law. For example, adoption is prohibited in most countries where the legal system is based on Islamic law. Those countries have other measures for protecting children, the best known being *kafala*. *Kafala* is generally defined as a voluntary commitment to take charge of the needs, upbringing and protection of a minor. As *kafala* does not create a legal parent–child relationship between the child who is taken into the charge of another, and the person holding the right to take care of him/her, it cannot be considered as adoption. In fact, *kafala* is not covered by the Hague Convention on the Protection of Children and Cooperation in Respect of Inter-country Adoption.

This chapter examines how English immigration law treats the admission of Islamic children under *kafala*. It specifically examines the Adoption and Children Act of 2002 which has introduced the institution of 'special guardianship' into the English legal system, in order to meet the needs of those children for whom adoption is not appropriate and to permit to all Muslims domiciled in the UK to be able to take care of children. This development also modernises the law, since it reflects and safeguards religious and cultural diversity. In particular, the aim of this chapter is to highlight how diffusion[1] within Western legal systems of legal models from outside the West arises from the movement of people. The example of the 'special guardianship' shows how Western legal systems have to deal with new institutions transplanted by people coming from foreign cultures; in other words, it is an example of legal diffusion.

---

1   On this form of diffusion see W. Twining, *General Jurisprudence: Understanding Law from a Global Perspective* (Cambridge University Press, 2009); W. Twining, 'Diffusion and globalization discourse' (2006) 47 2 *Harvard International Law Journal* 507.

Immigration and Legal Transplant

The notion of 'legal transplants',[2] formulated by Alan Watson, refers to: 'the phenomenon of circulation of legal models whereby a solution or a rule or a body of more solutions and rules that form a part of a definite model move themselves from a system to another'.[3] For Watson 'transplanting is the most fertile source of development' and 'the majority of changes is the result of loans obtained by different juridical systems'.[4] According to this theory a legal model can circulate thanks to its own prestige or by imposition,[5] through the activity created by the legislator, by the jurisprudence,[6] through legal writing or doctrine, or resulting from a combination of these last three activities.[7]

The notion of 'legal transplants' could be contextualised today within the sphere of multicultural societies, if it were ascribed a wider meaning.[8] In fact, the process of globalisation has aided the progressive increase in the last years of migration fluxes, and the ease of mobility on a global scale has certainly facilitated the circulation of legal systems. In Europe in particular, the massive arrival of immigrants who are workers, but also bearers of values, traditions and new rules has meant that Western legal models have had to deal with new institutions 'transplanted by a people from foreign culture'.[9] According to Alan Watson's notion, the legal transplant represents an advantage for those systems that 'import' a model from another system – and therefore there is a new and useful legal solution, however an alternative notion of legal transplant may be that the transfer of legal models occurs simply as an empirical fact with which the receiving countries have to deal, having no other choice.

---

2   The comparative literature offers several contributions on the issue. See A. Watson, *Legal Transplants: An Approach to Comparative Law* (University Press of Virginia, 1974); Rodolfo Sacco, *Introduzione al diritto comparato* (5th edn, UTET 1992) 43; U. Mattei, 'Efficiency in legal transplant. An essay in comparative law and economics' (1994) 14: 1 *International Review of Law and Economics* 3; P.G. Monateri, 'Methods in comparative law: An intellectual overview' in P.G. Monateri (ed.), *Methods of Comparative Law* (Edward Elgar, 2012) 51.

3   G.A. Benacchio, *Diritto Privato della Comunità Europea. Fonti, modelli e regole* (Luminis Cedam Wolter Kluwer, 2004) 146.

4   Watson (n2) 27.

5   Sacco (n2) 148.

6   G.A. Benacchio, *Diritto Privato della Comunità Europea. Fonti, modelli e regole* (Cedam, 2004) 147.

7   Sacco (n2) 43.

8   P. Shah, 'Globalization and the challenge of Asian legal transplants in Europe' (2005) *Singapore Journal of Legal Studies* 348.

9   M. Chiba, *Legal Pluralism: Toward a General Theory Through Japanese Legal Culture* (Tokai University Press, 1989) 179. Actually the author uses the idea of 'legal transplants' when referring to the third century BC wave of Koreans which, according to him, represented the first foreign legal transplant in Japan.

According to Watson's notion, the success of a legal transplant will depend on the ability of the host national legal order to adapt to the new decontextualised model. It is no coincidence that Watson uses the term 'transplant'; this concept inevitably reminds us of human organ transplants, where success or rejection depends on the body's ability to adapt to a new element. The success of a legal transplant of the new model imported by ethnic groups will depend not only on the way in which the host countries' legal systems will be able to deal with them, but also on the compatibility of these models with the values and principles that characterise the host countries' legal systems. Immigrants who come to Europe after an initial period of isolation looking for a job, tend to join their own community, so that immigration 'from individual becomes familiar and communitarian'.[10] This stabilisation of immigrants, with the consequent formation of families and communities, fosters the tendency to 'reproduce in a foreign country the institutions of the communities of origin and to apply traditional laws and practices'.[11] So, the regulatory framework which governs the lives of non-European citizens who live in Europe is established on a double track: one consisting of the rules and laws of the host country and the other consisting of rules and laws of the country of origin; there is therefore a dichotomy between 'official law' and 'unofficial law'.[12] This way, the behaviour of many people is shaped by a 'model after religious or ethnic identity [and they] follow laws that don't respect the national borders and sometimes they are discordant or in open conflict with the host Country's legal system'.[13] For this reason immigration inevitably causes a change in the legal environment of the host country, since immigrants, even though they are ready for dialogue and for the acceptance of the host country's law, do not renounce their expression of cultural life, of which law is a part, especially those aspects which they reproduce in their familial setting.

Family Law and *Kafala*

'Family is a fundamental social group, it is in every historically recognised society, which structure and functions change in the course of time and from a society to another',[14] and this is why family law is a field which is most vulnerable to cultural–ethnic effects, for '[...] both anthropo–sociological and legal reasons'.[15]

---

10 Among the early Italian researches who document this transformation process, see G. Costadoni, 'I limiti del relativismo culturale' in L. Mauri and G. Micheli (eds), *Diritti di cittadinanza e immigrazione straniera* (Franco Angeli, 1992) 102.

11 A. Facchi, *I diritti dell'Europa Multiculturale* (Laterza, 2008) 42.

12 W. Menski, *Migration, Diasporas and Legal Systems in Europe* (Routledge-Cavendish, 2006) 42.

13 Ibid.

14 N.A. Baarsma, *The Europeanisation of International Family Law* (Asser Press, 2011) 121.

15 Ibid.

Indeed, 'family' is a polysemous[16] concept, that is, it combines different meanings depending on the actors who turn to it and on the contexts in which it is used, and for this reason even the experts in civil law do not refer to 'family' but to 'families'.[17] In a multicultural society especially, a uniform social model of family does not exist, because when culture, religion and traditions change, 'families' will change as well, followed by, as a consequence, familiar relationships between man–woman and parents–children; the existential (e.g., educational, psychological, religion, medical) choices related to a minor: marriage; filiation; the conditions of dissolution of family unit, and so on.

This kind of social transformation requires 'a rethink of the entire Family law',[18] particularly in Western legal systems. These systems have to take into account not only new familial structures composed by immigrants, but also have to give attention to the identification and custody petitions required by these new families. It is in the context of this new background that the *kafala* will be analysed, a long-term foster care used in Islamic countries but unknown to Western legal systems.

In almost every Islamic country[19] the adoption of children is prohibited by a law that comes directly from the Koran.[20] The reason for this prohibition is due to the Islamic idea of family as an institution of holy origins, and the filial bonds are expressions of Allah's will.[21] For this reason, man cannot, through artificial juridical bonds, decide on the suspension or the foundation of new filial bounds beyond the biological generation within marriage.[22]

---

16   Polysemy (from Greek: πολυ-, *poly-*, 'many' and σῆμα, *sêma*, 'sign') is the capacity for a sign (e.g., a word, phrase, concept, etc.) or signs to have multiple related meanings.

17   In the 1980s the existence of several types of families was proposed by Vincenzo Scalisi, 'La "famiglia" e le "famiglie"' in *La riforma del diritto di famiglia dieci anni dopo. Bilanci e prospettive*, Acts from Verona's Conference, 14–15 June 1985 (Luminis Cedam Wolter Kluwer, 1986) 280.

18   A. Miranda, 'La privatizzazione del diritto di famiglia: il modello di Common Law' in *Alessandro Dagnino* (ed.), *Alambicco del Comparatista II: Matrimonio, Matrimonii* (Giuffrè, 2000) 370.

19   With the exception of Tunisia, Iraq, Turkey, Somalia and Indonesia. For an in-depth examination see R. Aluffi, *Le leggi del diritto di famiglia negli Stati arabi del Nord-Africa* (Fondazione Giovanni Agnelli, 1997).

20   'Allah hasn't placed for any man two hearts in his body [...] and he did not make your adoptive sons as your own sons'. *Koran*, Sura XXXIII, vers 4.

21   'Only Allah tells the truth and guides you on the right path' *Koran*, Sura XXXIII, vers 4.

22   The origin of the Islamic prohibition of adoption is uncertain. According to part of the doctrine it must be considered under a historical perspective: see P. Palermo, 'Ricongiungimenti familiari solo per gli stranieri e non per i cittadini: il caso della kafalah' (2010) *Diritto e Giustizia* 120, which refers to the doctrinal thesis that recognises in the Islamic prohibition the aim to interrupt those tribal connections which were traditional in the pre-Islamic society and to put into effect the idea of social innovation proposed by Mohammed. Indeed, the new prophetic message wanted to substitute the bond of

From this we can deduce that, since adoption is an institute with the aim of making a filial relationship created independently from natural procreation, according to Islamic culture it must be prohibited. The prohibition of adoption established by Allah's law, which in Islamic law systems has the same relevance as a source of right,[23] is also confirmed in the national legislation of different Islamic countries.[24]

The absence of institutions which may be used to create an 'unnatural' filial system does not mean, however, that minor orphans or abandoned children are left to their own destiny. The duty of brotherhood and solidarity towards abandoned minors, also exhorted by the Koran, is performed by every good Muslim through '*kafala*',[25] which is the only institute recognised by the Islamic system aimed at the guardianship and protection of abandoned or orphaned childhood.

From these considerations it emerges that this institute is strongly linked to the traditional social values that define Islamic society and to its religious values. Although the regulation of this institute has specific characteristics in every single Islamic system, it is possible to identify the essential and common features of this particular form of protection for abandoned children.

---

tribal fidelity – which gained strength through adoptions – with the sense of belonging to Islamic community at universal vocation that is *Umma*, characterised by faith. In fact for the author, Patrizia Palermo, 'the prohibition was functional to [...] the crossing of tribal system on which pre-Islamic society was built and on which adoption was often used to allow the subjects without sons to bequeath name and patrimony and to allow families to grow larger or shrink'. Another interesting and possible origin of the prohibition of adoption, which is related to the Prophet's life, is argued by Rebecca Gelli and it explains: 'the prohibition of adoption has its origins in Mohammed's life [...]. Adoption already existed, in the pre-Islamic era, on the model of the Roman *adopito plemna*: Mohammed, before the Revelation, adopted his slave Zayd and, with the intent to reform the social habit that would permit an enfranchised man to marry a free woman, he gave him as spouse his cousin Zaymab. When he repudiated his wife, he decided to get married to her and, through the divine law, he abolished adoption and also the hindrance in marriages between the one who adopts and the adoptee's spouse.' R. Gelli, 'Questioni relative al ricongiungimento del minore in Kafalah al cittadino italiano' (2010) 39: 4 *Famiglia e diritto* 787.

23   R. David, *I grandi sistemi giuridici contemporanei* (11th edn, Luminis Cedam Wolter Kluwer, 2004) 383: 'the Muslim law does not represent [...] an autonomous branch of Science. It is none other than one Islamic religious face. This religion includes, on one hand, a theology, that establishes dogmas and what a Muslim must believe, and on the other hand, *sharia*, that orders to religious what they must or cannot do.'

24   For example, the 'Algerian Family Code' of June 1984, art. 46, states that '*l'adoption (tabeni) est interdite par la Chari'a et la loi*' [adoption (*tabeni*) is prohibited by the Sharia and the law]; the Libyan Family Law Act of 1984; the Moroccan Personal Status Code of 1957, art. 83, point 3, where it is specified that 'adoption does not have any juridical validity and it does not produce any of the effects of filiation'.

25   The etymological meaning of the word, translated from Arab, is 'to add something to something else'.

Through *kafala*, a Muslim married couple (or a single adult) obtains the custody of a child who was not given to the custody of his/her biological relatives.[26] Specifically, *kafil* (a couple or a single adult),[27] commits him/herself to provide for the needs of a *makful* (abandoned child) through a contract signed before a judge or a notary, in a definitive way[28] until the child reaches the age of majority,[29] and undertakes to care for the child the same way as a 'good father' would do.[30] Although *kafil* has parental responsibility over the child, there is no kind of filiation with the minor:[31] *makful* does not take his/her *kafil*'s surname,[32] does not obtain any transmissible rights or expectancy,[33] nor does he/she interrupt the relationship with his/her family of origin.

From the procedural point of view it is firstly necessary to judge correctly the living conditions of the *makful* and the suitability of the *kafil*. Islamic law usually implies that the child has been previously declared 'abandoned' by the competent juvenile court, and if the biological parents are known, they are summoned to give their approval to *kafala*.[34] Moreover, in different Islamic countries,[35] it is necessary to listen to the opinion of the *makful* and to obtain his/her approval to *kafala*.

---

26   *Kafala* does not refer only to the abandoned child, but also to the minor for whom custody in an extended family is not possible. On this issue see A.M. Galoppini, 'L'adozione del piccolo marocchino ovvero gli scherzi dell'eurocentrismo' (2003) in *N giur civ comm* 143.

27   For example, Algerian law considers the possibility of couples and single people, becoming *kafil* regardless of whether they are male or female. In contrast, Moroccan law restricts this possibility only to couples with at least three years of marriage and who are considered morally and socially suitable.

28   A peculiarity of this institute is that *kafil*'s commitment is definitive. On this issue see N. Yousini Haddad, 'La kafala en droit algérien' in J. Poussot-Petit (ed.), *L'enfant et les familles nourricères en droit comparé* (Presse de l'Univerisitè des Sciences Sociales de Toulouse, 1997) 135–41.

29   In Moroccan law it is necessary to highlight the hypothesis according to which, if the foster child is female, *kafala* does not cease at the coming of age but continues until she gets married, as an example of enforcement of the different juridical position for women compared to that of men typical of Islamic systems.

30   On this issue see Haddad (n28) 133.

31   See C. Campiglio, 'Il diritto islamico nella prassi italiana' (2008) 1 *Riv Dir Intern Proc Priv* 46, 'Kafala does not interrupt the juridical bond with the family of origin and it does not have any personal effects on the child'.

32   With particular reference to the impossibility of transmitting the foster parent's name to the foster child see Sura XXXIII, verse 5, 'to the adoptive children you have to give their father's surname: this is right in front of God! If you will ignore the fatherhood, may they be brothers in religion; they are with us'.

33   As far as inheritance is concerned, however, the possibility is considered that *kafil*, through the declaration inserted into one's own will (*tanzil*), is equivalent to one of the legitimate heirs.

34   See Haddad (n28) 135–41.

35   This is stated, for example in Art 117 of the Algerian Civil law. See further Haddad (n28) 136.

Islamic law also requires some conditions that need to be satisfied to take care of the abandoned minor. The *kafil* must: be of age, believe in the Islamic religion,[36] be able to guarantee adequate care and good nurturing to the child, and finally be able to fulfill the parental role with dignity[37] and meet the responsibilities deriving from *kafala*. The competent authorities[38] have to verify the compatibility between the two subjects in addition to verifying the *makful*'s condition of abandonment and the *kafil*'s suitability. Once *kafala* is allowed, the public competent authority has the right and the duty of oversight and checks the evolution of the child's integration in the extended family and in the event of the *kafil*'s transfer of residence abroad it must authorise the *makful*'s transfer.

As one can deduce from the above, *kafala* is and must be considered as a form of protection of abandoned children provided for by legal orders based on Islamic law. For this reason *kafala* is, in international law, a valid alternative to the forms of protection of children provided for by Western laws, in particular as regards to adoption and custody. In particular, the United Nations Convention on the Rights of the Child[39] considers that state parties shall in accordance with their national laws ensure alternative care for such a child, 'such care could include, inter alia, foster placement, *kafalah* of Islamic law, adoption or if necessary placement in suitable institutions for the care of children. When considering solutions, due regard shall be paid to the desirability of continuity in a child's upbringing and to the child's ethnic, religious, cultural and linguistic background'.[40]

Furthermore, the 1996 Hague Convention on parental responsibility and the protection of children[41] specifically includes 'the placement of the child in a foster family or institute, that is its custody with *kafala* or with a similar custody'[42] (art. 3, lett. *e*) thereby assimilating *kafala* with the 'Western' child protection approaches concerning parental responsibility. On the contrary, *kafala* was not considered in the 1993 Hague Convention on International Adoptions despite one of the aims and purposes behind the convention being to harmonise the diverse laws on adoption. In the search for a uniform legal environment there was a marked absence of consideration of how Islamic *kafala* and other forms of adoption could co-exist.

---

36   In particular, a prerequisite of the *kafil*'s belonging to Islam must be framed in the effort to offer to the child the best family that also guarantees a good education. This prerequisite of Islamic faith is clearly in conflict with the principle of laity, accepted from Western law.

37   Regarding parental roles, women have to take care of children's growth (*hadana*), while men have the duty of feeding (*nafaqa*), as well as custody, care and parental authority.

38   In general this is a specialised judge regarding juvenile court at the civil courthouse.

39   Convention on the Rights of the Child (adopted 20 November 1989, entered into force 2 September 1990) UN GAORes 44/25 (1989).

40   Ibid. art. 20.

41   Hague Convention on Jurisdiction, Applicable Law, Recognition, Enforcement and Cooperation in respect of Parental Responsibility and Measures for the Protection of Children (adopted 19 October 1996, entered in force 1 January 2002) OJ EU 2003 L 48.

42   Ibid. art 3, lett. *e*.

Kafala and the English Legal System

English family law has had to broaden its horizons in recent years to deal adequately with the myriad of novel issues raised by migrant single adults, migrant families and migrant children. Indeed, there can be no doubt that for a significant minority of people either resident or domiciled in this country, the traditional boundaries of family law (at least so far as it is taught in English law schools) fail to accommodate or give adequate emphasis to what are now crucial international dimension.[43]

With these words Murphy has underlined how English family law, similarly to the legal systems of other European countries, is today required to extend its own borders and to confront problems related to the recognition of family law institutions of new minority ethnic groups. The legal institution of *kafala* has in particular raised some problems in English immigration law regarding the family reunification right. As a matter of fact, since 'Immigration control is not a neutral ground on which distinct cultural institutions are legitimated within British legal systems',[44] immigration law has become a sort of arena in which the main conflicts stemming from the contrast between the foreigner law systems and the host law systems are played out.

In English immigration law, like Italian and French immigration law, the *kafala* Islamic system is not mentioned among the prerequisites for the achievement of family reunification, since such an institute is unknown. This means that a *kafil* who lives in the UK has no right to remove the child from his own country and bring him into England. In English law, Immigration Rules sanction the acknowledgement of child adoptions occurring in a foreign country, dependent on whether the foreign country belongs to those considered as 'designated countries', and is included in the additional list to the 1976 Adoption Act, reconfirmed from the 2002 Adoption and Children Act.

Among all the countries excluded from this list, as well as the Southeast Asian countries of Hindu law, such as India, Pakistan and Bangladesh,[45] there are also most of the Islamic law countries such as Morocco, Tunisia, Iraq and Iran, with the consequent impossibility of recognising *kafala* as an adoption measure. However, part 8 at paragraph 309 (A) of the 2002 Adoption and Children Act regulates adoption de facto[46] as well as de jure, where, if it is proved that the connection

---

43   J. Murphy, *International Dimensions in Family Law* (Manchester University Press, 2005) 2.

44   P. Shah, 'Transnational Hindu law adoption: Recognition and treatment in Britain' (2009) 5(2) *International Journal of Law in Context* 107.

45   The exemption of the southeastern countries of Hindu law creates many difficulties, as the UK government does not recognise the consequences of these kinds of adoption, for a further insight see Shah (n44) 107–30.

46   Immigration Rules Part 8 – Family members – para. 309 (A). For a deeper analysis about immigration rules see the website of the UK Border Agency, available at <http://www.ukba.homeoffice.gov.uk/> accessed 15 October 2013.

between the *makful* and the *kafil* really exists, Islamic *kafala* could be included. The law that regulates this de facto adoption requires two essential requisites in order to be considered in this manner: the adoptive parents must prove that during the period spent abroad they have:

a. lived together for a minimum of 18 months, of which the 12 months immediately preceding the application for entry clearance must have been spent living together with the child;

b. assumed the role of the child's parents, since the beginning of the 18-month period, so that there has been a genuine transfer of parental responsibility.

If these two requisites can be established, English judges can verify the actual relationship between the *makful* and the *kafil*, thereby ensuring the best interest of the child and excluding any risk of recognising false adoptions, behind which human trafficking could possibly be concealed. For this reason, in a decision of the Asylum and Immigration Tribunal (AIT),[47] it has been emphasised how this law, which regulates de facto adoption 'is probably not intended to facilitate the entry of children by themselves: it is probably intended to ensure that, if a number of members of the family are to come to the United Kingdom together, a child who has been living as a child of the family with the parents for some time is not left behind'.

Although *kafala* can be compared to de facto adoption, the *kafil* may still have difficulties related to the achievement of reunification with a child under *kafala*, in particular if he needs to prove a 'genuine transfer of parental responsibility' as required by the regulations, since this would imply a severing the relationship with the child's family of origin. which *kafala*, on the contrary, does not assume.

Part of the English doctrine[48] has underlined the failure of these dispositions, which do not reflect the true intent of English law towards new foreign institutes as one of openness; on the contrary, the immigration policy appears to be restrictive. Beside these criticisms, it is important to underline how most difficulties probably arise because of the cultural differences between English norms and Islamic law countries on adoption. Indeed, O'Halloran points out 'In the UK adoption now exists only as a legal process, delineated and regulated by statute, culminating in proceedings that are judicially determined. Legislation addresses the rights and the obligations of the parties concerned, defines the roles of those mediating bodies with roles in the process, sets out the grounds for making an adoption order and states its effect'.[49] From this it is clear that the key aspect of the institution

---

47   *MN (Non-recognised Adoptions: Unlawful Discrimination?) India* [2007] UKAIT 00015, date notified 12 February 2007, para. 13.

48   See R. Mckee, 'Children' in D. Jackson and G. Warr (eds), *Immigration: Law and Practice* (Sweet and Maxwell, 2005); Shah (n44) 107.

49   K. O'Halloran, *The Politics of Adoption: International Perspectives on Law, Policy & Practice* (Springer, 2006) 8.

of adoption, which in England is governed by legislation and juridical control, is therefore a state-centred process.[50] The problems in respect of adoption arise when the different cultural approaches, such as those found in Islamic law, do not require the intervention of the state.

The centralised approach of English law that regulates adoption, in which agencies of the state play a major role, limits recognition of those obtained in the foreign countries that do not follow the same approach. This gives rise to the risk of falling in the straits 'of Eurocentric and legal imperialism'.[51] This risk, however, as revealed by Prakash Shah, has not been underestimated by the judiciary who, in a similar circumstance regarding forced marriage[52] have stated as follows:

> We must be careful to ensure that our understandable concern to protect vulnerable children (or, indeed, vulnerable young adults) does not lead us to interfere inappropriately – and if inappropriately then unjustly – with families merely because they cleave, as this family does, to mores, to cultural beliefs, more or less different from what is familiar to those who view life from a purely Euro-centric perspective.[53]

The institution of *kafala* is complex in regards not only to familial reunification but also to those Islamic couples residing in the UK who wish to take care of an abandoned child. In this case the couple residing in the UK should adapt to the English law, which, in line with the laws of countries following a Western legal tradition and with international treaties, considers adoption as to be the only institution dedicated to the care of abandoned children. Yet, as it has been said in this chapter, adoption is prohibited for Islamic believers. To solve this impasse and give Muslims residing in the UK the possibility of taking care of an abandoned child, a new institute of special guardianship[54] was included in the 2002 Adoption and Children Act.

Special guardianship seems to perfectly reproduce two of *kafala*'s essential characteristics: the special guardian has parental responsibility for the child until he/she reaches the age of majority; the child must not sever his/her parental connections, even though the latter have a very limited parental responsibility over the former. This new institute is the right answer to the needs of those who want to offer a stable family to a child, but they are not allowed to adopt him/her because of the prohibition imposed by cultural or religious regulations/provisions. This intention was clearly expressed in 2000 by the then-Prime Minister Tony Blair who, in the White Paper, preceding the reform of the adoption law, had

---

50   Shah (n44).

51   Ibid.

52   *NS v MI* [2006] EWHC 1646 (Fam), para. 37.

53   Shah (n44).

54   Adoption and Children Act 2002 s115, available at <http://www.legislation.gov.uk/ukpga/2002/38> accessed 16 October 2013.

specified that the new institute of special guardianship was proposed because 'some minority ethnic communities have religious and cultural difficulties with adoption as it is set out in law'.[55]

The attention paid to the problems of a multicultural society by the English government is also shown in a following point of the White Paper, where it is stated that 'in order to meet the needs of these children where adoption is not appropriate, and to modernise the law so it reflects the religious and cultural diversity of our country today, the Government believes there is a case to develop a new legislative option to provide permanence short of legal separation involved in adoption'.[56]

Werner Menski points out that there is no direct reference to *kafala* and there are no provisions that can specifically be applied to Muslin families in the Act. Indeed Menski observes that: 'The State shies away from admitting plurality-conscious awareness, or is this perhaps just technical legal language, trying to keep out of ethnic politics, while working on practical solution?'[57]

It could, however, be argued that the White Paper's title: *Adoption: A New Approach*, in which a choice has been made not to make any specific reference to an Islamic institute, is not attributable to a reluctance to admit the existence of a multiplicity of consciences within England and Wales, but, on the contrary, reflects a willingness to be open by using technical-juridical language, which is neutral.

Conclusion

The individualisation of the special guardianship's new institution, which was previously unknown in the English legal rules, represents the right compromise and dialogue between two very different legal systems, and perhaps one of the few examples of legal diffusion from the Islamic legal system to a Western legal system.

---

55 Department of Health, *Adoption: A New Approach. A White Paper*, Cm 5017, December 2000 London, para. 5.8, available at <http://webarchive.nationalarchives.gov. uk/+/www.dh.gov.uk/prod_consum_dh/groups/dh_digitalassets/@dh/@en/documents/ digitalasset/dh_4080512.pdf> accessed 16 October 2013.

56 Ibid.

57 W. Menski, 'Law, religion and culture in multicultural Britain' in *Law and Religion in Multicultural Societies* (DJOF, 2008) 58.

Chapter 5

The Judicial Committee of the Privy Council: Common Law and its Local Variations in the Commonwealth

Pamela Martino

Introduction

England 'has been the only rival to civilian systems based on Roman law in creating a legal Empire, in providing a model'.[1] In fact, it could be argued that common law is not only national law, but it belongs to the Anglo-Saxon 'community': 'Nearly one third of all the people alive today live in regions where the law has been […] marked by the Common Law. […] Great Britain was once the greatest colonial power in the world'.[2] As a consequence of imperial expansion and later membership of the Commonwealth, common law was no longer conceived of as an immutable set of rules, but as a form of legal reasoning the common basic principles of which were enhanced by the case law of the Privy Council.[3] This has led to a sense of cultural belonging that transcends national borders by encouraging the dialogue between courts of common law, the use of judicial precedents from outside the courts of England and Wales, mostly from the Commonwealth area, and only later from other Western countries, especially European.[4]

---

1   O.F. Robinson, T.D. Fergus and W.M. Gordon, *European Legal History* (2nd edn, Butterworths, 1994) 124.

2   K. Zweigert and H. Kötz, *An Introduction to Comparative Law* (3rd edn, Clarendon Press, 1998) 219; M. Rheinstein, 'Common law-equity', *Encilopedia del diritto* (Giuffrè, 1960) 914.

3   The definition of common law in legal thought and as a judicial system is provided by R. Pound in *The Spirit of the Common Law* (Marshall Jones Company, 1921) 1–31.

4   J. Allard and A. Garapon, *Les juges dans la mondialisation. La nouvelle révolution du droit* (Editions du Seuil et la République des Idées, 2005). This trend is both favoured and confirmed by the jurisprudence of the Privy Council 'which plays a crucial role in maintaining the harmony of the common law within the commonwealth world, laying down paths of cross-fertilisation': E. Örücü, 'Comparative law in British courts' in U. Drobnig and S. van Erp (eds), *The Use of Comparative Law by Courts* (Kluwer Law International, 1999) 273. In *Mercedes-Benz A.G.* [1995] 3 All ER, 929 (PC), the Privy Council preferred the approach of the Australian courts when deciding Hong Kong law; and displayed the same attitude in *Vasquez v R* [1994] 1 WLR 1304 and *O'Neill v R* [1994]

However, although a number of different legal systems have come under the influence of the common law, these differ in socio-cultural terms. Within the common law world the initial circulation of the model emanating from England and Wales has evolved through a process of bilateral interaction,[5] in which the jurisprudence of the Privy Council has been at the same time instrumental and an expression, influencing cases in countries such as New Zealand, Canada, Australia, India and Hong Kong.[6] The diffusion of the substantially uniform common law in reciprocal directions among the legal systems with Anglo-Saxon origins is shown by the frequent references made by the courts in England and Wales to the decisions of the courts of the Commonwealth as 'authorities'. This lack of distinction between national and Commonwealth jurisprudence suggests a trend towards uniformity which may arise from the reluctance of British courts to conceive of, for example, New Zealand law as foreign law: indeed, in *R v Horseferry Road Magistrates' Court ex p Bennett*,[7] Lord Bridge stated that 'Whatever differences there may be between the legal systems of South Africa, the United States, New Zealand and this country, many of the basic principles to which they seek give effect to stem from common roots'.[8]

The jurisprudence of the Privy Council appears to have confirmed the uniform application of the common law in the Commonwealth: in *Cheali v Equiticorp Finance Group Ltd. and another*,[9] where Lord Browne-Wilkinson stated that '[i]t is manifestly desirable that the law on this subject should be the same in all common law jurisdictions', and, again, in *Vasquez v R*, where the Privy Council held 'This conclusion will bring Belize into line with other Commonwealth countries of the Caribbean [...]'.[10] For a long time the English common law has been the only source of inspiration and the absolute interpretation parameter of foreign law in the Commonwealth.[11] It is only in the last few decades, that the

---

3 All ER, 674 (PC). The influence of the English courts on domestic and foreign precedents is stressed by G. Gorla, *Diritto comparato e diritto comune europeo* (Giuffrè, 1981) 543 ff and 651 ff.

5   For major insights on the subject in Italian doctrine see, F. Duranti, 'La nuova circolazione dei modelli costituzionali negli ordinamenti di matrice anglosassone', available at <www.forumcostituzionale.it> accessed 8 March 2014. And also E. Ceccherini, 'La funzione del giudice nel crescente processo di osmosi fra ordinamenti', available at <http://www.crdc.unige.it> accessed 8 March 2014.

6   The issue has been exhaustively analysed, with particular reference to the Canadian case, by T. Groppi, 'A user-friendly court: The influence of Supreme Court of Canada decisions since 1982 on court decisions in other liberal democracies' (2007) 36 *Supreme Court Law Review* 337.

7   [1994] 1 AC 42.

8   Ibid. [67F-H].

9   [1991] 4 All ER, 989 (PC).

10   [1994] 3 All ER, 674 (PC).

11   In an article dating back to the 1920s Symon wrote 'the appeal does tend to promote legal uniformity within the Empire. The Common Law of England is the heritage

Privy Council has become familiar with the 'localisation' of the common law, arising from the interpretation of the law provided by local judges 'in so far as they reflect the advantage which those judges enjoy of familiarity with prevailing local conditions, this with the proviso that the courts have used that advantage'.[12]

The Evolution of the Privy Council Case Law

The origins of the Privy Council date back to the Norman conquest of England in 1066 which led to the establishment of a feudal monarchy founded on strongly centralised judicial organisation. The *Curia Regis*, which was the forerunner of the Privy Council, performed a combination of administrative and judicial functions and was not conceived of as a mere court, but had rather a general vocation of *judicial administration*, that is to say, an activity which combined the judicial function with active administration. The *Curia* gradually specialised in settling disputes, and acted as the final court of appeal for all the imperial territories. In the twelfth century the *Curia Regis* divided into two separate entities: the Court of Common Pleas and the King's Bench, which inherited much of the *Curia Regis'* original jurisdiction.[13]

Established by the Judicial Committee Act 1833 as a Committee of the Privy Council with advisory powers in respect of the Crown, which could issue an order in council to give effect to the recommendations of the Committee, the Judicial Committee of the Privy Council was one of the highest courts of the United Kingdom as well as a court of final jurisdiction for appeals against the judgements of the Commonwealth, the British Overseas Territories and States that were independent from the British Crown.[14] On the basis of the Judicial Committee Act 1844, the Judicial Committee of the Privy Council was described

---

and pride of American Jurisprudence – so it is of ours. So long as Australia endures a free English-speaking community it will not lose its faith in the Common law. We are the children of the Mother-country'. J.H. Symon, 'Australia and the Privy Council' [1922] 4 *Journal of Comparative Legislation & International Law* 137, 150.

12   Örücü (n4) 273. See also *Hector v Attorney General of Antigua and Barbuda and others* [1990] 2 All ER, 303 (PC).

13   A. Fitzroy, *The History of the Privy Council* (John Murray, 1928).

14   It is important to emphasise that under the Constitutional Reform Act 2005 devolution cases from the regions of the United Kingdom are now heard by the Supreme Court. The Judicial Committee hears domestic appeals to Her Majesty in Council from the Disciplinary Committee of the Royal College of Veterinary Surgeons, against certain schemes of the Church Commissioners under the Pastoral Measure 1983, and from the Arches Court of Canterbury and the Chancery Court of York in non-doctrinal faculty causes, from Prize Courts, it decides disputes under the House of Commons Disqualification Act and it hears appeals from the Court of Admiralty of the Cinque Ports. Furthermore, Her Majesty has the power to refer any matter to the Judicial Committee for 'consideration and report' under section 4 of the Judicial Committee Act 1833.

as the supreme court of appeal in charge of settling disputes in all countries, as colonies or possessions, which were subject to the authority of the United Kingdom. Prior to the Colonial Laws Validity Act 1865, the legislative provision which governed leave to appeal to the Crown as a source of justice, meant that the selection of decisions which courts referred to the Judicial Committee of the Privy Council could be controlled. By contrast, once the Colonial Laws Validity Act 1865 came into force it became impossible for colonial legislatures to control the right of appeal. The Judicial Committee of the Privy Council was, therefore, the representation, at jurisdictional level, of British imperialism and operated as a channel to facilitate the uniform application of the common law in all the possessions of the Crown.[15] Moreover, at the head of the common law judicial system, powers were divided between the Judicial Committee of the Privy Council and the Appellate Committee of the House of Lords: the former had appellate jurisdiction for judgements from all the colonies and possessions of the Crown, the internal 'territorial' jurisdiction and the special jurisdictions (admiralty, ecclesiastical causes and issues raised in certain professional associations); while the latter was the supreme judicial institution of the United Kingdom, from which flowed gradually over time civil and criminal cases from England, Wales, Scotland (only civil cases) and Northern Ireland, distinguishing itself in cases concerning the protection of fundamental freedoms and, in recent years, disputes between national and European law.[16]

Since the late nineteenth century the Judicial Committee of the Privy Council has been charged with the task of resolving disputes related to territorial claims both in Britain[17] and in other British possessions and colonies. The spirit of its activity within the Commonwealth was essentially that expressed by Walter Bagehot in The English Constitution of 1867, when he described it as 'a great conspicuous tribunal' that 'ought to rule all other courts, ought to have no competitor, ought to bring our law into unity'.[18]

---

15   P.A. Howell, *The Judicial Committee of the Privy Council, 1833–1876* (Cambridge University Press, 1979).

16   A. Torre, 'La Corte Suprema del Regno Unito: la nuova forma di una vecchia idea', available at <http://www.astrid-online.it> accessed 8 March 2014, and 'La giustizia costituzionale nel Regno Unito; caratteri, istituzioni e prospettive', available at <http://www.astrid-online.it> accessed 8 March 2014.

17   Particularly in Ireland with reference to the nineteenth-century Irish home rule movement and to devolution issues in Scotland, Wales and Northern Ireland as a result of the devolution acts passed in the late 1990s of the twentieth century. See: R. Hazell, 'Judges left out – The role of the judicial committee of the privy council in resolving devolution disputes in the United Kingdom', available at <http://www.federalismi.it> accessed 8 March 2014; and T Groppi, 'Conflitti devolutivi: nuovi percorsi per il judicial review of legislation?' in C. Decaro (ed.), *Parlamenti e devolution in Gran Bretagna* (Luiss University Press, 2005).

18   W. Bagehot, *The English Constitution* (Chapman and Hall, 1867) 159.

In the nineteenth century the right to appeal to the Privy Council was essentially conceived of as 'the strongest bond of union between this country and the colonies'.[19] In 1875, the Privy Council pointed out with regard to its status as court of final jurisdiction, that:

> this power has been exercised for centuries over all the dependencies of the Empire by the Sovereign of the mother country sitting in Council. By this institution, common to all parts of the Empire beyond the seas, all matters whatever requiring a judicial solution may be brought to the cognizance of one court in which all have a voice. To abolish this controlling power and abandon each colony and dependency to a separate Court of Appeal of its own, would obviously destroy one of the most important ties connecting all parts of the Empire in common obedience to the courts of law, and to renounce the last and most essential mode of exercising the authority of the Crown over its possessions abroad.[20]

And in 1879, ruling on an appeal from New South Wales, the Judicial Committee of the Privy Council stated that 'it is of the utmost importance that in all parts of the Empire where English law prevails, the interpretation of that law by the courts should be as nearly as possible the same'.[21]

The jurisdiction of the Judicial Committee of the Privy Council, seen for a long time as a unifying element between the former British colonies which, after independence became members of the Commonwealth, is not limited in time to the interpretation/application of the laws and local Constitutions. Nor is it limited to the application of those common law principles and institutions which became part of the local legal systems, in countries which were formerly part of the British Empire, directed at guaranteeing individual rights and the principle of due process in civil and criminal litigation against the excessive power of the executive or State legislation.[22] Rather, the jurisprudence of the Privy Council was extended to

---

19   G.D. Faber, 83 Parliamentary Debates (4th) 85 (1900) [1892–1908]. The jurisdiction of the Privy Council embraced about a quarter of the world's territory, as emphasised by N. Bentwich in *The Practice of the Privy Council in Judicial Matters* (Sweet and Maxwell, 1937).

20   K.C. Wallace Nesbitt, *The Judicial Committee of the Privy Council*, paper presented at the Thirty-Second Annual Meeting of the New York State Bar Association, Buffalo, 28–9 January 1909, 15 <www.archive.org> accessed 8 March 2014.

21   *Trimble v Hill* (1879) 5 App. Cas. 342, 345.

22   See: *Jerusalem-Jaffa District Governor v Sulciman Murra* [1926] AC 321; *Edwards v Attorney General of Canada* [1930] AC 1924; *Attorney General of British Columbia v Attorney General of Canada* [1924] AC 203. On this point see N. Bentwich, 'The judicial committee of the Privy Council as a model of an International Court for Human Rights' (1948) 2 *International Law Quarterly* 392. Finally, on the role of the Judicial Committee of the Privy Council in managing the relation with Indian, Canadian and New Zealand courts, while ensuring the uniform application of English common

create a uniform system of common law throughout those countries coming within British influence.[23]

The dissolution of the British Empire, was, not unnaturally, followed by claims for greater autonomy by the Dominions which became members of the Commonwealth. As a result, a radical change in the position of the Privy Council occurred with regard to the binding authority of precedents emanating from English common law. The approach of the Privy Council to the rule of precedent was obsequious in respect of the spirit of the English Constitution but also aimed at the substantial preservation of local customs and laws to the extent that it could be said that: 'when an appellate Court in a colony which is regulated by English law differs from an appellate Court in England, it is not right to assume that the Colonial Court is wrong'.[24] Likewise the interpretation of a colonial law, even if modelled on English law, had to free itself from the English *ratio legis*.[25] The Privy Council did, however, point out that '[i]t is otherwise if the authority in England is that of the House of Lords. That is the supreme tribunal to settle English law, and that being settled, the Colonial Court, which is bound by English law, is bound to follow it'.[26]

The English common law was, therefore, the common heritage of all English people, including the settlers in new colonies, who, although not bound to follow the decisions of the English courts of common law, considered it appropriate to do so except when local conditions precluded the application of English precedent. The diffusion of the common law through the empire meant that local variants of English common law gradually evolved and in turn became an integral part of the common law. In the former colonies therefore the common law tradition gave rise to new applications and new forms.

In 1931, following the Imperial Conferences held between 1926 and 1930 on the relationships between the territories of the Empire, the Statute of Westminster was passed.[27] This Statute abolished the Colonial Laws Validity Act

---

law in accordance with the modulation resulting from the specific local conditions, see I. Richardson, 'The Privy Council as the final court for the British Empire' (2012) 43 *Victoria University of Wellington Law Review* 103; R.B. Haldane, 'The work for the Empire of the Judicial Committee of the Privy Council' (1921) 1 *Cambridge Law Journal* 143.

23   K. Roberts-Wray, *Commonwealth and Colonial Law* (Stevens, 1966) 461.

24   *Robins v National Trust Co. Ltd* [1927] AC 515, 519.

25   *Attorney-General for Ontario v Perry* [1934] AC 477, 487.

26   *Robins v National Trust Co. Ltd* [1927] AC 515, 519.

27   During the conferences, which would inspire the Preamble of the Statute of 1931, members of the British Commonwealth of Nations were defined as 'autonomous Communities within the British Empire, equal in status, and in no way subordinate one to another' ('Summary of Proceedings of the Imperial Conference', Great Britain, Cmd. Paper 2768, 1926, 14). In a conference report: 'It became clear that it was no part of the policy of His Majesty's Government in Great Britain that questions affecting judicial appeals should

1865,[28] granting full legislative autonomy to the Dominions,[29] thereby paving the way for the abolition of appeals to the Privy Council and the 'legal decentralization of the British Empire'.[30] During the second half of the twentieth century, when traditional political ties were dissolved because of the Second World War, the retention of a right of appeal to a court located overseas, composed of British judges who had little familiarity with local values, came to be seen as incompatible with notions of an independent nation's sovereign status. In many cases this was followed by the abolition of the appeal to the Privy Council as a court of last resort.[31] Further, following the ruling of the Privy Council in *Australian*

---

be determined otherwise than in accordance with the wishes of the part of the Empire primarily affected', in 'Summary of Proceedings of the Imperial Conference', 19. Finally, Lord Balfour, at the Imperial Conference of 1926, with reference to the Dominions spoke of 'autonomous communities within the British Empire, equal in status, in no way subordinate one to another in respect of their domestic or external affairs' (*The Royal Empire Soc.* [1931] 172 L.T. 392).

28   The law established the principle of the validity of colonial laws, as long as they were not in conflict with an Act of the Westminster Parliament, even though in breach of established principles of common law.

29   Despite the consequent recognition of the autonomy of the former British Dominions, some of them, such as Canada and Australia, retain the British monarch as head of state. See T.E. Frosini, 'Le derivazioni dirette del sistema inglese: Australia, Canada, Nuova Zelanda' in P. Carrozza, A. Di Giovine and G.F. Ferrari (eds), *Diritto costituzionale comparato* (Laterza, 2009).

30   See Anonymous, 'Decline of the Judicial Committee of the Privy Council. Current status of appeals from the British Dominions' (1947) 60 *Harvard Law Review* 1139. Canada, in particular, led the way in seeking emancipation from British paternalism. In 1875, a bill had been introduced in Parliament that, among other things, provided for the abolition of the right of appeal to the Judicial Committee of the Privy Council, although this provision was later removed from the final text of the draft to avoid being totally quashed in Parliament. The Supreme Court Act 1875 preserved the prerogative of the Assembly to judge in last resort on the appeals of the local courts. Conversely, confirmation of the intention to preserve the jurisdiction of the Privy Council, can be found in the decision *Nadan v The King* [1926] AC 482 (PC), which declared as unconstitutional an amendment to the Canadian Criminal Code which stated that the Canadian Supreme Court was the court of final jurisdiction in criminal cases. Only after the approval of the Statute of Westminster in 1931 was the path towards abolition of the appellate jurisdiction of the Judicial Committee of the Privy Council firmly established. On this point see 'Abolition of appeal to the Judicial Committee of the Privy Council by Canada and the Irish Free State' (1936) *Virginia Law Review* 342.

31   J.N. Matson, 'The Common Law abroad: English and indigenous laws in the British Commonwealth' (1993) 42 *International and Comparative Law Quarterly* 753; K.J. Keith, 'The unity of the Common Law and the ending of appeals to the Privy Council' (2005) 54 *International and Comparative Law Quarterly* 197; Anonymous, 'Decline of the Judicial Committee of the Privy Council. Current Status of Appeals from the British Dominions' (1947) 60 *Harvard Law Review* 1140.

Consolidated Press Ltd. v Uren it was made clear that 'the need for uniformity is not compelling', confirming the independence of local courts from having to always follow the common law as stated by the House of Lords and the Privy Council.[32] Even before this, in *Parker v The Queen*, the Australian High Court had departed from the reasoning of House of Lords in the earlier case of *Smith*,[33] holding in *Parker* that *Smith* was a decision that was 'misconceived and wrong'. Judge Dixon said on that occasion:

> Hitherto I have thought that we ought to follow decisions of the House of Lords, at the expense of our own opinions and cases decided here, but having carefully studied Smith's case I think that we cannot adhere to that view or policy. There are propositions laid down in the judgment [...] which I could never bring myself to accept [...] I think Smith's case should not be used as authority in Australia at all.[34]

Again, in *Skelton v Collins* Judge Windeyer highlighted the different British and Australian conditions suggesting that the Australian High Court should release itself from the House of Lords who made 'only reference to English decisions [...] and seemingly only to meet economic and social conditions prevailing in England'.[35]

The same approach was followed by New Zealand.[36] In *Hart v O'Connor*, while dismissing the appeal, the Privy Council, referring to the earlier case of *Archer v Cutler*, emphasised that:

> If *Archer v Cutler* is properly to be regarded as a decision based on considerations peculiar to New Zealand, it is highly improbable that their Lordships would think it right to impose their own interpretation of the law, thereby contradicting the unanimous conclusions of the High Court and the Court of Appeal of New Zealand on a matter of local significance. If however the principle of *Archer v Cutler*, if it be correct, must be regarded as having general application throughout all jurisdictions based on the common law, because it does not depend on local considerations, their Lordships could not properly treat the unanimous view of

---

32   [1969] 1 AC 590, 641. In other words, 'The Privy Council is thus recognizing that the common law may speak with different accents in different parts of the world. There is no assumption of universality and no necessary policy of the desirability of uniformity': G.W. Bartholomew, 'English law in *Partibus Orientalium*' in A.J. Harding (ed.), *The Common Law in Singapore and Malaysia* (Butterworths, 1985) 25.

33   *DPP v Smith* [1961] AC 290.

34   (1963) 111 CLR 610, 632.

35   (1966) 116 CLR 94, 135. See also *Malaysia Bin Jamil v Harum. Yang Kamsiah Bte Meor Rasdi* [1984] 1 AC 529, 535, the Privy Council held that it fell within the jurisdiction of the Courts of Malaysia, instead of the Privy Council, to decide when to depart from English law.

36   R. Cooke, 'Divergences-England, Australia and New Zealand' (1983) *New Zealand Law Journal* 297.

the courts of New Zealand as being necessarily decisive. In their Lordships' opinion the latter is the correct view of the decision.[37]

The arguments of the Privy Council, which supported the possibility that the common law could differ in countries such as Australia and New Zealand, should have been even more relevant when applying common law in Hong Kong. If this process of differentiation of law in the various areas of the Commonwealth was a response to needs arising from specific economic and social contexts then clearly there were greater similarities between British and Australian society than between the English and the Hong Kong societies. Despite this, in the *de Lasala* case the Privy Council, noting a trend to align with the common law as it is interpreted in England regardless of more or less marked specificities, made it clear that:

> Different considerations [...] apply to decisions of the House of Lords on the interpretation of recent legislation that is common to Hong Kong and England. Here there is no question of divergent development of the law [...] Since the House of Lords as such is not a constituent part of the judicial system of Hong Kong it may be that in juristic theory it would be more correct to say that the authority of its decisions on any question of law, even the interpretation of recent common legislation, can be persuasive only; but looked at realistically its decisions on such a question will have the same practical effect as if they were strictly binding, and courts in Hong Kong would be well advised to treat them as being so.[38]

The apparent inconsistency in the orientation of the Privy Council regarding uniformity in the application of the law in the Commonwealth is not due solely to historical reasons. Failure to achieve uniformity is partly attributable to the heterogeneous system of rules for the reception of common law at the local level and to the territorial structure of the complex map of the State appeals. The Privy Council's intent to maintain its traditional role as a promoter of cohesion in the Commonwealth is also not conducive to achieving uniformity, in so far as cohesion may require acknowledgement of differences and diversity. This is further complicated where there are 'mixed' areas of jurisdiction, where common law and civil law collide, as in the legal system of Hong Kong for example.[39] Instead,

> [t]he Commonwealth, widely thought to be an anachronism, survives intact, without any significant role for the Privy Council. The Privy Council has,

---

37 [1985] 1 AC 1000, 1017.

38 *de Lasala v de Lasala* [1980] AC 546, 558; [1979] HKLR 214, 220–21.

39 The Hong Kong Special Administrative Region, established in 1997 under Article 31 of the Chinese Constitution, has preserved the body of regulation of the common law in force before that date, while ensuring the reconciliation with the Chinese system based on the civil law model. With reference to the validity of common law after the passage of Hong Kong under the Chinese rule, see *HKSAR v Ma Wai Kwan David* [1997] 2 HKC 315.

however, played its part in creating the friendly atmosphere which keeps the Commonwealth together as a free association of sovereign States. The Privy Council's willingness and ability to respond to the changing political and constitutional background of the British Empire and Commonwealth have allowed the common law to continue to engender respect in the many jurisdictions where it has been adopted. As a result, in the Asia-Pacific region, the common law is seen not as a relic of alien imposition, but as the foundation of a variety of largely similar legal systems which serve their various jurisdictions well. Though they may no longer share a final court of appeal, the common law jurisdictions of the Asia-Pacific region, and indeed the whole Commonwealth, still have a great deal to learn from one another's experiences in the law.[40]

In conclusion, the receptivity of the Privy Council to social and political changes, while constituting an admission of the heterogeneity of national experiences within the Commonwealth, has given flexibility in time and space to the common law legal tradition, safeguarding its survival in related but alternative forms in the territories in which it was traditionally established.

The Paradox of the Common Law between Uniformity and Local Variants

The harmonising role of the Committee has been encouraged by the rule of precedent, according to which a principle or rule established in a previous legal case is either binding on, or persuasive for, a lower court. The judgements of the Privy Council have the force of binding precedent in any legal system that recognises the Privy Council as a court of final jurisdiction, and are binding not only on the courts of the country in which the judgement was issued, but on the courts of all the countries of the Commonwealth under its jurisdiction.[41] Even where a country has abolished appeal to the Privy Council as a court of final jurisdiction, precedents flowing from the Privy Council remain binding in respect of any cases pending at the time of abolition. A Judicial Committee of the Privy Council appeal decision concerning an overseas territory court judgement was also persuasive in respect of the domestic courts of England and Wales as stated in *London Joint Stock Bank v Macmillan & Arthur*.[42] Privy Council precedents were also regarded as binding in practice on the domestic courts of first instance in those matters for which legislation passed in Westminster

---

40   W.S. Clarke, 'The Privy Council, politics and precedent in the Asia-Pacific region' (1990) 39 *International and Comparative Law Quarterly* 741, 756.

41   See J.W. Harris, 'The Privy Council and the Common Law' (1990) 106 *Law Quarterly Review* 574 and supporting dicta in: *Trimble v Hill* (1879) 5 App. Cas. 342, 345 and *Breuer v Wright* [1982] 2 NXLR 77. Cf.: *Negro v Pietro's Bread Co. Ltd.* [1933] 1 DLR 490.

42   [1918] AC 777.

was extended to the English colonies, creating a shared legal framework.[43] As explained by Judge Lindley

> It is true that the decisions of the Privy Council are not theoretically binding in this court [i.e., the Court of Appeal in England]; but in case of mercantile or admiralty law, where the same principles are professedly followed in the colonies and in this country, it is, to say the least, highly undesirable that there should be any conflict between the decisions of the Judicial Committee and those of the High Court or Courts of Appeal in this country.[44]

Where there was a conflict between the precedents of the House of Lords and those of the Privy Council the law in force in one of the countries of the Commonwealth was derived from English legislation and jurisprudence, then the interpretation of that law by the House of Lords was binding on the Council and domestic courts.[45]

However, when ruling on the 1952 case of *Fatuma Binti Mohamed Bin Salim Bakhshuwen v Mohamed Bin Salim Bakhshuwen*,[46] which raised issues of 'Mohammedan' law, it became clear that when the Privy Council was cited as the authority for English law, this did not reveal the full picture. The law of the Commonwealth countries was not exactly English law, although it originated from it. Furthermore, because, for example, the *Mohammedan Law* as applied in India was different from that applied in East Africa the doctrine of binding precedent could only be valid for Privy Council's decisions related to the implementation of the law in the same Commonwealth country. In fact when ruling on an Indian appeal the Judicial Committee of the Privy Council acted as an Indian court, while when ruling on African appeals it acted as an African court.

---

43 See *Combe v Edwards* (1877) 2 PD 354.

44 *The City of Chester* (1884) 9 PD 182, 207.

45 *Robins v National Trust Co. Ltd.* [1927] AC 515, 519. See also *Tai Hing Cotton Mill Ltd. v Liu Chong Hing Bank Ltd.* [1986] AC 80, in which Lord Scarman claimed that: 'The Judicial Committee is not the final judicial authority for the determination of English law. That is the responsibility of the House of Lords in its judicial capacity'. The decision *Tai Hing* confirmed the decision *De Lasala v De Lasala* [1980] AC 546 declaring the essential uniqueness of interpretation provided by the House of Lords on all the English laws adopted in the territories forming part of the Commonwealth. See also, the decision in the case *Hart v O'Connor* [1985] AC 1000, in which the Privy Council insisted on the convergence between the common law of New Zealand and that of Australia and England. In *Jamaica Carpet Mills Ltd. v First Valley Bank* (1986) 45 WIR 278 the Jamaican Court of Appeal faced conflicting decisions of the House of Lords and of the Privy Council. It held that if the decision of the House of Lords exposes an error in the ruling of the Privy Council, even where a court is normally bound by the judgements of the Privy Council, it has to follow the decision of the House of Lords. See R. Cross and J.W. Harris, *Precedent in English Law* (Oxford University Press, 1991) 22 ff.

46 [1952] AC 1, 14.

A clear statement on this matter was made in the *Uren* case, which showed how the courts of the Commonwealth were not necessarily bound by the decisions of the House of Lords, thus the dictum of the *Robins* decision – that 'if the authority in England is that of the House of Lords. That is the supreme tribunal to settle English law, and that being settled, the Colonial Court, which is bound by English law, is bound to follow it'[47] – must be regarded as modified.[48] Moreover, the common law might be viewed as being one and indivisible, increasingly when acting as appeal court the Privy Council had to apply the domestic law of the country from which the appeal was being made, which created problems if it was also to be bound by the application of the House of Lords precedents relating to appeals against English court's rulings under the English common law.[49] While the Council considered, for example, it was 'regrettable that there should be any divergence between English and New Zealand law on a point of fundamental principle',[50] and might be reluctant to abandon its role of seeking to ensure uniformity of law across the Commonwealth, this uniformity was nuanced and not monolithic. Although the judgements of the Privy Council were binding on all courts within its jurisdiction and had persuasive authority in respect of the English courts, the Privy Council was not usually bound by the decisions of the House of Lords, although the latter had undoubtedly persuasive effectiveness.[51] So that while it can be concluded that the Privy Council has always opted for a substantial line of continuity between the law of the Commonwealth and the English law it has also had to accommodate, to a greater or lesser extent, local elements of specificity in its approach.[52]

The paradox therefore lies in the Privy Council's role in serving to establish uniformity in the various jurisdictions and to create a common (imperial) law,[53]

---

47   *Robins v National Trust Co. Ltd* [1927] AC 515, 519.

48   [1969] 1 AC 590.

49   See H.H. Marshall, 'The binding effect of decisions of the Judicial Committee of the Privy Council' (1968) 17 *International and Comparative Law Quarterly*, 743. See also: T.O. Elias, 'Colonial courts and the doctrine of Judicial Precedent' (1955) 18 *Modern Law Review* 356. It is an important step forward compared to the original powers of the Judicial Committee of the Privy Council that 'applies every variety of law – religious and secular, primitive native customs, English, French, Dutch, Spanish and Indian codes, decrees and ordinances of colonial governments, Turkish law which is maintained in Cyprus and Palestine, and the Moslem, Hindu and Jewish religious jurisprudence which is administered in religious courts within the British domain. It applies, too, to international conventions, and may be called upon to declare the law of nations and interpret it for the British realm'. Bentwich (n22) 392.

50   *Invercargill City Council v Hamlin* [1996] 1 All ER 756 (PC), 527.

51   P.F. Smith, S.H. Bailey and M.J. Gunn, *The Modern English Legal System* (Sweet & Maxwell, 1991) 397.

52   *Edward Wong Finance Co. Ltd. v Johnson, Stokes and Master* [1984] 2 WLR 1.

53   See A.P. Poley, 'The Privy Council and problems of closer union of the Empire' (1917) 17 *Journal of the Society of Comparative Legislation* 30.

which originates from the state of subjection to the British Empire of the various nations, and its need to evolve in the context of political, social and economic growth of those same jurisdictions as they have become emancipation from Britain.[54] The doctrine of precedent has exalted the paradox of common law, which on one hand, might be considered as an immutable set of rules, while on the other hand it has the capacity to evolve together with the social and economic contexts.[55] The Privy Council, in fact, enhanced the tendency to exaltation of national specificities, recognising the need to respect the diversity expressed by the judges of each country in their work of interpretation and implementation of the law. In making judgements the Privy Council has had to consider domestic realities. As observed in the New Zealand context:

> Although inheriting English common law, it did not follow that New Zealand common law would develop identically. The Court of Appeal should not be deflected from developing New Zealand common law merely because the House of Lords had not regarded an identical development as appropriate in England.[56]

In other words the Privy Council endorsed the harmonisation of the law in the Commonwealth while preserving the development of an autonomous national common law, as Martin emphasises:

> [...] the strength of the common law lies not in its conformity, but in its ability to adapt to changing circumstances. The common law of England has learned much from the development of law in Canada and Australia, where different but equally able minds have chosen to tackle difficult legal problems in different ways. The common law can only benefit from this plurality of approach.[57]

Emancipation from the Privy Council and its Subsequent Role

Where appeal to the Privy Council has been abolished the same courts have declared the authority of the Privy Council's decisions as purely persuasive. For example, in Guyana appeal to Her Majesty in Council in civil and criminal matters was abolished in 1970 (appeal on constitutional matters was abolished

---

54   R. Martin, 'Diverging common law: Invercargill goes to the Privy Council' (1997) 60 *Modern Law Review* 94.

55   On the rule of precedent and the acceptance of English common law by the British colonies: P. Stein, 'Common law (paesi di) I) Diritto inglese' and 'Common law (paesi di) II) Diffusione del Common Law', *Enciclopedia Giuridica Treccani* VII (1988).

56   *Invercargill City Council v Hamlin* [1996] 1 All ER 756 (PC) 513. The point had already been stressed by Lord Diplock in *Cassell & Co. Ltd. v Broome* [1972] AC 1027.

57   Martin (n54) 101.

in 1973). In *Persaud v Plantation Versailles & Schoon Ord Ltd.*, Judge Crane explained that

> consequent on the removal of the Privy Council as our final court of appeal, the doctrine of stare decisis, in so far as that court is concerned, is a dead letter with us; its former judgments are now only of persuasive authority. Of course, we shall regard them as we have always done in the highest esteem; we shall continue to cite, apply and to follow them and, when we do so, they will thereafter speak with our authority [...] It seems to me that it is only the natural consequence of its abolition as the final court of appeal for Guyana that the Privy Council should lose its place as a binding force in the hierarchy of authority. Ipso jure, its pronouncements have ceased to be authoritative.[58]

In some countries of the Commonwealth, such as Australia, the High Courts have on several occasions departed from precedents of the House of Lords, and with the abolition of appeal to the Privy Council local judges have acquired the necessary degree of autonomy to ensure a more appropriate application of local law. This has led to the start of a process of reference to English precedents not as part of a legal system to which all legal systems of the Commonwealth belong, but as foreign law from a comparative perspective.[59] This has been particularly noticeable in the newly established Supreme Courts. In fact, many recent research studies on the dialogue between Supreme Courts have pointed out that in the area of civil law the citation of foreign precedents is sporadic and less articulated, while in the area of common law there is a frequent cross-fertilisation. Foreign precedents are used in the cognitive phase of interpretation in order to define the orientation of the law, as an element of evidence in the phase of decision-making, and as an argumentative line of reasoning in judgements. Sometimes the use of foreign and supranational case law is also employed to support arguments to the contrary.[60] Furthermore, belonging as they do to the family of common law, it has

---

58   *Persaud v Plantation Versailles & Schoon Ord Ltd.* (1970) 17 WIR 107, 132. The virtual independence declaration of the Guyana courts was echoed in the decision *Viro v R* (1978) 141 CLR 88 where Judge Gibbs claimed that the High Court of Australia would no longer be bound by the judgements of the Privy Council as 'Part of the strength of the common law is its capacity to evolve gradually so as to meet the changing needs of society. It is for this court to assess the needs of Australian society and to expound and develop the law for Australia in the light of that assessment'.

59   It has been stated in the case of Australia that: 'The history of this country and of the common law makes it inevitable and desirable that the courts of this country will continue to obtain assistance and guidance from the learning and reasoning of United Kingdom courts just as Australian courts benefit from the learning and reasoning of other great common law courts' (*Cook v Cook* [1986] HCA 73).

60   See T. Groppi and M-.C. Ponthoreau (eds), *The Use of Foreign Precedents by Constitutional Judges* (Hart Publishing, 2013).

been almost unavoidable to local courts to refer to English and Commonwealth precedents, in particular when adopting a comparative approach for the protection of fundamental rights.[61] It is true that the emancipation from English precedents has led the courts of the Commonwealth to have a creative role in the development of the common law and contribute to the localisation of the common law as well as its diffusion.[62]

Conclusion

The composition of the Judicial Committee of the Privy Council is an indicator of its role.[63] It is composed of members of the Supreme Court of the United Kingdom (the former Lords of Appeal in Ordinary, or members of the Appellate Committee of the House of Lords), members of the Privy Council that have held a 'high judicial office',[64] by the Lords Justices of Appeal, members of the Court of Appeal, and the higher judges from the countries of the Commonwealth for which the Judicial Committee of the Privy Council operates as a court of appeal. There is, consequently a clear the link between the Judicial Committee of the Privy Council and the organisation of the courts of common law.[65] This composition has, on the one hand, fostered the circulation of uniform interpretation within the Commonwealth territories, on the other hand, in recent decades it has also symbolised the localisation of the law of the British Commonwealth. The establishment, among others, of the Eastern Caribbean Supreme Court, instead of the Privy Council, as a court of final jurisdiction, is a clear example of a reaction against this, although the fact that its members are trained in British universities and Inns of Court means that they continue to be carriers of the English common law, legal heritage. Similarly in countries such as New Zealand, released from the ties of the harmonising role of the Privy Council – although it remains a symbol of the persistence of the link with the former mother country – there has been a noticeable trend towards localisation in implementing the law, which is evidence of New Zealand's constitutional maturity process. The approval of the

---

61   M. Gobbo, 'L'utilizzo giurisprudenziale della comparazione negli ordinamenti australiano e neo-zelandese' in G.F. Ferrari and A. Gambaro (eds), *Corti nazionali e comparazione giuridica* (Edizioni Scientifiche Italiane, 2006) 207 ff.

62   *Mabo v The State of Queensland* (No 2) [1992] 175 CLR 1. See the remarks made on this decision by Gobbo (n61) 221–4.

63   'The composition of the Judicial Committee […] denotes the character (and, as it were, the mission) of a "transnational court"'. L. Moccia, *Comparazione giuridica e diritto europeo* (Giuffrè, 2005) 559.

64   See Schedule 16, s. 2(2), Constitutional Reform Act 2005. One effect of the reform is that Lord Chancellor is no longer a member of the Committee.

65   R.M. Jackson, *The Machinery of Justice in England* (Cambridge University Press, 1977).

Supreme Court Act 2003 which provided for the establishment of the Supreme Court of New Zealand, as a court of final jurisdiction, consisting of judges who are responsible for implementing the law on the basis of the essential knowledge of New Zealand's history and context,[66] marks a clear break from appeal to the Judicial Committee of the Privy Council and its perceived incapacity in making a proper assessment of the social and legal context of New Zealand.[67] Even so, the attitude in New Zealand, which, compared to Canada, India, Pakistan, Australia and Malaysia, has only recently decided to abolish the appeal to the Privy Council, has been ambivalent because of a substantial academic, political and judicial mistrust of the local courts which led in the past to greater respect being afforded to the jurisprudence of the Privy Council.[68]

The recent localisation of the common law in the Commonwealth confirms the observations of E. Örücü according to whom:

> grouping legal systems into legal families separates the members of one grouping from another. Although the significantly similar are put together, even in that similarity one is also highlighting the difference to make them distinctive. [...] within the groups difference is still of value although there is similarity. Originality, derivation and common elements surface behind the efforts of classifications. [...] The relationship between a legal system and its

---

66   See: F. Duranti, 'L'istituzione della Corte suprema e l'evoluzione del costituzionalismo neozelandese' (2004) 3 *Diritto Pubblico Comparato ed Europeo* 1557; P. Nevill, 'New Zealand: The Privy Council is replaced with a domestic Supreme Court' (2005) 3 *International Journal of Constitutional Law* 115; M. Olivier, 'Judicial diversity in New Zealand' (2010) 2 *Public Law* 241. According to section 3 of the Supreme Court Act, the Court is established 'to recognise that New Zealand is an independent nation'.

67   *Wallis v Solicitor General* (1903) NZPCC 730. In this case Judge Edwards noted: 'The Judges of this court are not unaccustomed to have their decisions upon the statute laws of the Colony reversed by their Lordships with something akin to contempt, although their Lordships might well reflect that trained lawyers who have spent their lives in the Colony, who know and understand its genius, its laws and its customs, as they cannot hope to know and understand them; who have spent anxious days and much thought and reflection in the elucidation of the laws of their country, to which their Lordships themselves can give but a brief and hurried consideration; who have the assistance of an able and zealous Bar (many of whose members are also members of the English Bar), well-versed in the laws of the Colony, while their Lordships themselves must depend as a rule upon such assistance as they can get from members of the English Bar, who know nothing of such laws – their Lordships might well reflect, I say, that the Judges of this Court are under those circumstances at least as likely to arrive at the correct conclusion as to the meaning of the statute law of the Colony as they are themselves' (759).

68   See: M. Richardson, 'The Privy Council and New Zealand' (1997) 46 *ICLQ* 908; J. Mc Soriley, 'New Zealand's link with the Privy Council and the proposed Supreme Court', available at <http://www.parliament.nz> accessed 8 March 2014.

socio-cultural context does not stand in the way of its relationship with other legal systems or even with other socio-cultural contexts. [...] legal systems can never be placed in fixed positions for all time and in all areas of law.[69]

The establishment of local Supreme Courts shows the willingness of national experiences to free themselves from the juridical imperialism of the Privy Council. At the same time, however, the Privy Council has endorsed the dialogue between different jurisdictions. The abolition of appeal to the Privy Council as the court of final jurisdiction, has allowed new 'leaders' to emerge in this process. For example, the jurisprudence of certain Supreme Courts, especially the Canadian, has become a benchmark for the interpretation of constitutional provisions or Charters of Rights,[70] in spite of the on-going development of precedents by other national supreme courts within the Commonwealth. Indeed, the Canadian Supreme Court is the main source of inspiration for the Constitutional Court of South Africa and in some cases the Canadian case law is the best example to follow.[71] The Canadian case law is considered to be helpful in many cases not only because of the similarities between the Canadian Charter of Rights and Freedoms and the South African Bill of Rights, but because of the persuasive reasoning of the Supreme Court of Canada.[72] The New Zealand Bill of Rights and the Basic Laws of Israel in matters of rights are also inspired by the Canadian Charter, provoking a broad use of the Supreme Court precedent. Even following the establishment of the Supreme Court in 2003, the Canadian case law continues to be the reference point for the interpretation of section 5 of the New Zealand Bill of Rights about the 'justified limitations'.

Moving away from the legal imperialism of the Privy Council's led therefore, to a process of circulation of models with a persuasive, but rather extended, authority which has moved beyond the original focus on harmonisation. Commonalities can still be found arising from the historical bonds with the parent legal system and are illustrated by the frequent citation of precedents drawn from the law of England and Wales.[73] At the same time, this evolution has led to different scenarios due to

---

69   E. Örücü, 'Looking at convergence through the eyes of a comparative lawyer' (2005) *Electronic Journal of Comparative Law* 3–4.

70   T. Groppi, 'La circolazione della giurisprudenza canadese sulla Carta dei diritti e delle libertà', available at <www.unisi.it> accessed 8 March 2014.

71   See *S v Zuma and others* (CCT5/94) [1995] (2) S.A. 642 (S. Afr. Const. Ct.), and J. Sarkin, 'The effect of constitutional borrowings on the drafting of South Africa's Bill of Rights and interpretation of human rights provisions' (1998) 1 *University of Pennsylvania Journal of Constitutional Law* 176.

72   See S. Choudry, 'Globalization in search of justification: Toward a theory of comparative constitutional interpretation' (1999) *Indiana Law Journal* 819, 848.

73   N. Olivetti Rason, 'La comparazione nella giurisprudenza della Corte suprema del Canada' in G.F. Ferrari and A. Gambaro (n61), 345. See also, C.L. Ostberg, M.E. Wetstein and C.R. Ducat, 'Attitudes, precedents and cultural change: Explaining the citation of

the changing constitutional assets in an area characterised by common origins but heterogeneous growth.

It is possible to regard the Privy Council as an instrument that has contributed to the development of localised common law that is today articulated through national supreme courts where appeal to the Privy Council has been abolished, and by the Privy Council where it has not, underpinning which there are shared legal traditions. Looking at the Constitutional Reform Act 2005,[74] the institution of the Supreme Court of the United Kingdom could be considered the inevitable culmination of a trend towards the localisation of the interpretation of the law.[75] Although the new Supreme Court of the United Kingdom has taken over the judicial functions performed by the Judicial Committee of the Privy Council in respect of devolution issues, it is also important to emphasise the role of the Supreme Court in picking up the baton of the Judicial Committee of the Privy Council and its harmonising role, through its use of the comparative method with particular reference to the jurisprudence of common law countries.[76] While the Supreme Court is also potentially a place of comparison with the courts of civil law countries and supranational courts, familiarity is a main determinant in the choice of foreign precedents selected for comparative interpretation by the British judges.[77] Unsurprisingly most of the cited cases have come from the courts of the Commonwealth, including Australian, Canadian and New Zealand Supreme Courts, with the majority of cross-referencing being to cases involving guarantees of fundamental rights.

The Supreme Court of the United Kingdom, described as a substantially Constitutional Court,[78] has already shown a marked openness to dialogue and may become the means whereby there is renewed circulation of common law case law, following in the footsteps initiated by the Judicial Committee of the Privy Council.

---

foreign precedents by the Supreme Court of Canada' (2001) 34 *Canadian Journal of Political Science* 377.

74   Following the 2005 reform, the Supreme Court has inherited the judicial functions of the Judicial Committee of the Privy Council and the Appellate Committee of the House of Lords, becoming a court of final jurisdiction in civil matters for England, Wales, Scotland and Northern Ireland, and in criminal cases for England, Wales and Northern Ireland. For a comment on the law and its stated objectives see: D. Woodhouse, 'The Constitutional Reform Act 2005 – Defending judicial independence the English way' (2007) 5 *International Journal of Constitutional Law* 153; F. Gandini, 'Brevi note sulla istituzione della Corte suprema per il Regno Unito' (2009) V *Il Foro italiano* parte 238.

75   Constitutional Reform Act 2005, s 40.

76   See A. Torre, 'Regno Unito: giustizia costituzionale e comparazione in un paese "senza costituzione"' in G.F. Ferrari and A. Gambaro (eds), *Corti nazionali e comparazione giuridica* (ESI 2006) 167 ff.

77   Choudhry (n72) 838.

78   This was the expression used by Lord Clarke answering the questions of an Italian research delegation visiting the Supreme Court in June 2013.

Chapter 6

'Lease, *Locazioni* and *Kera*': Merging Legal Concepts in Postcolonial Malta

David Zammit and Kurt Xerri

Diffusion within the Maltese Jurisdiction

This chapter explores an example of internal diffusion, in which legal concepts have migrated from one sector to another of the Maltese legal system, leading to a merging of civilian, common law and indigenous concepts of rent law, which reflects a rare moment of political consensus in Malta following independence from Britain. As an example of internal diffusion within a small mixed jurisdiction, it serves to problematise and challenge many of the orthodox assumptions about diffusion which were critiqued by William Twining in a leading article on the topic.[1] Specifically, Twining invited legal scholars to consider how diffusion may operate outside and beyond the framework of a standard colonial and neo-colonial context, where the sources of importation of legal concepts are diverse and where diffusion can occur horizontally and across levels of ordering. He also showed how diffusion may occur through complex and indirect pathways which bypass the legislator, for instance via a judicial decision or even more informal routes. Agents of diffusion can be jurists or legal elites, not necessarily governments and the process of reception may be a long drawn out process which belies imperialist 'top down' models of transmission and transforms the legal concepts involved in the process. We shall see how most of these features of diffusion can be exemplified by this Maltese case and we shall focus particularly on:

> how importation of and resistance to foreign legal ideas, laws and institutions often forms part of some broader local political struggle.[2]

---

1   W. Twining, 'Diffusion of law: A global perspective' (2004) 49 *Journal of Legal Pluralism & Unofficial Law* ix.
2   Twining, ibid. 28.

The Historical Background

The British, that assumed de facto control of the Maltese islands in 1800,[3] tried for a long time to introduce elements of their language and culture into Maltese society. This process of cultural exportation, however, encountered strong resistance, especially due to the fact that the alert Maltese political class had been advocating autonomy since the very advent of the colonisers. Consequently whatever was Anglo-Saxon in nature was held to be both alien to Malta as well as threatening to its identity.[4] The spirit of the times is best summed up by Fenech:

> As for Maltese ethnicity, the vanguard of the Maltese political and educated class placed its locus in "Latin Europe" and did everything they could to hold it there.[5]

The Italian-speaking law courts, therefore, represented an eminent symbol of Maltese resilience and most of all the hub of the nationalist sentiment.

The Origins of Tenancy Law

Until 1925, rents had been regulated exclusively by the liberal provisions of the Maltese Civil Code.[6] In fact, despite decades of colonial rule, the Maltese system remained firmly rooted in the civilian tradition and, as underlined by Attard, it was, ironically, the British colonial administration that introduced the first Civil Code of the island.[7] The process of codification in fact reached its culmination with the enactment of Ordinance VII of 1868;[8] the new code was largely based on the *Jus Commune* and the *Code Napoléon* along with other continental codes and prominent juridical opinions.[9] The specific provisions on leases (*locazioni*)[10] had been previously introduced through Ordinances I, VII and XI of 1857.[11]

----

3   The island's status of Crown Colony would only become official in 1814 pursuant to the Treaty of Paris.

4   D. Fenech, *Responsibility and Power in Inter-war Malta – Book One: Endemic Democracy (1919–1930)* (San Gwann: Publishers Enterprises Group, 2005) 24.

5   Ibid.

6   Now indexed as chapter 16 of the Laws of Malta.

7   D.J. Attard, *The Maltese Legal System* (Malta University Press, 2012) 24.

8   Promulgated on the 11 February 1870.

9   Attard (n5) 24; P. De Bono, *Sommario della storia delle legislazione in Malta* (Tipografia del Malta, 1897) 293.

10   The Civil Code was introduced in the Italian language since Maltese was not yet recognised as an official language.

11   De Bono (n7) 293.

The Origin of the Special Statutes

The enactment of the first special law on leases arrived during a very promising moment in Malta's history. The Maltese had, in fact, just obtained an unprecedented degree of autonomy from the British colonisers and, as of 1921, all internal matters had fallen under the responsibility of an elected bicameral Parliament consisting of a Legislative Assembly and a Senate. The implications of the new scenario were that Maltese politicians had to amplify the political scope of their activities beyond the constitutional aspect. The plight of the tenants was brought to the fore by the Labour Party (LP) that, in turn, counted on the lower, vulnerable classes for electoral support.

As documented above, when the first rent control measures were introduced in 1925, tenancies had not known regulation for over 100 years. Until the housing crisis felt in the aftermath of the First World War, there was a certain complacency regarding the housing situation, probably stemming from the belief that if left alone, the market would provide adequate housing.[12] This changed soon after the introduction of self-government when the local administration was suddenly faced with a waning supply of dwellings and a mounting anxiety that landlords would exploit this tight situation.[13] Landowners formed a key part of the electorate and the membership of the major political parties and they were hostile towards any legislation that aimed to cap their profits or limit their absolute rights to property. The LP had, on the other hand, been advocating the enactment of a regulatory bill as early as 1921.[14] After a first failed attempt that was met with considerable scepticism on the part of the local legislative body, a second bill was approved in September 1924; not because the Assembly had become suddenly convinced of the impending need to safeguard tenants but rather as it was the price the MLP had put on their vote of confidence to the government.[15]

Despite superseding the Civil Code, this new rent law still remained true to civilian concepts. The author of the first draft legislation (that was dropped by the Assembly), Pier G. Frendo, had both quoted the German Civil Code[16] and declared the influence of Italian legal decrees on the Maltese Bill;[17] specifically

---

12   U. Mifsud Bonnici, 'Housing rights in Malta' in S. Leckie (ed.), *National Perspectives on Human Rights* (Nijhoff, 2003) 253–7.

13   Ibid.

14   G. Bonnici, *Storja tal-Partit tal-Ħaddiema* (*Sensiela Kotba Soċjalisti*, 1990 (reprint)) 40.

15   Ibid. 83.

16   Frendo quoted Article 138 of the German Civil Code: 'in particular a legal transaction is void by which a person, by exploiting the predicament, inexperience, lack of sound judgment or considerable weakness of will of another, causes himself or a third party, in exchange for an act of performance, to be promised or granted pecuniary advantages which are clearly disproportionate to the performance'.

17   A.M. Saliba, *First Labour Party Legislative Initiatives under the 1921 Self-government Constitution*, dissertation submitted to the Faculty of Laws, University of Malta, 2012, 104.

the Italian laws No. 477 of 18 April 1920,[18] No. 331 of 3 April 1921,[19] and No. 1561 of 8 November 1921.[20] Upon closer examination of the latter Italian texts, however, one instantly perceives a certain severity – some clauses even prohibited the landlord from terminating the lease unless he could prove that he needed the premises for himself or that he was demanding them back due to some other grave reason[21] – and such provisions would never have formed the object of a consensus in the particularly bourgeois Assembly of Malta. Other Italian notions that Frendo had included in the first Bill were, however, taken up, such as the setting up an Arbitral Commission responsible for matters of increases in rent,[22] and proposed afresh in the second Bill.

The Control of Rents of Immovables Act[23] was therefore the first rent law to be passed by the Legislative Assembly. In comparison to the previous Bill, which had remained on the drafting board, this law contained significant concessions to the demands of the more conservative party in power. Clauses that had been included by Frendo in 1922, such as those guaranteeing security of tenure, had been abandoned and instead the new Bill sought only to protect tenants from excessive rents. The law, in fact, gave tenants the right to take any claim regarding orders of eviction, notices of rent increases or changes in conditions of tenancy to the newly set-up Arbitral Commission. The purpose of this body was to decide on extensions of tenancy and fix a reasonable rent for a maximum of three years – which was the established lifetime of the Act. The latter aspect is important since it effectively meant that tenants would only be given a fixed extension and they would not be guaranteed permanent security of tenure. The Act was in general very lenient with the landlords, especially when considering that elsewhere,

---

18 *Regio Decreto Legge 18 Aprile 1920, N. 477 – Contenente nuove disposizioni per gli affitti e le pigioni delle case di abitazione e degli edifici urbani ad uso di bottega, negozio, magazzino, studio, ufficio e simili* (Royal Legal Decree of 18 April 1920, Number 477 – Containing new provisions for rents and leases of dwelling houses and urban edifices used for shops, stores, workshops, studies, offices and such like).

19 *Regio Decreto Legge 3 Aprile 1921, N. 331 – Che proroga i contratti di locazione di appartamenti o di case di abitazione, contemplati nei numeri 1, 2, 3, 4, 5 dell'Art. 1 del decreto n. 477 del 1920, e stabilisce altresi nuove norme per le locazioni dei negozi* (Royal Legal Decree of 3 April 1921, Number 331 – Which extends the contracts of lease of the apartments or dwelling houses envisaged in numbers 1, 2, 3, 4, 5 of Article 1 of decree number 477 of 1920 and further establishes new norms for the letting of shops).

20 *Regio Decreto Legge 3 Novembre 1921, n. 1561 – Concernente la proroga di contratto di locazione di appartamenti o case ad uso di abitazione* (Royal Legal Decree of 3 November 1921, number 1561 – Concerning the extension of the contract of lease of apartments and dwelling houses).

21 *Regio Decreto Legge 18 Aprile 1920*, n. 477 § 11 (Royal Legal Decree of 18 April 1920, number 477 § 11).

22 *Regio Decreto Legge 3 Aprile 1921*, n. 331 § 5 (Royal Legal Decree of 3 April 1921, number 331 § 5).

23 Act I of 1925.

in England[24] and Italy[25] increases were being capped. A new provision sought to introduce some protection in that unless the proprietor gave one month's notice[26] to the tenant through an official letter, renewal would have taken place tacitly, based on exactly the same conditions of the previous agreement.[27]

Therefore it emerges how, even at this stage, it was Continental sources that were relied on in drafting Maltese rent legislation. In the United Kingdom, in fact, the concept of a specialised adjudicatory body would only be given due consideration after the end of the Second World War,[28] when the actual Rent Tribunal, regarded as an instrument of price-fixing, came into force through the enactment of the Landlord and Tenant (Rent Control) Act 1949.[29] The British seemed to have resisted this idea of arbitration because of the fear that these tribunals would have assumed competences which were not lodged in their hands, thus encroaching on the powers of the ordinary courts. It is interesting how Frendo, in the presentation of his first Bill in 1922, had shown a similar concern regarding a specialised 'tribunal' (in fact the term he had used in the Bill was 'Commission'), since he claimed that modern procedural law was against the establishment of such bodies. The Arbitral Commission, however, proved to be particularly successful and its status was soon raised to that of a 'Rent Regulation Board', just four years later in 1929. It would eventually be granted a wider competence through the Rent Restriction (Dwelling Houses) Ordinance[30] of 1944.

Act I of 1925 was renewed for another term in 1927 through the Re-letting of Urban Property Continuance Act and then replaced by the Urban Rent Regulation Act of 1929.[31] This new rent law followed the general lines of the first one, but it brought about a significant increase in tenants' rights. First of all, it provided for the establishment of a Board that could permit, and establish, an increase in rent in the case of properties where the landlord needed to carry out major structural

---

24   In the United Kingdom increases had been controlled according to the rateable value of the property since 1915 (Increase of Rent and Mortgage Interest (War Restrictions) Act).

25   *Regio Decreto Legge 18 Aprile 1920,* n. 477.

26   The initial proposition was that of 15 days, however, it was extended in order to give the tenant sufficient legroom to find an alternative accommodation. Saliba (n15) 109.

27   Saliba (n15) 108.

28   'Rent Control extension for 10 years after war', *The Glasgow Herald* (20 April 1945) 4, available at <http://news.google.com/newspapers?nid=2507&dat=19450420&id=b0BAAAAAIBAJ&sjid=eFkMAAAAIBAJ&pg=4060,5838017> accessed 18 July 2014. The first panel that advocated its introduction was the Inter-departmental Committee on Rent Control under the chairmanship of Viscount Ridley. It was proposed that the tribunals would be set up to determine fair rents for controlled houses and adjust all disputed rents in their respective jurisdictions, dealing first with rents that vary most from the average for houses of the same class.

29   'Statues: Landlord and Tenant (Rent Control) Act, 1949' (1950) 13 (1) *The Modern Law Review* 76.

30   Currently indexed as chapter 116 of the Laws of Malta.

31   Act XXIII of 1929.

repairs at his own expense. Moreover, the lessor needed prior permission from the board in cases of eviction, and he could only avail himself of three grounds for this: default in payment, non-observance of any conditions or the need of the property for himself or for his immediate family. The Act was effective until the end of 1933; therefore, once again, the law limited its protection and fell a step short of ensuring permanency of tenure. Despite not having based themselves on the English texts, the Maltese Members of the Assembly were nevertheless very much aware of what was happening in England. In fact, whilst Malta was tightening its control on leases, in the United Kingdom the trend was completely the opposite since rent control had hindered the construction industry significantly.[32] This point was even raised by Prime Minister Gerald Strickland in one of his speeches to the Assembly.[33]

The Colonial Intervention

The first stint of Maltese self-government was short lived and following a row between the governing party and the Church in 1930, the Constitution was suspended. This effectively meant that all internal matters reverted to being under British control. Interestingly, one of the laws which was retouched by the Governor during this brief period[34] was the rent law. The Re-letting of Urban Property (Regulation) Ordinance[35] was enacted through an Order-in-Council[36] with the specific aim of ameliorating the functioning of the 1929 Urban Rent Regulation Act. This legislation represented a step backwards in what concerned tenant protection and this was probably owing to the decontrolling trends that had developed in England following the first bout of post-war rent control measures. In fact, the calamitous effects of these restrictive provisions on the English housing supply had already given rise to the Rent and Mortgage Interest Restrictions Act 1923 and further decontrol subsequently would take place through the Rent and Mortgage Interest Restrictions (Amendment) Act of 1933.[37] Article 7 of the

---

32   J.F. Brenner and H.M. Franklin, *Rent Control in North America and Four European Countries: A Survey, Part 3* (Potomac Institute (Washington DC), Council for International Urban Liaison, Volumes 1–77 of International Urban Reports, 1977) 6–7.

33   Saliba (n15) 117.

34   The Constitution granting self-government was reintroduced in 1932 although the further degeneration of Anglo-Maltese relations led to Malta's return to the Crown Colony status in 1933. This situation was going to persist until the end of the war.

35   Ordinance XXI of 1931.

36   Under the colonial system an order-in-council was a regulation issued by the sovereign on the advice of the Governor.

37   Brenner (n30) 6: in 1923 a number of premises were decontrolled as soon as the landlord obtained vacant possession. In 1933, controlled dwellings were divided into three groups according to their rateable value. Those with the highest rate were decontrolled at once; those with the lowest ceased to be decontrollable; whilst those in the middle continued

Re-letting of Urban Property (Regulation) Ordinance, for instance, was amended to lay down that unless the tenant replied to the lessor's official letter within 15 days, he would have been considered to have accepted any new conditions of the tenancy proposed by the latter.

This move meant that the British had intruded in the Maltese legislative sphere and their intention to introduce Common Law concepts emerges clearly in the Explanatory Report of the Ordinance where it was further explained that 'the rights and duties of landlord and tenant during the lease (be this an agreed lease or a tacitly renewed one) [were to be] governed by the Common Law'.[38] This particular phrase clearly indicated a certain tactlessness towards Maltese nationalist sensitivities, although it could arguably have been interpreted to cover Roman law, understood as the Common Law of Malta and it probably reflected the new Governor's lack of preparation on local matters. When this Ordinance was enacted, on 19 June 1931, Sir David Campbell had only been in office for a fortnight[39] and this note appears to have gone unnoticed.

The revocation of the Constitution[40] nevertheless meant that Maltese politics reverted to concentrating solely on their struggle for autonomy. Other issues, such as rent regulation, took second stage and this gave an absolutely free hand to the Colonial government on all internal issues. British influence on Maltese tenancy law had not yet manifested itself fully; this was only going to occur after the Second World War.

Post-war Developments

Although the problem of housing shortages had been haunting Malta since the aftermath of the First World War, the devastation brought about by the second global conflict was to alter the scenario completely. The most densely populated areas of the island had not been spared by the conflict and the supply of housing had been reduced significantly. This prompted the British administration to adopt new measures designed to deal with the problem; these came in the form of rent freezes and the indefinite protection of tenants. The elements of the Rent Restriction (Dwelling Houses) Ordinance enacted in 1944[41] reflected most elements of the statutes being enacted in England.

---

to be decontrolled on vacant possession (although security of occupancy still applied). This liberalising process continued further in 1938.

38   Explanatory Report by the Treasury Counsel on Ordinance No. XXI of 1931, *The Malta Government Gazette* (19 June 1931) 525.

39   General Sir David Campbell had been appointed Governor of Malta on 4 June 1931.

40   It was going to be reintroduced for a brief period between July 1932 and November 1933.

41   Chapter 116 of the Laws of Malta.

In the meantime, British influence was also evident in the enactment of a number of emergency laws that authorised the government to requisition any building for re-allocation. The colonial administration had introduced the Land Acquisition Act of 1947, through which it speeded up the procedure involved in the governmental acquisition of land needed for reconstruction and town planning.[42] Two years later, in 1949, these powers were embodied in the Housing Act.[43] Requisitioning under emergency powers had been part of the British housing system since 1939 when it was made necessary, first by the war, and subsequently by the housing shortage.[44] In the meantime, self-government in Malta was finally reintroduced in December of 1947 and the first local post-war government proceeded to lower the 'fair rent' thresholds of leased premises even further.

These rent control measures, however, proved to be disproportionately harsh on landowners. According to the amended Rent Restriction (Dwelling Houses) Ordinance, dwellings erected prior to the war were to remain pegged to their 1939 prices whilst the cap on the rent of new buildings was fixed at 3 per cent of the freehold value of the site and 3.25 per cent of the capital outlay on construction.[45] Furthermore, a landlord needed the permission of the Board in order to raise the rent or alter the conditions of the agreement. The last former tenant along with his ascendants, descendants and other relatives by consanguinity or affinity also enjoyed a right of preference over any other tenant. These measures accompanied the new restrictive measures of the amended Re-letting of Urban Property (Regulation) Ordinance, which prohibited the lessor from refusing to renew the lease upon its expiration, if not with the consent of the Board.[46]

These provisions evidenced an emerging trend in the drafting of rent legislation. Unlike previous Acts, which had always been intended as temporary measures, the new statute made no reference to its intended demise and the future of rent control as a permanent fact of life was thereby assured.[47] In fact, even after the housing problem had subsided, most of these immediate post-war legislative measures survived.[48] Despite being aware of the grievances of landlords, the local government never made any attempt to amend the highly criticised rent law.[49]

It was precisely this problem that led to a very widespread practice, amongst Maltese landlords, of either letting houses furnished – thus exacting an extra

---

42   Ibid. 29.

43   Chapter 125 of the Laws of Malta.

44   W.I. Jennings, 'The Emergency Powers (Defence) (No. 2) Act, 1940' (1940) 4 (2) *The Modern Law Review* 132.

45   Rent Restriction (Dwelling Houses) Ordinance, § 2(ii).

46   Reletting of Urban Property (Regulation) Ordinance, § 3.

47   J. Rose, *The Dynamics of Urban Property Development* (Routledge Library Editions, 1985) 109. (Rose was dealing with the English Rent and Mortgage Interest Restrictions Act of 1939.)

48   Attard (n5) 35.

49   A. Camilleri, *Building Trends and Policies 1943–1981*, dissertation submitted to the Department of Architecture and Civil Engineering, University of Malta, 1982, 42.

sum for the furniture – or resorting to temporary emphyteutical[50] grants that enabled them to circumvent the restrictive measures imposed by the rent statutes.[51] Maltese tenants, particularly newly-weds, did not have much choice and they were constrained to enter these emphyteutical contracts for prices which were usually as high as those paid for market rents. Although being in evident breach of the intention of the law, the Courts seemed to turn a blind eye on this evasive avenue contrived by landowners. The evolution of tenancy law in Malta, set against the historical context of the time, thus seems to suggest that this reluctance on the part of the judicial organs to extend the reach of the special statutes to cases deriving from emphyteusis had its roots in a much deeper concern on whether to let an institute of civil law slip under the regulation of a colonial statute. At the heart of it all there lay the essence of the Maltese struggle for autonomy.

This state of affairs was never questioned, until in 1969 – only five years after the acquisition of Maltese independence from Britain in 1964 – the Court of Appeal finally seemed to grasp the nettle in the case of *Caterina Zahra v Saverio Frendo.*[52]

The Facts of the Case

The plaintiff's father had granted a property under temporary emphyteusis for a period of 32 years back in 1934. Ms Zahra ended up as the sole owner of the said premises and she claimed that with the expiration of the term of the emphyteusis there had been an 'ipso jure' consolidation of the title. She therefore filed a case in order to obtain a judgement that declared the defendant's prolonged occupation of the premises as wrongful. The defendant, on the other hand, opposed this claim by invoking the protection of the special rent statutes that were applicable by virtue of the valid title of lease (*lokazzjoni*) he had contracted with the emphyteutas[53] of the same premises some 13 years earlier. The essence of the question was whether a lease that had been granted by a temporary emphyteuta was deserving of the same protection as any other contract of lease. The argument of the defendant was, in fact, that the provisions of the Civil Code were in this case superseded by the

---

50   Emphytheusis is defined to mean ownership against an annual payment (*ċens*) for a defined period of time of any property. The contract which constitutes this right can be considered as one of almost complete transfer of ownership; the original owner, as a matter of fact, retains only the ground rent which is paid to him in recognition of his right, and the possibility of an eventual consolidation. From V. Caruana Galizia, 'Civil law notes: Law of things', unpublished copy obtained from the Malta University Library.

51   Ibid. 21.

52   Decided by the Court of Appeal (Malta) on 21 February 1969, Cit. 310/66.

53   The persons who had the 'utile dominium' of the property i.e. right of occupation as owner; as this is regarded as conferring a real right, it was perfectly legal for the emphyteutas to lease the property held in emphyteusis to third parties.

Re-letting of Urban Property (Regulation) Ordinance[54] that guaranteed security of tenure to the lessee.

This was not the first time the Maltese Superior Courts had confronted such a legal quandary. However, previous jurisprudence had consistently denied tenants of properties let out by emphyteutas the same level of protection granted to those who contracted their tenancies directly with the owner. Several judgements quoted the current Article 1530 of the Civil Code, which states that when the lessor would be in possession of the urban tenement under a temporary or dissoluble title, the lease would only remain valid if made on fair conditions until the expiry of the agreed term, for a maximum period of an additional four years.[55] Another judgement[56] had similarly confirmed that once the emphyteusis came to an end, the juridical position of the parties to the contract would be altered completely. The reasoning behind these decisions was that the direct owner could at no point be held to be a 'lessor' and consequently bound by the special statute. Behind this question, therefore, there seemed to lie an underlying sentiment of resistance to the possibility of allowing a colonial statute to supersede the Civil Code.

The Decision

The First Hall initially followed the prevailing opinion in the previous judgements and found in favour of the plaintiff. The defendant, however, took the matter before the Court of Appeal where he found a forum that was willing to expound a different theory from that which previous compositions of the Court had upheld. The court of second instance, in fact, contested the affirmation made in previous judgements that there existed no binding juridical relationship between the direct owner and the lessor of the property. It evidenced, on the other hand, that the reversion of the property in the hands of a direct owner was irrelevant to the special statute.

The Court of Appeal quoted a previous judgement[57] that presented an analogous circumstance deriving from a contract of usufruct. This judgement had held that the special law imposed on the owner the same obligations that had previously bound the usufructuary *qua* lessor, since the lease remained in place by virtue of the statute. The Court also relied on Italian doctrine and jurisprudence on similar questions arising out of usufruct; in Italy special laws were in fact held to prolong contracts beyond the title that the original lessors enjoyed over the property.[58]

---

54   Then indexed as chapter 109, now as chapter 69 of the Laws of Malta.

55   *Vella v Cuschieri*, decided by the Court of Appeal on 10 March 1948, vol. XXXIII.i.625.

56   *Magro v Pace*, decided by the Court of Appeal on 24 May 1954, vol. XXXVIII.i.319.

57   *Gabriele v Zahra*, decided by the Court of Appeal (Inferior) on 26 June 1957.

58   Amongst other sources the Court of Appeal quoted the judgement *Carrieri v Marsan* decided by the Court of Cassation on 19 June 1962 a. 1550: '*La ragione della decisione è semplicissima: in regime di proroga no è la volontà delle parti, ma quella della*

The Court of Appeal then veered into the wider argument regarding the scope of the special law. It remarked that the Ordinance's undisputed bias towards the tenant was the consequence of a serious housing shortage that had required the law to guarantee security of tenure for lessees. The Court therefore leaned toward a liberal interpretation of the scope of the Ordinance and held that leases contracted by 'temporary' owners were clearly intended to fall within the protective ambit of this statute:

> [...] Chapter 109 [now 69] did not give any definition of the word "landlord" or "lessor" and in the Court's opinion, this was done because its objective was to control renewal of leases; in this case one only had to look at who occupied the juridical position of "lessor" at the moment when renewal was to take place.

This judgement lays a particular emphasis on the special law's objective of derogating from the Civil Code's provisions, subtly inferring that all contrary decisions had disregarded the spirit of its enactment. The Court was of the opinion that direct owners had no reason to enjoy any exemptions since by the operation of the Statute the position of the direct owner would be 'transfused' into that of the lessor.

Merging Laws and Languages

Through *Zahra v Frendo,* the Court of Appeal effectively extended the scope of the term 'lease' as provided for in the Ordinance, to cover contracts originating from civil law concepts such as emphyteusis, that had until then, been regulated solely by the provisions of the Civil Code. The Court had therefore superimposed a statute inspired by common law sources and terminology upon an institute that was civilian in nature, thus conceptually fusing the two legal traditions. Until that point, in fact, the Maltese Courts had allowed common and civil law to sail parallel to each other and whilst bringing the special rent laws to bear on leases as understood in the strict meaning of the term, they precluded their applicability

---

legge che determina il protrarsi del rapporto' (The reason for the judgment is very simple: as regards the legal regime providing for the extension of the contract, it is not the will of the parties, but that of the law which determines the extension of the relationship). It also made use of G. Pescatore, 'Della Proprietà', 156: *'Non si contesta [...] l'applicabilità del regime della proroga legale anche alle locazione stipulate dell'usufruttuario: la conseguenza che ne deriva è che, in caso di cessazione dell'usufrutto, il regime di proroga ha la prevalenza su quello ordinario stabilito dall'articolo 999'* (The applicability of the regime of legal extension of the contract even to a contract of lease stipulated by the usufructuary is not contested: the consequence which derives from this is that, in cases where the usufruct terminates, the regime of legal extension prevails over the ordinary rules defined by article 999).

to other tenancy contracts governed by the Civil Code. *Zahra v Frendo*, on the other hand, captured the wider picture and brought every 'lessor', whatever the derivation of his or her title, under the protection of the Ordinance.

This decision seems to be imbued with further significance since it came at a fundamental turning point in Maltese constitutional history. The appeal was in fact decided just five years after the country's acquisition of independence from Britain, which is when the Maltese constitutional struggle against colonialism had finally been rewarded. During this immediate post-colonial period, the time must have seemed ripe to merge these two concepts and unify Maltese tenancy laws. This decision appears to represent a real moment of convergence; when a united national consciousness transcended the anti- and pro-British sentiment that had divided the Maltese political arena during the previous decades. It comes as no coincidence that such a ground-breaking case was decided by Chief Judge, Sir Anthony Mamo, a distinguished jurist who appealed to both major political parties and who would later be chosen by mutual agreement between them as the first President of the Republic of Malta.

Another noteworthy aspect is the fact that the Court of Appeal did not just perform an abstract analysis of the law applicable to the case. A *leitmotif* of this case is the way in which the Court, in the process of blending juridical concepts, also operated in the linguistic sphere, by equating the varied terminology which, due to the three languages being employed by Maltese law, had created another barrier to its holistic interpretation. After the mid-1930s, in fact, Maltese and English replaced Italian as the official language of legislation and Maltese replaced Italian as the language of the Court. Unlike subsequent statutes, which were increasingly pervaded by English legal terminology, the Civil Code, however, still relied very heavily on Italianate terminology and this seemed to create uncertainty. Moreover, the 'Italianate' Maltese which is still used by the Courts does not always enjoy an easy correspondence in meaning to the 'Semitic' Maltese which had been endorsed by the pro-British party. As a result of this culturally and linguistically hybrid context, Maltese legal discourse contained at least three different expressions referring to contract of lease and the person of the lessor (see Table 6.1).

The Court of Appeal made it clear that all these terms were referring to the same concept and that none of them implied any disassociation from either the Code or the Statute.

Table 6.1   Different expressions: Same concept

'Italianate' Maltese	English	'Semitic' Maltese
'lokazzjoni'	lease	'kera'
'lokatur'	lessor	'sid il-kera'
'inkwilin'	lessee	'kerrej'

Consolidation of This Approach in Subsequent Legislation

This decision also seems to have triggered particular amendments to the rent law. In fact, following the deliberations of the Court of Appeal in this particular judgement, Parliament proceeded to ratify the necessary changes to the Housing (Decontrol) Ordinance.[59] Act XXIII of 1979, which constituted the last major set of amendments to the Maltese rent statutes, stipulated that on the termination of any emphyteutical grants signed after 21 June 1979 there would be an automatic conversion of the emphyteutical contract into a lease. There was going to be the same effect on 17–30-year grants, signed prior to the said date.[60] Grants that were similarly contracted before 1979 but for periods longer than 30 years could be converted into perpetual concessions subject to certain conditions.[61]

Conclusion: Diffusing Laws and Languages

The Maltese case reproduced in this chapter serves to exemplify many of the points made by Twining and referred to in the Introduction. While the background of the case could be rendered as the straightforward exportation of legal concepts by a colonial power from the common law world into the colony's legal system, the judgement itself is clearly an example of a post-colonial court acting as a cultural broker between different legal concepts and discourses which, albeit stemming from different cultural universes, are blended and made to correspond to one another. The court, not the legislator, was the effective agent of horizontal diffusion in this case and it relied upon Italian judgements to justify rendering post-war Maltese legislation with a clear common law orientation applicable to contracts of emphyteusis governed by a Maltese Civil Code inspired by Roman and French law and enacted in the late nineteenth century. The judgement is one culminating point of a drawn out process in Maltese law by which common law concepts and vocabulary come to be aligned with civilian ones and required the court to connect two different dialects of legal Maltese. It thus clearly illustrates how the study of diffusion and that of normative hybridity in the broad sense in which these terms are defined by Sean Donlan are interlinked, such that: 'hybridity, understood in this way, has gone hand in hand with diffusion, the movements that generate legal-normative

---

59   Chapter 158 of the Laws of Malta. This statute had been enacted by the British administration in 1959 with the objective of decontrolling all the dwellings built after that date. Act XXIII of 1979 re-introduced tenant protection to contracts that were regulated by this Ordinance. In doing so, it allowed the same degree of protection to emphyteutas.

60   Ibid. § 12(2).

61   Ibid. § 12(4).

complexity'.[62] At the same time, consideration of the political context is critical. This judgement was only possible in the context of a rare moment of national unity following independence, in which significant socio-political divides were temporarily bridged.

---

62   S.P. Donlan, 'To hybridity and beyond: Reflections on legal and normative complexity', Working Paper, downloaded from Academia, page 7, <https://www.academia.edu /2078759/To_Hybridity_and_Beyond_Reflections_on_Legal_and_Normative_Complexity>.

Chapter 7

Legal Capital is Out – EEIG is Cool! How the Evaporation of Legal Capital in EU Private Companies might Provide a Revival Opportunity for EEIGs

Alessio Bartolacelli

Introduction

The concept of 'diffusion' in company law, and in particular in EU company law, is often related to a more complex system of rule harmonisation and/or to the competition between legal systems. In this chapter a specific form of diffusion will be analysed in terms of both its importance, and the consequences it is believed to lead to.

The diffusion discussed here has had as its main target the reduction of the minimum legal capital required for private companies throughout Europe over the past 10 years. This chapter considers how such a process arose within the traditional Private Limited Companies of the UK, to then diffuse to inform French, Spanish, German, Belgian, Portuguese, Dutch and, lastly, Italian approaches in the regulation of companies.

Competition and Freedom of Establishment: The Legal Framework of EU Company Law, the Role of Fundamental Principles and ECJ Decisions

It is well known that in the European Union each member country maintains law-making competence in company laws; this means that throughout Europe different company models can be found. Nevertheless, several core points of their structures are common, or quite similar: first of all, there is the main division between partnerships (or *sociétés de personnes, società di persone, Personengesellschaften, sociedades de personas*) and companies (*sociétés de capitaux, società di capitali, Kapitalgesellschaften, sociedades de capitales*); and, secondly, between public (*société anonyme [SA], società per azioni [SPA], sociedad anonima [SA], sociedade anónima [SA], Aktiengesellschaft [AG]*) and private companies (*société à responsabilité limitée [SARL], società a responsabilità limitata [SRL], sociedad limitada [SL], sociedade por quotas [SQ], Gesellschaft mit beschränkt Haftung*

[*GmbH*]). Each national model however, possesses specific features, which are an obvious result of the legal tradition of the country where it was established.

In addition to national authority, from 1968 on, Member States of the former European Economic Community, also witnessed a new, ever increasing law-making competence of the EEC with regard to company law. Such an authority, first as the EEC and now as the European Union, mainly exercised its powers through Directives, legal tools not setting out detailed provisions on a given subject but providing general guidelines (and sometimes even various options among which national lawmakers are free to choose) to be applied by each country within its local legal framework and traditions.[1]

By these means, in the last 50 years, Europe has acquired several main guidelines for the harmonisation of national company laws. This has included, among other things, the regulation of filing of company documents in Trade Registries, legal capital requirements, annual balance sheets, takeover bids and so on; the scope of the framework, however, has almost always only been focused on public companies, leaving member countries substantially free to regulate the organisation of private ones. This means that, while public companies are, in many ways, very similar throughout the European Union (EU), private ones can be significantly different.[2]

This situation is extremely interesting from an economic point of view. Small and medium sized enterprises (SMEs) are widespread throughout the EU and represent the main feature of the economies of countries such as Italy, France, Spain and up to a point, even Germany. In the case of SMEs, private companies (or closed corporations) are the preferred way to run business, mainly due to the benefit of limited liability enjoyed by members. Moreover, in the last few years, EU fundamental principles of freedom of establishment and movement within the Union have been strongly reasserted by several significant judgements of the European Court of Justice; the trend started with the *Centros* case in 1999[3] and continued with the *Überseering* (2001),[4] *Inspire Art* (2003),[5] *Sevic* (2005),[6] and *Cartesio* (2008) decisions.[7]

This trend follows a pathway towards establishing real competition between company models. As public companies are characterised by common features

---

1 For a critical approach to the issue see L. Enriques, 'EC Company Law directives and regulations: How trivial are they?' (2006) *University of Pennsylvania Journal of International Economic Law* 1, spec. 8.

2 Ibid. 11.

3 Case C-212/97 *Centros Ltd v Erhvervs- og Selskabsstyrelsen* (1999) ECR I-01459.

4 Case C-208/00, *Überseering BV v Nordic Construction Company Baumanagement GmbH* (2002) ECR I-09919.

5 Case C-167/01, *Kamer van Koophandel en Fabrieken voor Amsterdam v Inspire Art Ltd* (2003) ECR I-10155.

6 Case C-411/03, *SEVIC Systems AG* (2005) ECR I-10805.

7 Case C-210/06, *Cartesio Oktató és Szolgáltató bt* (2008) ECR I-09641.

throughout the EU, due to the process of harmonisation, the focus here will be on those company types where competition may be less restricted: that is, basically, private companies.[8]

In this scenario, different national rules regarding the establishment and the regulation of private companies cease to be a disadvantage, and can be seen as providing opportunity for improved competition.

Where it All Began: The Private Limited Company of the UK

It is no coincidence that almost all the national company law modifications I am going to describe were introduced from 2006 onwards. That year, the Companies Act was enacted in the United Kingdom, providing new rules regarding, among other aspects, the repeal of the prohibition of financial assistance by companies; the simplification of legal capital reduction procedures – that now no longer have to go before a court for approval; the simplification of the procedures if directors avail themselves of the possibility of handling the share capital of the company; and, most important of all from a symbolic point of view, a significant deregulation of the minimum legal capital regime.[9]

This special situation, entailing a strong Private Limited Company and an enhanced freedom to establish this model in every EU member country, caused an impressive phenomenon of emigration of UK Limited Companies to neighbouring countries; as of August 2005 (and thus even before the modifications entailed by the 2006 Companies Act), indeed, in 2010 more than 27,000 Limited Companies were reported to have their registered offices in Germany alone: the Limited Company had been recognised as the best choice when establishing a new company.[10]

Continental European lawmakers had to ask themselves, at this point, *why* UK Limited was better than its comparable domestic solutions such as *GmbH*, *SARL*, *Limitadas*, *SRL* and so on. Although legal literature has not always been unanimous on this point,[11] the answer seems to be that establishing a Limited Company was

---

8   T.H. Tröger, 'Choice of jurisdiction in European Corporate Law: Perspectives of European corporate governance' (2005) *European Business Organization Law Review* 3; D. Zimmer, 'Corporate law competition in Europe' (2010) *The Journal of Interdisciplinary Economics* 29.

9   P. Davies, *Gower and Davies Principles of Modern Company Law* (London: Sweet & Maxwell, 2008) 261.

10   Data appears in G.B. Portale, 'Società a responsabilità limitata senza capitale sociale e imprenditore individuale con "capitale destinato" (Capitale sociale quo vadis?)' (2010) *Rivista delle società* 1237, 1239.

11   U. Noack and M. Beurskens, 'Modernising the German GmbH – Mere window dressing or fundamental redesign?' (2008) *European Business Organization Law Review* 97, 105 maintain that 'hidden costs' related to the constitution of a new UK Limited by German shareholders 'work in favour of the long-established and well accepted domestic form', that is, *GmbH*.

(and in most cases, still is) cheaper, faster and smarter than using classic domestic solutions. The main features of the UK Private Limited Company are:

a. a minimum legal capital which need be no more than a mere 1 penny;[12]
b. non-cash contributions are allowed;[13]
c. there is no obligation to pay cash contributions before registration;
d. setting up the company can be done using standard forms, both for the memorandum of association and articles, provided by Companies House;[14]
e. there is no need for notarisation, so the costs for setting the company up are lower and the time needed is shorter. Only a simple written statement is required;
f. Companies House offers the possibility of a online incorporation, which can also be a same day incorporation;[15]
g. the internal structure of the company can be organised very freely; directors can be both natural and legal persons (but at least one legal person director is needed). Shareholder decisions can also be taken via electronic means.

Most of these features were available for private limited companies already prior to the Companies Act of 2006, but the joint effect of the Act and of the ECJ decisions referred to above created the need for the remaining European jurisdictions to find countermeasures to use against the ever increasing number of Limited Companies operating outside the UK.[16]

Other EU Countries' Countermeasures

Changes to the General Model (France, Portugal and the Netherlands)

These countermeasures, a sort of 'answer' by continental lawmakers to the UK Limited Company option, can be divided into two main groups. On the one hand,

---

12   Section 765 2006 Companies Act only provides a rule regarding *public* companies' initial minimum requirements, due mainly to the Second European Directive.

13   Arguably *ex* s90 2006 Companies Act et seq.

14   Model articles can be found online: <http://www.companieshouse.gov.uk/about/model Articles/modelArticles.shtml> accessed 10 May 2014, Section 19(3) *Companies Act 2006*: 'A company may adopt all or any of the provisions of model articles'; s20(1) Companies Act 2006: 'On the formation of a limited company (a) if articles are not registered, or (b) if articles are registered, in so far as they do not exclude or modify the relevant model articles, the relevant model articles (so far as applicable) form part of the company's articles in the same manner and to the same extent as if articles in the form of those articles had been duly registered'.

15   See <http://www.companieshouse.gov.uk/infoAndGuide/faq/sameDayServices. shtml> accessed 10 May 2014.

16   J. Payne, 'Legal capital and creditor protection in UK private companies' (2008) *European Company Law* 223.

some countries decided to change several features of the original model of Limited Companies operating within their borders; on the other hand, other EU members resolved to create new company types (or, better, sub-types) that were thought to be a stronger competitive option. In both cases it is quite clear that the minimum legal capital has been seen by national lawmakers as a possible *barrier to entry* to the specific market constituted by incorporation within their borders, and almost every solution mirrors such a belief.

Concerning the first kind of solution, general models of private companies were changed in France from 2003 onwards, in Portugal in 2011 and in the Netherlands in 2012.

French *sociétés à responsabilité limitée*, and Portuguese *sociedades por quotas* now have a minimum legal capital requirement of just one euro in the case of one-person companies,[17] while Dutch *besloten vennootschappen (BV)* have removed any explicit minimum legal capital requirement, merely ruling that at least one share with voting rights must be held by a party other than the *BV* itself.[18] The French law was modified in this sense in 2003, while the Portuguese one in March 2011. Dutch civil code modifications (so called *Flex-BV* reform), on the other hand, have only entered into force since October 2012, although they were first approved by the upper House of the Dutch Parliament in December 2009.[19] In the French and Portuguese cases provisions relating to capital maintenance have been kept unchanged, so it is possible for general meetings to raise capital (and, if necessary, reduce it) according to the usual rules applicable to those company

---

17   As for France: art. L 223–1 *Code de commerce*, modified by *Loi* 2003–721 of 1 August, now states: '*Le montant du capital de la société est fixé par les statuts. Il est divisé en parts sociales égales*' (A company's legal capital amount is set by company's articles. It is divided in shares having the same par value). In Portugal, art. 219, third paragraph, *Codigo das sociedades comerciais* stated, before being reformed in 2011, that the minimum capital requirement for a *SQ* was 5,000 euro and each share had a minimum par value of 100 euro; after that reform, 'new' art. 219, *CSC*: '*Os valores nominais das quotas podem ser diversos, mas nenhum pode ser inferior a € 1*' (shares' par value may be different from one share to another, but none can be under one euro). This means that minimum capital for a *SQ* with two shareholders amounts to two euro, while just one euro will be enough for a one-person company, according to art. 270-A *CSC*; see P. de Tarso Domingues, 'O novo regime do capital social nas sociedades por quotas' (2011) *Direito das sociedades em revista* 97, 98 and 107.

18   M. Kroeze and J. Berend Wezeman, 'Reform of Dutch private company law' in J.A. McCahery, L. Timmerman and E.P.M. Vermeulen (eds), *Private Company Law Reform. International and European Perspectives* (TMC Asser Press, 2010) 181, 185: 'before the EEC harmonization programme and the second EEC Directive on capital maintenance, the concept of a minimum capital requirement was unknown in Dutch law'.

19   '*Wet vereenvoudiging en flexibilisering bv-recht*'; complete text and all data regarding the procedure can be found online: <https://zoek.officielebekendmakingen.nl/dossier/31058> and <https://zoek.officielebekendmakingen.nl/dossier/32426> accessed 10 May 2014.

types. Dutch law, on the other hand, provides creditor protection tools that are different from legal capital and are based on the duty of directors to perform a form of solvency test (distribution and balance sheets test) before approving the distribution of dividends to shareholders, the repayment of shares and the purchase of shares themselves.[20]

The regime regarding contributions has not been changed in the French *SARL* or in the Portuguese *SQ*: in the first case, one can donate cash or provide both in-kind contributions and work or service contributions;[21] in the second, only in-kind contributions are allowed, while work or service ones are explicitly prohibited by Art. 202 of *Codigo das sociedades comerciais*; in Portugal shareholders are now no longer required to deposit cash contributions in a bank, but just to give these to the directors at the time the company is being set up.[22] In the Netherlands, legal capital can also be denominated in foreign currency[23] and no bank certificate is required for cash contributions. While work and service contributions continue not to be allowed by law, an auditor's report for in-kind contributions' valuation is not required.[24]

These three company types can be established by natural and also legal persons. In 2008 the French law created the possibility of using a standard form to establish a company if it is a one-person company and the only shareholder is also the only director.[25] Participation in general meetings via electronic means was also made possible in the same year.[26]

As far as Portugal is concerned, several reforms in 2005 and 2006 permitted the establishment of companies with a one-day constitution (*Empresa na hora*)[27] and by means of online procedures.[28] Apart from the *Empresa na hora*, there is at the moment in Portuguese company law no hint of further model articles. No mention of these aspects are provided by the Dutch Civil Code, even after

---

20   H. Boschma, L. Lennarts and H. Schutte-Veenstra, 'The reform of Dutch private company law: New rules for the protection of creditors?' (2007) *European Business Organization Law Review* 567, 598 and following.

21   According to Arts. 1843–2 e 1843–3 of French *Code Civil* work and service contributions cannot be the sole contributions to the company.

22   Literally, 'in the company's coffers': *nos cofres da sociedade*.

23   Dutch Civil Code art. 2:178 states that, if it is so provided, legal capital's value can also be expressed in a currency other than the euro; the same rule is also in force in the UK, see Davies (n 9) 266 and following.

24   Art. 2:203a, now repealed by the reform, stated that cash contributions had to be assessed by a bank's statement.

25   Art. D 223–2, third paragraph, *Code de commerce*: '*ces statuts types s'appliquent à moins qu'il n'ait été joint des statuts différents lors de la demande d'immatriculation de la société*' (these model articles apply unless different articles have been used as of a company's request of filing).

26   Art. L 223–27, third paragraph, *Code de commerce*.

27   *Decreto lei* 111, 8 July 2005.

28   *Decreto lei* 125, 29 June 2006.

the private companies' reform of 2012 came into force, but such a model is also already believed to be extremely competitive.

The Creation of New Company Sub-types (Spain, Germany and Belgium)

The second group of solutions is perhaps more interesting. New private company sub-types were developed by at least four national lawmakers between 2003 and 2012. This is the case of the *sociedad limitada nueva empresa* (*SLNE*) in Spain (2003),[29] the *Unternehmergesellschaft* in Germany (2008),[30] the *société privée a responsabilité limitée – starter* in Belgium (2010)[31] and the *società a responsabilità limitata semplificata* (and a *capitale ridotto*) in Italy (2012).[32]

SLNE is a special case and deserves to be dealt with separately. It is the oldest of the new models and seems to be the prototype of entry-level companies (since its name: '*nueva empresa*' means 'new enterprise').[33] It is a sub-version of the *sociedad limitada*[34] where, somewhat curiously, no modification to the minimum legal capital requirements has been made. Minimum capital is now 3,000 euros (the same as 'normal' *sociedad limitada*), but there is a cap at 120,000 euros.[35] Its main features (as compared to a *sociedad limitada*) are the possibility of an extremely wide range of objects of the company; a maximum of five shareholders (all natural persons) at the moment of constitution; a register of shareholders is unnecessary; a simplified procedure for internal organisation: in particular shareholders' meetings

---

29　SLNE was implemented by *Ley* 7, 1 April 2003, and its regulation is now found within the *Texto refundido de la ley de sociedades de capital*, approved by *Real decreto legislative* 1, 2 July 2010, Arts. 434 onwards. When this article was under review Spain introduced (*Ley de apoyo a los emprendedores y su internacionalización*, nr. 14 of 27 September 2013) a new regime of progressive capital formation for *Limitadas* (*Sociedad Limitada a Formación Sucesiva*), which can now be registered with a legal capital usually under 3,000 euro.

30　Created by the Act for *GmbH* modernisation and the fight against abuses, better known as *MoMiG*, approved by the German Parliament on 23 October 2008, and in the GmbH Act at s 5a.

31　Created by *Loi* 12 January 2010.

32　The Simplified SRL was created by *decreto legge* 1/2012, Art. 3, later modified by law 27, 24 March 2012, and again by *decreto legge* 76/2013, finally amended by law 99, 9 August 2013. The Reduced Capital SRL, on the other hand, was created by *decreto legge* 83/2012, amended by Law 134, 7 August 2012, and finally repealed by already mentioned *decreto legge* 76/2013.

33　This was part of a wider project, named 'Proyecto Nueva Empresa': see A.J. Viera González, 'Algunas consideraciones sobre el "Proyecto Nueva Empresa"' (2002) *Revista de Derecho de Sociedades* 445.

34　Art. 434 *Texto refundido*: '*La sociedad nueva empresa se regula en este título como especialidad de la sociedad de responsabilidad limitada*' (the *SLNE* is considered under the present title as a sub-species of the *SL*).

35　Art. 443 *Texto refundido*.

can be made via electronic means as well as through conventional arrangements and if there is more than one director, creating a – properly speaking – board of directors is not allowed, due to the complexity of such a system of administration.[36]

In a similar way to the Limited Company in the UK, standard forms are also provided for the *SLNE*; although they are still defined as *orientativos* (indicative), so that shareholders are meant to be free to modify them.[37] An incentive not to do so is the possibility of a quicker procedure of incorporation that is reserved to companies using standard form articles.

Finally, since it is defined as a sub-type of the *SL*, changing from *SLNE* to the former company model is not subject to the strict rules provided for other types of conversion.[38]

As far as remaining company types are concerned, all of them opted to lower minimum capital requirements: the *Unternehmergesellschaft* (*UG*) in Germany can be set up with a minimum legal capital of just one euro, but even the maximum legal capital must be less than the 25,000 which is the minimum required for its 'parent' model: the *GmbH*.[39] The Belgian *SPRL-Starter* was created in 2010 with the same feature, but with a lower limit, set at 18,50, that is, the minimum capital requirement for the constitution of a 'normal' *SPRL*.[40] The limit is even lower in Italian *SRLS* and *SRLCR*, where the minimum capital is one euro, while the maximum may only reach 10,000.[41] Returning to legal capital, only cash contributions are allowed in *UGs* and *SRLS* and *SRLCR*,[42] and they have to be

---

36   Art. 447 *Texto refundido*.

37   Model articles are provided by *Orden Jus/1445/2003*, issued by Spanish Ministry of Justice on 4 June 2003 and published in the *BOE* nr. 134, 5 June 2003, 21819 *seq.*; the preamble to the *Orden* states as follow: '*los socios pueden elaborar otro tipo de estatutos sociales, con los límites de derecho imperativo establecidos en la Ley, como consecuencia lógica del principio de autonomía de la voluntad, tan esencial en todos los tipos de negocios jurídicos, pero muy especialmente en los societarios, en cuyo caso el plazo para calificar e inscribir será el general contemplado en la legislación específica*' (members can develop different company's articles, according to limits given by mandatory laws, as a logical consequence of the principle of freedom of will, so essential in every kind of contract, and even more in company ones; in this event general terms given by specific rules for constitution and filing apply). For more info see A.J. Viera González, 'Anotaciones a los estatutos orientativos de la sociedad limitada. Nueva empresa y posibilidades de configuraciones diversas' (2003) *Revista de Derecho de Sociedades* 207.

38   Art. 454 *Texto refundido*.

39   See s 5a(1) GmbH Act (*GmbHG*).

40   According to art. 223, *Code des sociétés*, the minimum capital is equal to one euro; the denomination of 'starter' is required as long as the company's capital is not increased beyond the threshold set for an 'ordinary' *SPRL*.

41   Art. 2463 *bis* Italian Civil Code for s.r.l.s.; art. 44, *decreto legge* 83/2012, now repealed, stated that rules applicable to *SRLCR* were the same as for *SRLS*.

42   This rule was very strongly criticised by several German scholars: see R. Veil, 'Die Unternehmergesellschaft im System der Kapitalgesellschaften' (2009) *Zeitschrift*

fully paid as of the moment of constitution of the company, while these limitations are not laid down by the Belgian legislature.

Among these company models, only the German *UGs* can be set up by both natural and legal persons, while the founders of the Italian and Belgian companies may only be natural persons.[43] In the case of the Belgian *SPRL-Starter*, there is also a limit to the number of employees, which cannot be more than five. In all the models considered here, however, a company is allowed to have just a single member from the moment of its constitution.

The pivotal and most interesting point however, is analysing how local models compensate for the almost complete absence of legal capital. Similar solutions have been enacted by both German and Belgian company law, with a more detailed regime for the latter; and in Italy, although the Italian case deserves to be dealt with separately.

In the German *UG*, the threshold of 25,000 euros has to be reached, but not as legal capital, rather as the company's overall equity: a part of the annual profits, amounting to 25 per cent has to be kept in the company as a special reserve, called the 'accumulation reserve', until this reserve, added to the actual legal capital, will at least amount to the minimum legal capital required for a 'normal' *GmbH*. The 'accumulation reserve' may only be used to increase legal capital, or to absorb company deficits before these affect what remains of the legal capital.[44]

In the Belgian *SPRL-Starter*, the same measure was adopted, in order to reach, by adding such a reserve to the actual capital, the minimum legal capital threshold required for an *SPRL*, that is, 18,550 euros.[45] In addition to such a provision, other features, starting with the name itself, bear witness to the specific 'entry level' hallmark of the *SPRL-Starter*. First of all there is a dimensional barrier: such a company, after increasing its legal capital above the minimum required for *SPRL*, has to convert to a 'normal' *SPRL*; if not, the *SPRL-Starter* must be wound up. Nevertheless, the Belgian legislature also laid down a peculiar rule concerning the period after the third year from the constitution of the company. During this time, shareholders are liable to creditors for company obligations for the amount of the difference between its actual legal capital and 18,550 euros.[46] It can be said that this is a statutory provision that modifies the extent of the limited liability granted to each shareholder.

Secondly, even if the theoretical minimum capital requirement amounts to only one euro, Art. 229, line 1, n. 5 of the *Code des sociétés* also applies to the *SPRL-Starter*. This rule establishes that, if a company files for bankruptcy procedure

---

für Unternehmens- und Gesellschaftsrecht 623, 630; C.-H. Witt, 'Verdeckte Sacheinlage, Unternehmergesellschaft und Musterprotokoll' (2009) *Zeitschrift für Wirtschaftsrecht* 1102.

43   Art. 2463 *bis*, Italian Civil Code, for Italian *SRLS* and Art. 249, para. 2, *Code des sociétés* for Belgian *SPRL-S*.

44   S 5a(3), *GmbHG*.

45   Art. 319 *bis*, *Code des sociétés*.

46   Art. 214, para. 2, line 3, *Code des sociétés*.

within three years after its constitution, the founders are liable with the company to creditors if the company's equity (i.e., legal capital, reserves and subordinated loans) was clearly not suitable for at least two years of its normal exercise of planned activity. It is important also to stress that legal capital cannot be reduced while the company maintains the form of *SPRL-Starter*.[47]

Hybrid Solutions: The Italian Case

As for Italy, after several modifications (at least six between January 2012 and August 2013) the Italian Parliament eventually decided to pursue both described lines of action. On the one hand, a new company sub-type (*SRL semplificata*: a simplified private limited company) was created, following both the German and Belgian examples; on the other hand, rules regulating all *SRL* were changed in order to also allow their incorporation with a minimum legal capital on a par with one single euro.

The main features of the 'new' *SRLS* are a minimum legal capital of just one euro (with a limit of 9,999.99 euros) and a restriction on the constitution of such companies to natural persons.[48] In addition, costs relating to the constitution process were cut by granting shareholders exemption from the payment of both notary public fees and some registry fees.[49] The price for such a benefit is that the deed of incorporation must be drawn up according to a standard model elaborated by the Italian Ministry of Justice.[50] This rule is obviously in contrast to the Italian *SRL*'s general principle of freedom which is accorded to shareholders regarding the provisions to be included in the deed of incorporation;[51] nonetheless we must consider two more aspects.

First of all, the latest amendments, as of August 2013, explicitly state that the standard form is mandatory both in its use and contents.[52] This means that a simplified *SRL* can be incorporated only by means of the standard form, and that the provisions therein cannot be modified by the shareholders' will: shareholders can only decide upon the company's object and directors, while the whole governance system is regulated by the model form.[53]

---

47   Again art. 214, para. 2, *Code des sociétés*.
48   Art. 2463 *bis*, Italian Civil Code.
49   Art. 3, *decreto legge* 1/2012.
50   Issued by Italian Ministry of Justice's decree (*decreto ministeriale*) nr. 138 of 23 June 2012.
51   Likewise, for instance, in the Spanish *SLNE*, where, although model articles were said to be just '*orientativos*', Viera González (n37) 208, maintains that '*escaso margen de configuración estatutaria*' [the narrow room left for articles' customisation] is one of the hallmarks of such a company sub-type in respect of the 'ordinary' *SL*.
52   Art. 2463 *bis*, para. 3, Italian Civil Code.
53   Although in my personal opinion such a conclusion was also possible without the amendment. For diverging views see M. Cian, 'S.r.l., s.r.l. semplificata, s.r.l. a capitale ridotto. Una nuova geometria del sistema o un sistema disarticolato?' (2012)

Secondly, and similarly, the standard model is extremely 'slight' (less than 10 paragraphs long) and indeed not very accurate. More specifically, when not regulated by the model, the standard default rules of *SRL*s apply, and this means, inter alia, that in the case of more than one director, a board has to be constituted, with all the rules that the presence of this body entail. This is despite the fact that the possibility of an alternative (and much simpler) governance system was provided for the standard *SRL* by the 2003 reform.

With reference to the standard model, however, the governance system does not seem to be the greatest problem. Rather it is the consequences of the lawmakers' consistent indecision that is of greater concern. The standard model was issued in June 2012, when the rules governing *SRL*s were quite different from those currently in force. Specifically, at the time only natural persons under the age of 35 could legally create an *SRL* and as an obvious consequence of such a general rule, the transfer of shares to natural persons over 35 was also forbidden. Violation was punished by establishing that the transfer was null and void, according to Art. 2463*bis*, paragraph 4, then in force; the same rule was repeated almost word for word in the model articles, at paragraph 4. Unfortunately, these model articles were not changed after the latest amendments to the rules regulating *SRL*s. Consequently this means that although the under 35 age limitation was repealed by the law, some echoes of the old rules remain in the model articles, which now do not seem to be fully applicable, at least as far as paragraph 4 is concerned, despite the fact that the use of the model articles is expressly required by the law, as 'mandatory'.

A final, extremely serious problem regarding the model articles arises as a result of uncertainty as to the meaning of 'mandatory'. Although the lawmaker obviously meant that the use of model articles was compulsorily required in order to create an *SRL* the wording of the rule does not make it clear whether extra provisions, not in opposition to the content of the model articles, may be lawfully added to the articles.[54]

As for rules applicable to *SRL*s but not stated expressly in article 2463*bis*, the 'ordinary' *SRL* regulatory framework is applicable 'as far as compatible'.[55] This last cross reference now allows us to take into consideration the second, newer, solution provided by Italian legislature.

Besides creating a new company sub-model, in August 2013, general rules regarding minimum legal capital requirements were changed for all Italian *SRL*s.

Rivista delle società 1101, 1113 et seq; A. Busani and C.A. Busi, 'La s.r.l. semplificata (s.r.l.s.) e a capitale ridotto (s.r..c.r.)' (2012) *Società* 1305; cf. M. Rescigno, 'La società a responsabilità limitata a capitale ridotto e semplificata' (2013) *Le nuove leggi civili commentate* 65, 66.

54   Regarding those profiles please see A. Bartolacelli, '"Novissime" modifiche alla disciplina della s.r.l.s.: saggio minimo di diritto transitorio' (2013) *Il nuovo diritto delle società* 7, 15 et seq.

55   Again Art. 2463*bis*, last paragraph, Italian Civil Code.

According to the wording of Article 2463, constituting a company with a legal capital of under 10,000 euros is now possible, provided that contributions are fully paid up and are in cash. In this case, shareholders can be both natural and legal persons, and the use of model articles is not required, as well as cost-cutting benefits not being granted. The main capital related amendment announced in August 2013, however, concerns the legal capital regime for companies whose legal capital is under 10,000 euros.

The solution found by Italian lawmakers almost perfectly follows the path previously set by the German *UG* and Belgian *SPRL* that is that: one fifth of the company's annual net profits shall be kept by the company itself in a reserve until such a reserve, added to actual legal capital, will be at least par to 10,000 euros, that is, the 'traditional' minimum capital threshold for a 'common' *SRL*.[56] Although there are similarities, in Italy, once again the trend towards a lower minimum legal capital has been accepted in a very singular way. The latter provisions concerning legal capital are not the same as those considered above in respect of the French, Portuguese and Dutch cases; in those occurrences, once the legal capital threshold has been reduced to a single euro or so, no countermeasure had been taken to safeguard the idea that maintaining the legal capital is a way of protecting creditors. Italian lawmakers did not dare to go that far, or at least, not fully. Consequently, a brand new 'two-and-a-half-gear' system has been set out, in which simplified limited (penalised by the compulsory use of model articles) and 'common' limited (with the *sui generis* version with reduced capital, and the 'classic' *SRL*) companies coexist freely and, perhaps, even happily.

More Minimum Legal Capital Threshold Lowering Experiences

Throughout Europe there have been other developments in company models. For example, a new company sub-type was created in Latvia in 2010 (*Micro SIA*) and in Denmark in June 2013 (*IVS*); while minimum capital requirements were lowered in Finland (2006: from 8,000 down to 2,500), in Hungary (2007: 3M florins down to 0.5M); in Poland (2009: 50,000 down to 5,000 zloty); in Bulgaria (2009: 5,000 down to 2 lev); in Denmark (2010: 125,000 down to 80,000 krone; and again in 2013, 80,000 down to 50,000); and in Sweden (2010: 100,000 down to 50,000 krone). This trend is also happening outside the EU: minimum capital reductions were decided in China and Japan, too, and LLCs in USA need a minimum capital (of just $1,000) only in three states.[57]

All these reforms in a relatively short time are evidence of a significant change regarding the idea of a legal capital as a means for protecting creditors; or, at least that a minimum legal capital system can be, by itself, a good way to guarantee

---

56   Art. 2463 para. 4, Italian Civil Code.

57   For these data, see: F. Dias Simões, 'Legal capital rules in Europe: Is there still room for creditor protection?' [2013] *International Company and Commercial Law Review* 166, 170.

stakeholders of limited companies. This diffusion nevertheless needed, in order to be fully implemented at least at a European level, the already mentioned set of ECJ decisions. As for extra-European countries, their domestic company models cannot be used freely by EU citizens due to the limited extent of the principle of freedom of establishment. It cannot, however, be ruled out that this could be one of the next streams of development in international economic law.

A Practical Implementation: Limited Liability for European Economic Interest Groupings Too?

The developments described above are quite interesting in themselves, but a further application can be found on a different level too, if the combined means of exercising entrepreneurial activity without restricting the limitation of members' liability are considered. The fact that nowadays creating a new limited liability company is almost costless, can lead to a second level liability limitation for members, especially where a capital company (if permitted by the domestic legal system) is a member of a partnership, or a '*società di persone*', '*Personengesellschaft*', and so on. In this way natural persons may then enjoy the benefits of limited liability via a capital-less company, created as a sort of special purpose vehicle, just in order to take part in the desired partnership without suffering from its usual disadvantageous characteristic of unlimited liability.

Such a solution may not always be attractive, in particular if general partnership models are available there is easy and cheap direct access to liability limitation by means of an almost capital-less company, without the need to create a partnership. There are cases, nevertheless, where the above device can be usefully exploited due to the impossibility of otherwise achieving the goal of limited liability. More specifically, this may be attractive to European Economic Interest Groupings (hereafter: EEIG).[58] The EEIG is a means of joint exercise of entrepreneurial activity between economic subjects (professionals, firms, companies, sole entrepreneurs and so on) coming from different EU countries. It was created in 1985 by the European Community, but during it's almost 30 years of existence it has not reached a huge level of success; on the contrary, it can be said that it has been a big failure: fewer than 2,000 established groupings throughout EU are too small a figure to state otherwise.[59] The potential of EEIGs nonetheless seems to be great: its structure is extremely light; there are only a few imperative rules to follow; it is completely mouldable by its members; it is transparent as far as taxes are concerned. All these observations lead one to wonder why this tool has not been more widely used.

The answer to such a question can be found in one of its few imperative rules: EEIG members always have unlimited and joint liability for the EEIG's

---

58   This chapter is part of wider research into EEIGs.

59   Data available in LIBERTAS – European EEIG Information Centre's website: <www.ewiv.eu> accessed 10 May 2014.

obligations.[60] This means that, in a world where limited liability is, more or less, a benefit people that can now be granted free of charge, or almost, this possibility is largely unavailable for EEIG members.

In order to remove the obstacle of unlimited liability for EEIG members, in theory, two different paths can be followed. The first requires an interpretation of Regulation 2137/1985 in an expansive way so that EEIG members may acquire direct limited liability; this is not the place to discuss such an option, which furthermore can be very hard to pursue due to the apparently unequivocal wording of the rule.[61]

The second option fits perfectly with the aims of this chapter, as it consists in providing EEIG members with an indirect limited liability, by asking them to wear the clothes of limited liability by other means. These means can be a private company, as in most cases, as has been indicated above, the use of the private company can guarantee limited liability of members, without having to pay high costs. In the case of an EEIG, therefore, 'indirect' liability limitation is made increasingly easier exactly because of the diffusion of almost capital-less companies throughout Europe. EU Regulation 2137/1985, in fact, specifically states that members shall be attributable to at least two EU countries.[62] This means

---

60   Although there are several little 'corrections to such a rule', this is the mainstream criteria under Art. 24, para. 1, EEC Regulation 2137/1985.

61   As just said, Regulation 2137/1985 imposes, at Art. 24, unlimited liability for a grouping's members: '1. The members of a grouping shall have unlimited joint and several liability for its debts and other liabilities of whatever nature. National law shall determine the consequences of such liability. 2. Creditors may not proceed against a member for payment in respect of debts and other liabilities, in accordance with the conditions laid down in paragraph 1, before the liquidation of a grouping is concluded, unless they have first requested the grouping to pay and payment has not been made within an appropriate period'. The only way to overcome this members' unlimited liability could be by means of what was stated in the second part of the tenth *Whereas* of the Preamble: 'whereas the members of a grouping have unlimited joint and several liability for the grouping's debts and other liabilities, including those relating to tax or social security, *without, however, that principle's affecting the freedom to exclude or restrict the liability of one or more of its members in respect of a particular debt or other liability by means of a specific contract between the grouping and a third party*'. It is nonetheless true that such an option is extremely narrow and it is hard to imagine it being applicable to wider hypotheses.

62   According to Regulation 2137/1985, Art. 4:
      1. Only the following may be members of a grouping:
      (a) companies or firms within the meaning of the second paragraph of Article 58 of the Treaty and other legal bodies governed by public or private law, which have been formed in accordance with the law of a Member State and which have their registered or statutory office and central administration in the Community; where, under the law of a Member State, a company, firm or other legal body is not obliged to have a registered or statutory office, it shall be sufficient for such a company, firm or other legal body to have its central administration in the Community;

that as far as companies are concerned, as members they are required to have their registered offices and central administration within the EU, but it is not mandatory they are in the same country. In addition, and most importantly, there is no specific requirement that the company actually carries on any real activity in the EU.

The combination of all these possibilities means that as creating limited companies throughout the EU is so simple and quick, or at least in its larger member states, the limitation of the liability of members can be a consequence of the kind of enterprise organisations have chosen, even if this choice is only made specifically for taking part in an EEIG. And it is quite evident that such a system is able to remove the biggest obstacle to the more widespread use of the European Economic Interest Grouping.

It would nonetheless be very naïve to think that such a scheme solves every problem. If it is true that the biggest drawback to the constitution of an EEIG is the unlimited liability of its members, it is likewise true that the most important advantage is its light structure, the hallmark of the Grouping. The creation of ad hoc companies just to be able to take part in an EEIG could be regarded as a burden weighing against that benefit.

Although, the use of private limited companies usually and normally grants limited liability to their members; nonetheless, in every EU country there are different rules regarding the possibility of finding ways to bypass liability limitation in order to hold shareholders liable in an unlimited measure. This is done by 'piercing of the corporate veil'.[63]

In each EU country such an option finds different variations. As far as the EEIG is concerned, because there is no compulsory link between a real activity and the place where the company has its registered offices and/or central administration, this specific topic can be pivotal, along with the applicable tax law, in choosing the country where the limited company is to be incorporated. This is also true for non-EU economic subjects interested in being full members of an EEIG. The changing corporate climate of Europe suggests that a way now exists to reinvigorate the EEIG, and prevent its great potential from turning into 'a former promising future'.

(b) natural persons who carry on any industrial, commercial, craft or agricultural activity or who provide professional or other services in the Community.

2. A grouping must comprise at least:

(a) two companies, firms or other legal bodies, within the meaning of paragraph 1, which have their central administrations in different Member States, or

(b) two natural persons, within the meaning of paragraph 1, who carry on their principal activities in different Member States, or

(c) a company, firm or other legal body within the meaning of paragraph 1 and a natural person, of which the first has its central administration in one Member State and the second carries on his principal activity in another Member State.

63   Regarding this specific profile, under a comparative point of view, see: H. Ito and H. Watanabe, 'Piercing the corporate veil' in M. Siems and D. Cabrelli (eds), *Comparative Company Law. A Case-Based Approach* (Hart, 2013) 165.

Final Remarks

To sum up, it can be said that at least two models of diffusion are currently in use in Europe as far as private companies' legal capital is concerned. Both of them expressly aim to reduce new companies' start-up costs, and it would be interesting to find out whether the states that eventually adopted them made an explicit reference to the prototypes.

On the one hand, what can be called the 'general reductive model' can be traced back to the English company model, where legal capital was not a mandatory requirement for a constituting a company. When France decided to lower the minimum legal capital for a *SARL* to just one euro in 2003, it did not explicitly make references to the English model, and the same happened when in 2008 model articles (typically used in the UK in order to make a company's constitution easier and quicker) were developed by French lawmakers for one person companies under certain conditions. The same happened with Portugal's decision to change the minimum legal capital to 1 euro in 2011; no specific mention was made regarding this reform being inspired by the English example, and the same can be said for the Dutch '*flex-BV*' reform in 2012.

Despite the lack of a specific reference, it can nonetheless be said that all these cases were inspired by previous UK experience, and aimed to create a more competitive national environment when the principles of freedom of establishment and movement within the EU began to have a wider implementation due to the above mentioned ECJ decisions.

A very strong English law reference can be found in the second stream as well. Although it involves the creation of new sub-models (that are not to be found – and are not even necessary – in the UK) along with the persistence of the main ones, when German lawmakers in 2008 decided to implement the *UG*, which serves as the typical example of these sub-models, they did so basically as an alternative to lowering a *GmbH*'s minimum capital requirement. We have seen that the need for such a development came from the fact that UK Limited Companies were much more attractive to German investors, who began to use that model instead of the domestic *GmbH*. Nonetheless, *GmbH* was and still is, a successful model and the German parliament, instead of lowering its legal capital requirements, opted for the creation of a 'mini-GmbH'.

Every country that did not want to make changes to the main model, preferring instead to introduce variations, has eventually followed this approach. In the academic commentaries there is some consensus that the German *UG* served as a prototype for the Belgian *SPRL-S* that were eventually created,[64] the Italian *SRLS*,[65] and for the very recently created *SLFS* in Spain and *IVS* in Denmark. Each one of these models can somehow be traced back to the earlier German *UG*. In most

---

64   S. De Dier, 'De S-BVBA: een minimalistische aanzet tot hervorming van het besloten vennootschapsrecht' (2010) *Tijdschrift voor Rechtspersoon en Vennootschap* 194, 218.

65   Cian (n53) 1101.

cases additional features were added to it (additional liability for shareholders in the *SPRL-S*; a capital ceiling in Italian *SRLS*, and so on), but the *UG* is still the core model for states interested in creating a variation to their domestic limited companies. In this sense, it is interesting to highlight that one of the German *UG*'s weaknesses was the possibility of a 'hidden' profit distribution by means of an increased remuneration to directors. This weak point was later overcome in the Spanish *SLFS*, where a limit on directors' salaries was established in 2013; in the same way, additional and auxiliary personal liability for a company's members established in the Belgian *SPRL-S* was also adopted by Spanish *SLFS*.[66] From this point of view it looks like every state at least tried to take on board suggestions emerging from previous foreign experiences; indeed it appears that a veritable diffusion and merging of experiences has been taking place in recent years, and is likely to continue during the next ones.

A concluding observation can be made: continental Europe's classic system of mandatory minimum legal capital requirements currently appears to be in some sort of crisis. It is no longer seen as necessary, but a strong tradition of reliance of economic systems on banking credit has not allowed, at least up to now, the development of alternative means of protecting creditors, such as solvency tests. This can be very dangerous, especially in times of financial crisis, when the banking credit crunch is harder, and there is lack of experience with regards to alternative means of funding. The rise of costless companies may be a way of enhancing the success of European Economic Interest Groupings, but, at the same time, presents challenges to the function and the purpose of 'classic' unlimited liability, and perhaps of partnerships themselves, in today's commercial law.

---

66 More details can be found in A. Bartolacelli, 'Società chiusa e capital sociale minimo: tendenze Europee' (2014) *Giurisprudenza Commerciale*, 519–51 and Id., 'Nuove esperienze europee in tema di costituzione "semplificata" e "a basso costo" di società con responsabilità limitata' (forthcoming) *Giurisprudenza Commerciale*.

Chapter 8

The Urban Diffusion of Local Direct Democracy between Switzerland and the United States

Thomas Favre-Bulle

Introduction

'Similar but different' is how Nicolas Von Arx compares direct democracy in Switzerland and in California.[1] They are in fact the two places in the world with the most intense use of direct democracy.[2] Twenty American states, mostly in the West, have implemented some form of direct democracy. In Switzerland, studies are abundant on ballots at federal level. In the United States, studies are numerous at state level. In both, the local level is only sporadically looked at. Yet, the local is where the ballot originates from, and its use prevails in municipalities.

Nowadays, there are many debates in Switzerland and in the United States on the way that direct democracy influences democratic governance in general. Many scholars engage in public debate expressing contrasting opinions on how the system dysfunctions and how it should evolve. Furthermore, discussions on the ballot are deeply enshrined in the continuous debates on the spatial political organisation of these places. Looking at how the spatial phenomenon of urbanisation played a key role in the emergence and use of direct democracy informs our way of devising the evolution of this form of democracy.

The three instruments of ballot-based direct democracy – initiative, referendum and recall – are the same in Switzerland and the United States.[3]

---

1 N. Von Arx, Ähnlich, aber anders. Die Volksinitiative in Kalifornien und in der Schweiz (Schulthess, 2002).

2 A. Auer, Le référendum et l'initiative populaire aux Etats-Unis (Economica, 1997).

3 I will not describe in detail the procedure in this chapter. See J.F. Zimmerman, The Initiative: Citizen Law-making (Greenwood Press, 1999) for the legal provisions in the United States, and S. Duroy, 'Les Landsgemeinden Suisses' in R. Drago (ed.), Les Procédés de la démocratie semi-directe dans l'administration locale en Suisse, vol. 15 (Presses Universitaires de France, 1987) for Switzerland. I look only at these instruments when they are triggered by a citizen's petition, not by a legal obligation or a government sponsor. An initiative is a vote on a legislative proposal drafted by citizens. A referendum

Switzerland and the United States both knew some form of assembly-based direct democracy prior to their adoption of ballot-based direct democracy. Between the end of the nineteenth and the beginning of the twentieth century, accelerating urbanisation raised issues that led in both cases to the adoption of the ballot-based form. Switzerland has been the main reference in the United States for the implementation of this form of direct democracy. Today, urban trends are still leading the use of local direct democracy, more intensely in large, urban and diverse communities than in rural, small and homogeneous ones. Moreover, metropolitan areas present new challenges to local democracy. These challenges of size and accountability are analogous to the issues that led to the adoption of the local ballot.

There are two forms of direct participation to law making and public administration labelled as direct democracy. One is the attendance, in person, at assemblies where those decisions are taken. The other is voting on legislative matters, as opposed to voting to elect a representative. The former is the oldest in both countries and continues to function in certain areas. This assembly-based form of direct democracy developed independently in Switzerland and in New England. The second form, direct democracy through the ballot was implemented in the United States between the end of the nineteenth century and the beginning of the twentieth century by reference to Switzerland, the 1848 Constitution of which included legal provisions for it. Many authors see both types as contrasting, if not competing, forms of direct democracy. Joseph Zimmerman, in his synthetic work on direct democracy in the United States published in 1999, describes them in two separate books.[4] He does not integrate the two into a single narrative of direct democracy.

The two countries differ in their way of implementing ballot-based direct democracy. As will be seen, in Switzerland, the ballot was introduced as a solution to keep direct democracy active as it was challenged by urbanisation. Urban communities were getting larger, and could not hold direct assemblies anymore. The ballot was a substitute ushered in around the middle of the nineteenth century. Conversely, in the United States, there was a clear rupture between the Town Meetings and the ballot-based direct democracy. The first ones date from the colonies, the second was inspired by Switzerland as a remedy to corruption and the unresponsiveness of representatives during what became recalled as 'the Progressive Era', at the dawn of the twentieth century.

---

is a vote to challenge a piece of legislation adopted by the legislative body. A recall is a vote to repeal an elected official before the end of his mandate. In all three, a petition must be signed by a sufficient number of citizens to place the matter on the ballot. In Switzerland, this number is fixed, while in the United States it is usually defined as a proportion of the electorate.

4   J.F. Zimmerman, *The New England Town Meeting: Democracy in Action* (Greenwood Publishing Group, 1999); Zimmerman (n3).

Before the Ballot, Assembly-based Direct Democracy

Assembly-based direct democracy, that is people gathering together in one place to discuss and take public decisions, developed independently in the United States and in Switzerland.

The Swiss *Landsgemeinde* – the legislative popular assembly – has been traced to the old German institution of the Thing – the judicial assembly of free men – and the *Allmend* – the exclusivity of jurisdiction of a community within its domain.[5] As cantons and communities gained more independence with charters, especially with rights of jurisdiction, the *bailiff*, representing the Lord of the land in the administration of public justice, were replaced by the *Landamann*, elected by the assemblies.[6] These public administrations of justice have progressively gained more legislative and administrative competences to develop into proper assemblies with extensive political power. The *Landsgemeinden* only subsists in two cantons today, Glarus and Appenzell Innerrhoden, both of which have a small population. The direct assembly, however, is still the form of legislative power in 80 per cent of Swiss municipalities today, mainly in the German-speaking part of the country.[7]

In the United States, assembly-based direct democracy started in the English colonies, before Independence,[8] and worked in a way very similar to the Swiss assemblies. Established from 1620 by Puritans, Town Meetings were from the beginning law-making bodies, contrary to the Swiss *Landsgemeinden* that only became so later. Today, Town Meetings are confined to New England and were never implemented further than in the original colonies. Scholars such as Frank Bryan,[9] as well as journalists, such as Amy Crawford,[10] sometimes describe Town Meetings as the 'true form of direct democracy' and even as the 'true form of democracy', in contrast to elected representation. The opposition between assembly and ballot in the United States can be understood because there is no continuity between the two.

On the one hand, Andreas Ladner presents empirical evidence demonstrating that smaller Swiss municipalities are significantly more likely to experience higher

---

5   S. Duroy, 'Les Landsgemeinden Suisses' in R. Drago (ed.), *Les Procédés de la démocratie semi-directe dans l'administration locale en Suisse*, vol. 15 (Presses Universitaires de France, 1987) 11.

6   L. Carlen, *Die Landsgemeinde in der Schweiz: Schule d. Demokratie* (Thorbecke, 1976).

7   A. Ladner, *Politische Gemeinden, kommunale Parteien und lokale Politik: eine empirische Untersuchung in den Gemeinden der Schweiz* (Seismo Verlag, Sozialwissenschaften und Gesellschaftsfragen, 1991) 81.

8   Zimmerman (n4).

9   F.M. Bryan, *Real Democracy: The New England Town Meeting and How It Works* (University of Chicago Press, 2003).

10   A. Crawford, 'For the People, by the People' (2013) *Slate*, available at <http://www.slate.com/articles/news_and_politics/politics/2013/05/new_england_town_halls_these_experiments_in_direct_democracy_do_a_far_better.single.html> accessed 2 September 2013.

participation rates in assemblies.[11] The turnout of voters tends to be higher at both ends of the demographic scale, in municipalities with assemblies and no ballot, typically small ones, and in municipalities with no assemblies but with ballot, typically large ones.[12] On the other hand, Frank Bryan presents empirical evidence that small communities are significantly more active in the number of meetings they hold.[13] Consequently, in Switzerland as well as the United States, the vigour of assembly-based local direct democracy is inversely correlated with size. The smaller the community, the more frequent meetings will be (US) and the stronger the attendance will be (Sw).

Too Many to Congregate: Urbanisation and Adoption of the Ballot in Switzerland

Joëlle Salomon-Cavin explains the uprising of direct democracy, first in assembly, and then unassembled by the ballot, by the struggles between urban and rural communities.[14] In the *Ancien Régime*, the political situation in Switzerland was a loose confederation of largely independent communities organised through feudal networks. Unlike the rest of feudal Europe, fealty hierarchies were dominated by cities, and not by lords or *seigneurs*, although wealth was largely generated in the countryside. *Landsgemeinden* appeared in the more independent mountainous rural communities, while cities were largely ruled by corporations. The participation was at first limited to a selective number of burghers,[15] and only progressively extended to the larger number of citizens. It is to be noted that the *Landsgemeinde* of Appenzell Innerrhoden only allowed female participation in 1991, and only as a result of an injunction from the Federal Supreme Court.[16]

---

11   A. Ladner, 'Size and direct democracy at the local level: The case of Switzerland' (2002) 20(6) *Environment and Planning C: Government and Policy* 813–28.

12   A. Ladner and J. Fiechter, 'The influence of direct democracy on political interest, electoral turnout and other forms of citizens' participation in Swiss municipalities' (2012) 38 *Local Government Studies* 437, 450.

13   Bryan (n9).

14   J. Salomon Cavin, *La ville, mal-aimée: représentations anti-urbaines et aménagement du territoire en Suisse: analyse, comparaisons, évolution* (PPUR (Presses Polytechniques Universitaires Romandes), 2005) 41.

15   W.E. Rappard, *L'évolution économique et politique des villes et des campagnes suisses depuis la fin de l'ancien régime jusqu'à nos jours: Conférence faite le 3 février 1916 à l'Université de Genève sous les auspices de l'Union des Femmes* (Stæmpfli and Cie, 1916).

16   *Theresa Rohner und Mitbeteiligte gegen Kanton Appenzell* (1990). ATF 116 Ia 359, available at <http://relevancy.bger.ch/php/clir/http/index.php?lang=fr&type=show_document&highlight_docid=atf://116–1A-359:fr> accessed 18 July 2014.

Between 1830 and 1900, Switzerland transitioned from a regime of assemblies to a regime of ballot.[17] Parallel to the French Revolution, Switzerland experienced a period of political turmoil leading to the creation of a short-lived centralised Helvetic Republic. As in France, the creation of the Republic carried debates about a radical levelling of political competence with new and equal political wards that would eliminate the relative power of cities on the countryside.[18] But more than the Republic, the revolution of 1830 and the new federal constitution of 1848 consecrated ballot-based popular rights in Switzerland. With the 1830 revolution, suffrage was extended and citizens gained veto rights in many cantons. The constitution of 1848 created the right of initiative and referendum at the federal level. Most of the experimentations in the cantons took place between these two milestones, with the adoption of veto and initiative rights.[19]

Ballot-based direct democracy originated in Switzerland in the urban growth that made the continuation of assemblies of new bodies of citizens impossible because they were too large Switzerland exhibited a steady growth in the number of larger municipalities from 1800 and throughout the nineteenth and twentieth centuries.[20] But for Joëlle Salomon-Cavin, the initiative and referendum also contributed to the shaping of new urban societies by preventing the establishment of a dominant minority ruling the cities.[21] Formal equality of rights deactivated formal dominations and empowered the working classes. Labour laws, for example, are thus an urban product in Switzerland: they were passed by the ballot.

Autonomy of Local Governments in the United States

Direct democracy started locally in the United States and was driven by urban issues. It was then implemented at state level in 20, mostly Western, states. However, it never made its way to the federal level. In California, San Francisco and Vallejo, in the Bay Area, were the first cities to introduce popular initiatives as early as 1898. They had the power to do so because towns and cities were granted municipal home-rule by California in 1879, only preceded by Missouri in 1875.[22]

---

17   P.-A. Schorderet, 'Elire, voter, signer: pratiques de vote, luttes politiques et dynamiques d'institutionnalisation de la démocratie en Suisse au dix-neuvième siècle', doctoral thesis (Université de Lausanne, 2005).

18   F. Walter, 'Echec À La Départementalisation. Les Découpages Administratifs de La République Helvétique (1793–1803)' (1990) 40 *Revue suisse d'histoire* 67.

19   Schorderet (n16).

20   F. Walter, *La Suisse urbaine, 1750–1950*, vol. 3 (Editions Zoé, 1994) 36.

21   Cavin (n14).

22   J.J. Richardson, M. Zimmerman Gough and R. Puentes, 'Is home rule the answer? Clarifying the influence of Dillon's Rule on growth management' (The Brookings Institution Center on Urban and Metropolitan Policy, 2003) 10, available at <http://www.brookings.edu/ES/urban/publications/dillonsrule.pdf> accessed 25 March 2009.

Similarly to Switzerland, municipal law is not a federal matter in the United States: it is defined by the states themselves. Fifty states thus hold 50 different municipal statuses with different levels of autonomy. These statuses have been shaped by urban issues and in return determine the possibility for municipalities to engage in direct democracy. Between 1850 and 1914, the United States experienced a fierce 'urban competition',[23] a race of demographic growth and economic development that profoundly changed the organisation of American cities and urban environments. They became more polarised, between city centres sheltering the lower classes along with old factories and entertainment areas, and newly developed suburban areas with the rising middle class and the new industrial development. This 'reversed exodus'[24] was partly the result of the new services provided by new urban corporations, such as mass public transport, leading to what Samuel Warner identified as the 'streetcar suburbs'.[25] Local government was already overtaken by systematic patronage in utility franchising to private companies.[26] The shift to publicly operated utilities indeed only happened in the twentieth century.[27]

John Dillon, a judge of the Iowa state court in the 1860s, was particularly concerned with the collusion between private companies managing public utilities and local government. He perceived local government autonomy as the major problem. In order to solve it, he ruled in 1868 that every competence that was not explicitly granted to local authorities by the state legislature remained in the hand of the state and municipalities had no legal ground to intervene in it whatsoever. Local governments are thus creations of states, and as such states retain all authority over them.[28] This rule of zero autonomy for local government made its way to other states and is now referred as *Dillon's Rule*.

Almost at the same time, in 1871, Judge Thomas Cooley, of the Michigan Supreme Court, expressed a diametrically opposed view on local autonomy. Local governments have for him an inherent right of self-administration.[29] From 1875 to 1912, 13 Western states adopted the *Home Rule*, granting greater autonomy to local government.[30]

Dillon's Rule and *Home Rule* are two extremes of a scale and not a nominal distribution. Zimmerman makes an ordinal classification of the 50 states ranked by

---

23   Z.L. Miller, *Boss Cox's Cincinnati: Urban Politics in the Progressive Era* (Ohio State University Press, 2000) 5.

24   Ibid. 8.

25   S. Warner, *Streetcar Suburbs: The Process of Growth in Boston, 1870–1900* (Harvard University Press, 1962).

26   Richardson, Zimmerman Gough and Puentes (n21) 7.

27   S.E. Masten, 'Public utility ownership in 19th-century America: The "aberrant" case of water' (2011) 27 *Journal of Law, Economics, and Organization* 604, 605.

28   *City of Clinton v Cedar Rapids and Missouri River Railroad Co* 24 Iowa 455 (1868).

29   *People v Hulburt* 24 Mich 44 (1871).

30   Richardson, Zimmerman Gough and Puentes (n21).

their degree of municipal autonomy,[31] as all states know some forms of local autonomy but in none of them are municipalities completely independent from the state. The localisation of the state on this scale can be defined by its state constitution and municipal law, as well as with the ruling of the state supreme court.[32] So, in practice, the legal foundations for municipal autonomy rests on provisions by the state, even though, placed in the state constitution, it can lack impact for the legislature.[33]

With reference to the local autonomy scale, California holds an intermediary position, where charter cities are granted *Home Rule* and general-law cities are submitted to *Dillon's Rule*.[34] On Zimmerman's scale of local autonomy, the state ranks 18th out of 50.[35] Interestingly, states with *Town Meetings* fall to the bottom of the list. *Town Meetings* are described as the only 'true democracy' because of their assembled character by scholars like Frank Bryan.[36] But in these states local governments remain limited in their autonomy from the state and as Charles Péguy remarked of Kantianists, '[they have] pure hands. But [they have] no hands'.[37]

Two different paths led to the adoption of initiative and referendum at the local level, depending on where the state was on the *Dillon's Rule* and *Home Rule* scale. In some states, cities and counties were granted this right by a statute. Nebraska passed such a law for its municipalities in 1897. California passed a similar one for its counties in 1893. In other cases, *Home Rule* provisions afforded a space for cities to experiment with these new instruments of self-government. This is what happened in California where, in 1898, Vallejo and San Francisco were the first in the country to implement ballot-based direct democracy.[38] Municipal initiative then spread quickly and by 1911, cities in 19 states had initiative and referendum at the local level, either granted by the states (in 10 states) or by their own initiative. John Matsusaka recalls that the historical details of the adoption of initiative by the cities, are largely undocumented, compared to the states.[39] However, there is a clear indication that cities were at the core of the initiative adoption trend.

---

31   J.F. Zimmerman, *Measuring Local Discretionary Authority* (Advisory Commission on Intergovernmental Relations, 1981), available at <http://www.getcited.org/pub/10227 1059> accessed 1 October 2013.

32   B.A. Garner and others, *Black's Law Dictionary* (West Group (Law), 2011).

33   C.A. Novak, 'Agriculture's new environmental battleground: The preemption of county livestock regulations' (2000) 5 *Drake Journal of Agricultural Law* 429; D. Krane, P.N. Rigos and M. Hill, *Home Rule in America: A Fifty-State Handbook* (Congressional Quarterly Books, 2000).

34   Richardson, Zimmerman Gough and Puentes (n21) 41; M. Albuquerque, 'California and Dillon: The times they are a-changing' (1997) 25 *Hastings Constitutional Law Quarterly* 187.

35   Zimmerman, *Measuring Local Discretionary Authority* (n30).

36   Bryan (n9).

37   C. Péguy, *Solvuntur objecta* (Cahiers de la quinzaine, 1910) 246.

38   J.G. Matsusaka, *For the Many or the Few: The Initiative, Public Policy, and American Democracy* (University of Chicago Press, 2008) 6.

39   Ibid. 7.

Circumventing Elected Officials by Direct Democracy in American Cities

Dillon's Rule provided a framework to limit the opportunities for local corruption. But in the West and in the centre, local governments were granted more autonomy and this autonomy continued to fuel collusion and corruption. This corruption and patronage became organised in a resilient system under the protection of a local political *boss*. In return, at the end of the nineteenth century, opponents of this system, mainly coming from the residential outskirts of cities, also became organised in a *Progressive Movement*. This movement advocated and implemented a new form of direct democracy to circumvent unresponsive elected representation.

On the one hand, from 1850 the growth of cities deeply disturbed the existing political structures and offered new opportunities for the creation of local urban political systems of corruption, patronage and nepotism.[40] Under the protection of a local political figure, the *boss*, this system became known as *bossism*. On the other hand, big corporations arose from cities. Rapidly up-surging needs and technical opportunities for new services – mass transit, water, electricity – created a favourable environment for big corporations managing these services. The size of these corporations made it difficult for any local government to regulate. The conjunction of these two effects created local environments where public services and governments were in the hands of a limited number of people and organisations, with strong incentives to favour each other and to be irresponsive to the demands of the electorate.

As a result, by the beginning of the twentieth century, the political leaders of cities had turned into bosses and created a system of corruption, nepotism and patronage.[41] For Zane Miller,[42] the emergence of bosses and the reform committees trying to solve or circumvent their operations was a consequence of the reshaping of cities, an urban phenomenon. As the old city centres were being abandoned by new middle classes who were building new suburbs, he sees *bossism* as a way of renewing order in a deeply disturbed urban environment. *Bossism* created organised political systems. By contrast, the reform movement was coming from the new residential outskirts of the city.

One of the Progressive Movement's goals was the reformation of the citizen as a means of restoring popular government. Direct democracy was a way of circumventing corrupt representation – the instrumental dimension – but also a way to educate citizens to debate and engage in legislation – the educational dimension. Smith and Tolbert have found evidence for this educational effect.[43] This 'education to citizenship' has been largely driven by urban trends.

---

40   Miller (n22).

41   N. Solomon, *When Leaders Were Bosses: An Inside Look at Political Machines and Politics* (Exposition Press, 1975).

42   Miller (n22).

43   D.A. Smith and C. Tolbert, *Educated by Initiative: The Effects of Direct Democracy on Citizens and Political Organizations in the American States* (University of Michigan Press, 2004).

Ballot-based Direct Democracy in the United States, the Swiss Reference

As the United States knew some form of direct democracy with the New England *Town Meetings*, this could have served as a reference for the ballot. On the contrary, I will show in this subsection that Switzerland was the main reference.

In the Federalist Paper no. 10, published in 1787, James Madison explicitly considered and rejected direct democracy.[44] His main argument concerned the importance of representation as a protection from the rule of factions. Madison compared Republican and Democratic forms of governments. These forms are respectively representative democracy, with elected delegates of the people, and direct democracy, where the people in assembly make the law themselves. Madison advocated that the latter presented no escape from the tyranny of the majority while the former provided mutual institutional control as well as control by the voters. Although New England *Town Meetings* were well known by the founding fathers, they explicitly discarded these in favour of representation. By the time the Progressive Movement was looking for a way to circumvent corrupt elected representatives in the cities, it had two possible references for modern direct democracy. New England and Switzerland, but no obvious nationwide solution.

To evaluate which of the two possible references was the most influential in the advocacy of a new form of direct democracy in the United States, a quantitative analysis of the Google Books Corpus is relevant. I calculated the proportion of books mentioning 'direct democracy' and 'United States' and which were also mentioning 'New England' or 'Switzerland'. Figure 8.1 shows that references to Switzerland predate mentions of New England by at least 30 years. References to Switzerland peak between 1890 and 1910, appearing in 70 per cent of the books on direct democracy and the United States. Most American states introduced the popular initiative, referendum and recall, during that time (Figure 8.2). Mentions of New England start to occupy a significant proportion – 50 to 60 per cent – of these books from 1910 to 1960 only, after most states had adopted direct democracy. These findings demonstrate that the reference for the diffusion of ballot-based direct democracy in the United States was Switzerland much more than New England. In effect, if New England were a reference for the Western States, we would see at least a proportion of these books mentioning it. Instead, almost no book mentions New England until 1910. The reference to New England found in direct democracy related literature is used after the implementation in the Western States either as a contrasting example, a non-influential precedent or in a synthesis of the various forms of direct democracy.[45]

---

44   J. Madison, 'The Federalist No. 10' (1787) 78 *The Federalist Papers* 80.

45   M. Luehrs Tripp, *The Swiss and United States Federal Constitutional Systems: A Comparative Study* (Librairie sociale et économique, 1940) 43; B.N. Banerjea, *Introduction to Politics* (Jijnasa, 1962).

In 2004, Thomas Gliozzo[46] identified two main sources of inspiration for ballot-based semi-direct democracy in two books published by Nathan Cree[47] and J.W. Sullivan,[48] describing the system recently implemented in Switzerland. For Thomas Gliozzo,[49] the latter is more influential than the former, but the metrics of citations in Google Books points the other way with six times more mentions in the 1900–1910 decade and 31 times more mentions in the 1910–1920 decade (Figure 8.3).

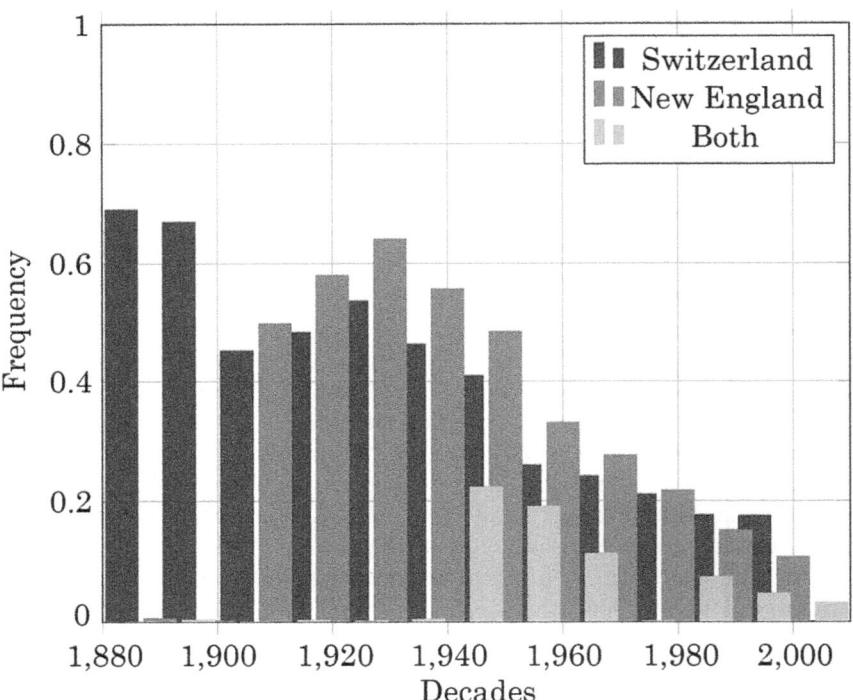

Figure 8.1   Frequency of books in English mentioning 'Switzerland' or 'New England' in the books mentioning 'direct democracy' and 'United States'

46   T. Gliozzo, *L'état Fédéré Américain* (Atelier National de Reproduction des Thèses, 2004) 471.

47   N. Cree, *Direct Legislation by the People* (A.C. McClurg and Company, 1892).

48   J.W. Sullivan, *Direct Legislation by the Citizenship Through the Initiative and Referendum* (True Nationalist Publishing Company, 1893).

49   Gliozzo (n47) 471.

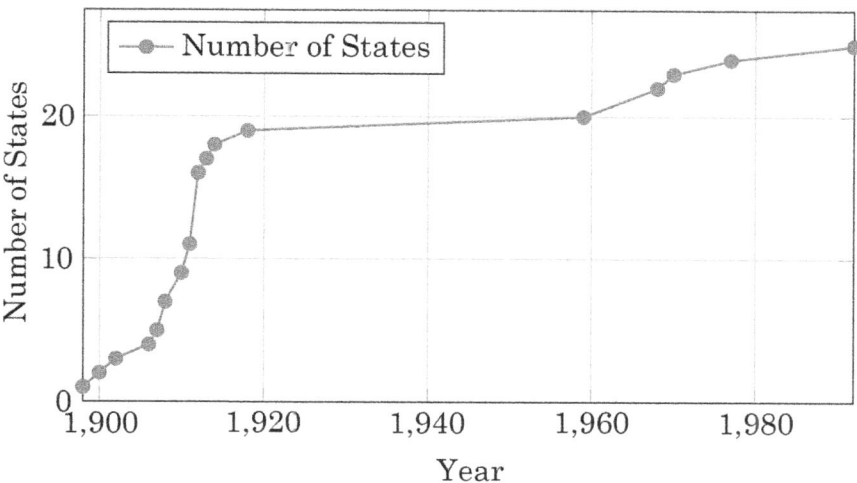

Figure 8.2   **United States: Number of states with state-wide initiative**
Source: D.A. Smith, *Tax Crusaders: And the Politics of Direct Democracy* (Routledge, 1998) 5.

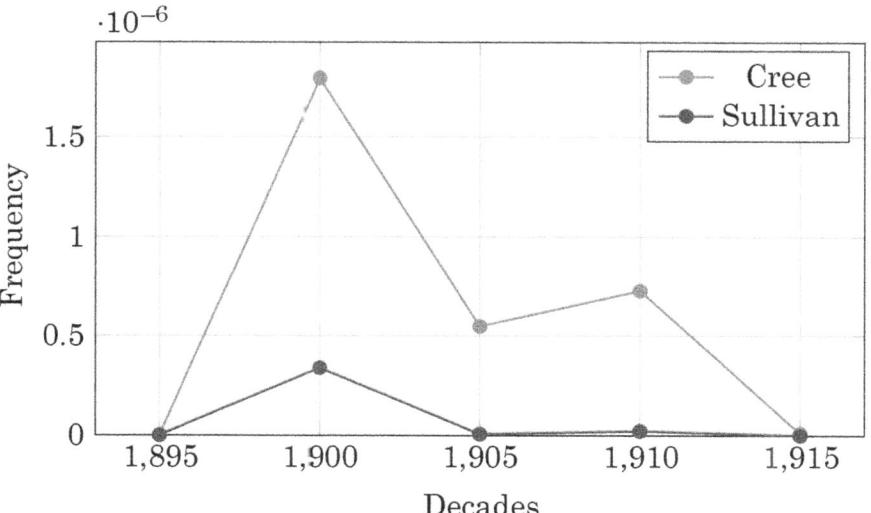

Figure 8.3   **Frequency of books in English mentioning Cree and Sullivan books on the Swiss model of direct democracy in all the books published in English**

The Urban Gradient of Local Direct Democracy Today

Both in Switzerland and the United States, specifically urban issues drove the adoption of a local form of direct democracy by the ballot. Data on local direct democracy is sparse today in these two countries. Nevertheless, existing studies demonstrate a common pattern, with a use of this form of democracy concentrated in urban environments. After a first rush following its adoption at the beginning of the twentieth century, direct democracy use remained low during most of its history since then. Only from the 1970s has the use of initiative and referendum gained significant momentum, at both local and federal/state levels. However, the number of local initiatives, contrary to the federal/statewide ones, has plateaued since the 1990s.[50] Taking election cycles into account, the number of local measures has been stable in California since 1995. The fact that two comparable trends between Switzerland and the United States can be observed tends to rule out purely local causal explanations that are only present in one of the cases, as for instance the tax revolt in the United States.[51] On the contrary, these comparable trends reinforce the plausibility that urban trends, which are themselves similar in these two cases,[52] feed local direct democracy. Local initiatives are more frequent in bigger, more diverse municipalities. This size and diversity effect exists in California,[53] as well as in Switzerland.[54] Moreover, a large proportion of local initiatives are dedicated to providing or restructuring urban public utilities – water, transport, public facilities – supporting the idea that initiatives are used to keep up with changing urban conditions, especially after growth phases. This interpretation is buttressed in California by the fact that residential mobility is correlated with the use of initiatives,[55] as if changes in population created a need for public policies to realign with people's preferences. In Zürich Canton, municipalities that have experienced population growth in the past years are more likely to see popular initiatives proposed.[56] This urban effect is found only in municipalities. Urban

---

50   J. Meyland, 'Modalités et pratiques de la démocratie semi-directe dans les communes suisses' (Office d'études socio-économiques et statistiques, Ville de Lausanne, 1981) 13–14; S. Grodecki, *L'initiative populaire cantonale et municipale à Genève* (Schulthess, 2008) 423–30; T.M. Gordon, *The Local Initiative in California* (Public Policy Institute of California, 2004), available at <http://www.ppic.org/content/pubs/report/ R_904TGR.pdf> accessed 17 March 2009.

51   J.B. Weatherby and S.L Witt, *The Urban West: Managing Growth and Decline* (Greenwood Publishing Group, 1994) 6.

52   M. Schuler et al., *Atlas des räumlichen Wandels des Schweiz / Atlas des mutations spatiales de la Suisse* (1st edn, Neue Zürcher Zeitung, 2007).

53   Gordon (n51).

54   Ladner and Fiechter (n12).

55   Gordon (n51).

56   Kanton Zürich, *Direktion der Justiz und des Innern, Statistisches Amt*, available at <http://www.statistik.zh.ch/internet/justiz_inneres/statistik/de/wahlen_abstimmungen. html> accessed 1 October 2013. Schuler et al. (n53) 84–5.

cantons[57] (CH) and counties[58] (US) do not exhibit any more intensive use of direct democracy than their rural counterparts. Therefore, the *urban gradient* – as Jacques Lévy[59] calls the conjunction of density and diversity – and its evolution in time is a good predictor of the use of local direct democracy.

The Metropolitan Challenges of Direct Democracy

Local direct democracy has gained momentum in the past decades. Acknowledging the urban trends that led to the diffusion and rise of this mode of democracy can help to understand the challenges facing it today. Scholars compete on two different interpretations as to why local direct democracy is so linked to bigger, more urban communities.

The first interpretation is simply that direct democracy is extensively used where the other form, namely representative democracy, fails to respond to the policy preferences of citizens. The main reasoning behind this interpretation is that representative democracy is unable to aggregate properly and be responsive to voters' preferences and therefore these voters feel the need to legislate by the ballot.[60] As urban places are more diverse in income, education and race, voters' preferences are also more diverse.[61] They are therefore more difficult to aggregate.[62] Indeed, Swiss elected officials report more consensus in smaller municipalities and deeper differentiation in larger ones.[63] This model is at the core of political prescriptions promoting smaller competing local jurisdictions,[64] in a context where people could 'vote with their feet' and move to another place when they are dissatisfied,[65] thus incentivising local governments to comply with aggregated preferences.

---

57   A.H. Trechsel, *Feuerwerk Volksrechte: die Volksabstimmungen in den schweizerischen Kantonen 1970–1996* (Helbing and Lichtenhahn, 2000) 23.

58   Gordon (n51).

59   S. Duroy et al., *Les Procédés de La Démocratie Semi-Directe Dans L'administration Locale En Suisse*, vol. 15 (R. Drago ed, Presses Universitaires de France, 1987) 180.

60   Matsusaka (n38) 138.

61   R.S. Erikson, 'Economic conditions and the presidential vote' (1989) 83 *The American Political Science Review* 567; A.G. Greenwald et al., 'Implicit race attitudes predicted vote in the 2008 U.S. Presidential Election' (2009) 9 *Analyses of Social Issues and Public Policy* 241.

62   N. McCarty and A. Meirowitz, *Political Game Theory: An Introduction* (Cambridge University Press, 2007) 68.

63   T. Huissoud and D. Joye, 'Participation, Insertion Locale et Démocratie Directe Dans Les Espaces Urbains' (1991) 31 *Annuaire Suisse de Science Politique* 109, 126.

64   B.S. Frey and R. Eichenberger, *The New Democratic Federalism for Europe: Functional, Overlapping and Competing Jurisdictions* (Edward Elgar Publishing, 2004).

65   C.M. Tiebout, 'A pure theory of local expenditures' (1956) 64 *Journal of Political Economy* 416.

The second interpretation is that larger communities generate more public debate, and local direct democracy is especially good at determining decisions that are worth a public debate. In Swiss cities, political issues get more complex and this complexity leads to more political activity and a greater use of direct democracy.[66] Following this model, local direct democracy is an efficient system for allocating limited resources (time, campaign money, volunteers) to the most valuable problems. John Matsusaka distinguishes between decisions that have 'Pareto-comparable outcomes'[67] – decisions that do not imply depreciating the position of some actors,[68] which he calls 'good government decisions' – taken by the legislature, and ones affecting distribution of wealth or personal opinions which are resolved through initiatives.[69] A direct democracy system allows consensual issues to take the faster and less resource-consuming track of representative democracy while the less consensual issues that require a more public debate are brought out in a more open public sphere. Consequently, initiatives are the sign of a well-functioning deliberative democracy.

The challenges of size and accountability that led to the diffusion of local direct democracy in Switzerland and the United States from 1848 to 1910 are analogous to the challenge presented to metropolitan governance today: a challenge of scale. Since 1950, metropolitan areas, through commuter and suburban spread, have grown to out-scale existing local governments.[70] How could these two states use the sorting and public sphere enhancing ability of direct democracy to address the scale of metropolitan policies? In Switzerland, proposals have been made to merge cantons together to align their territories with the metropolitan regions.[71] The quest for the perfect scale of governance has a long history.[72] Evolutions of local direct democracy have been largely driven by urban mutations. The rise of cities in the nineteenth century created problems of scale and political functioning

---

66   M. Bützer, *Direkte Demokratie in Schweizer Städten: Ursprung, Ausgestaltung und Gebrauch im Vergleich* (Nomos-Verlagsgesellschaft, 2007) 32.

67   Named after the Italian economist Vilfredo Pareto, 'Pareto optimality' is a game theory concept. An outcome is said 'Pareto optimal' when it cannot be improved without hurting at least one player. In the policy context described by John Matsusaka, a decision is said to be 'Pareto comparable' when it improves something without making anybody worse off. Hence, these decisions do not require arbitration between conflicting interests; they are 'good government decisions'.

68   A. Chinchuluun, *Pareto Optimality, Game Theory and Equilibria* (Springer, 2008).

69   J.G. Matsusaka, 'Economics of direct legislation' (1992) 107 *Quarterly Journal of Economics* 541, 569.

70   J.E. Oliver, *Democracy in Suburbia* (Princeton University Press, 2001) 35.

71   P.-A. Rumley, *La Suisse demain: de nouveaux territoires romands, un nouveau canton du Jura: utopie ou réalité?* (Presses du Belvédère, 2010).

72   D. Kubler, *La métropole et le citoyen: les agglomérations urbaines en Suisse vues par leurs habitants* (Presses Polytechniques et Universitaires Romandes, 2005); J. Blatter, *Governance – theoretische Formen und historische Transformationen: politische Steuerung und Integration in Metropolregionen der USA (1850–2000)* (Nomos, 2007).

that led to the adoption of popular initiatives and referendums. In the twentieth century, the growth of urban agglomerations beyond city limits changed the pattern of use of initiatives. The phase being experienced today, since the 1980s, is characterised by less attachment to territories and growing importance of networks in urban functioning.[73]

Joint initiatives could be used in order to transfer the qualities of direct democracy into this new urban environment. The National Tariff System of the Netherlands' public transport system is a good analogy for how joint initiatives could function. The whole country is divided in contiguous zones. A passenger buys a single ticket for all the zones he intends to cross to get to his destination. Local direct democracy today, functions as if a passenger would have to get off the train every time he crosses a zone to buy another ticket, wait for the next train, and board it again. Using joint popular initiatives between several jurisdictions would allow citizens to buy a single policy ticket for several zones.

73   J. Levy, 'La Ville, Concept Geographique, Objet Politique' (1996) *DEBAT-PARIS-* 111; G. Pflieger and C. Rozenblat, 'Introduction. Urban networks and network theory: The city as the connector of multiple networks' (2010) 47 *Urban Studies* 2723.

Chapter 9

The 'Margin of Appreciation' in ECHR Case-law as a Boundary Line to Legal Transplants

Alessandra Pera

Introduction

This study investigates the influence of the European Human Rights Court on State 'margin of appreciation' on the diffusion of accepted or rejected cultural and political choices through the jurisprudence of the case-law.

The margin of appreciation is an interpretative argument, a criterion, a parameter, which allows the Court to preserve rather than censure national State policies and choices on difficult issues which, involving moral and ethical questions, and which do not receive common answers in the European legal systems.[1] Recent examples are decisions on *in vitro* insemination in UK legislation, such as *Evans v United Kingdom*;[2] on the non-recognition of same sex marriage in Austrian legislation (*Schalk and Kopf v Austria*).[3] on the criminalisation of abortion except when the mother's life is in danger in Irish legislation (*A. and others v Ireland*);[4] on the Austrian prohibition of *in vitro* fertilisation with gamete donation (*S.H. and others v Austria*);[5] and on the Italian prohibition of prenatal diagnosis on *in vitro* formed embryos (*Costa and Pavan v Italy*).[6]

However, a particular hermeneutic approach can be open or closed to peculiar solutions, as proved by the debate on the scope of the notion of 'family life' under Articles 8 and 12 of the European Convention on Human Rights. This notion, which is undefined in the Convention, has been interpreted and applied to include

---

1   On different patterns for diffusion, see W. Twining, 'Diffusion of law: A global perspective' (2004) 49 1 *Journal of Legal Pluralism 34*, 35; by the same author, more recently, W. Twining, *General Jurisprudence: Understanding Law from a Global Perspective* (Cambridge University Press, 2009).

2   *Evans v United Kingdom* App no 6339/05 (ECHR, 10 April 2007).

3   *Schalk and Kopf v Austria* App no 30141/04 (ECHR, 24 June 2010).

4   *A. and others v Ireland* App no 25579/05 (ECHR, 16 December 2010).

5   *S.H. and others v Austria* App no 57813/00 (ECHR, 1 April 2010 and 3 November 2011).

6   *Costa and Pavan v Italy* App no 54270/10 (ECHR, 28 August 2012).

various kinds of interpersonal relationships, inside and/or outside marriage. It admits the coexistence of the Scandinavian family model alongside the conservative definition provided by the Irish Constitution and the Italian refusal to legally recognise same-sex unions. In fact, the broad notion of 'family life' and the recourse to the 'margin of appreciation' determine the existence of solutions and models which are really heterogeneous, but at the same time are all within the framework of the general concept of family life. As a result family life protected under these provisions include: the family based on marriage, de facto family, same-sex marriage and unions, relationship between child and legitimate or natural or adoptive parents, step-families and every kind of relationship occurring between people who are linked together by a peculiar affective bound, according to their way of feeling and perceiving personal relationships and also in the light of each State's cultural, traditional, religious and social backgrounds.

In considering the margin of appreciation the European Court of Human Rights has to take into account political choices and perceptions of social differences among the contracting States, and adopt a case by case approach, which it is able to do because its decisions are binding only among the parties to the case. Consequently in ECHR case law there are many examples of the coexistence of different hermeneutic solutions of the same legal rule, of the same principle, and/or of the same sentence, because some notions are extremely general and comprehensive, for example, in *Keegan v Ireland*,[7] a natural father applied for custody of his child, who had been placed for adoption by the mother shortly after the birth without his knowledge. In such a situation the Court has held that, even if the parents were not married, there existed a bond of family life between the child and his father, which must be protected. There was, therefore, no scope to allow for the Irish 'margin of appreciation' and for its restrictive conception of family.

In contrast is the case of *Johnston and others v Ireland*,[8] where Irish law was again scrutinised. This case involved a child born from the union of a man and a woman who were respectively married to other spouses. This child had many problems in getting recognised by his natural parents, as the marriage contract cannot be dissolved according to Irish law. In fact, the institution of marriage is considered the foundation of the family under the Irish Constitution. As the child was born after his parents' respective marriages, they could not recognise their common son because he was an adulterine child and there was no bond of family life between the child and his natural parents – unlike the bond arising between children and their parents in families where the parents were married. In this case the court held that the distinction between these two types of family and the bond between parent and child fell with the margin of appreciation. Here, the use of margin of appreciation (argument) operated in favour of the Irish conception of the legitimate family instead of a broad notion applied in *Keegan v Ireland*.[9]

---

7   *Keegan v Ireland* App no 16969/90 (ECHR, 26 May 1994).
8   *Johnston and others v Ireland* App no 9697/82 (ECHR, 18 December 1986).
9   *Keegan v Ireland* App no 16969/90 (ECHR, 26 May 1994).

The above mentioned two Irish cases are just a paradigmatic example of two different ways of using the margin of appreciation argument in the same area of law, limiting or broadening the notion of family life and its dimensions, discouraging or promoting one model instead of another, providing a juridical solution instead of the opposite one and, in particular addressing the issue of atypical or non-traditional family bonds or 'others family relationships' in comparison to those arising from the 'legitimate' (conventional) family.

In what follows this chapter considers some decisions of the Court on abortion, ovum donation, pre-implant embryo analysis and artificial procreation techniques, to find out if, in such subjects, which are all strongly connected to ethical, moral and social values, the case law of the Court is diachronically coherent in its various decisions or if there are considerable and relevant incoherencies and interpretative mismatches among them.

In this latter hypothesis, the explanation for these contradictions lies in the different use of the margin of appreciation argument and in the single rules and models being scrutinised by the Court. An examination of these suggests that sometimes the ECHR intends to preserve a certain national model through the margin of appreciation and at other times prefers to substitute it with another one, using different arguments, such as the general consensus of contracting States. Indeed, it seems that in the decision-making process the Court's approach is firstly, to consider the choice of the model, and particularly that of the rule or the value that has to be promoted or discouraged among the contracting States and secondly, the choice of the hermeneutic argument that can be adopted in order to achieve this goal, according to an anti-formalistic hermeneutic approach. The consequential outcome can be very different, depending on which argument is adopted.

A first type of consequence can be that of a policy oriented programme, whereby the consensus of the majority of the contracting states can determine the need for law reforms in those states where a certain model is not known, envisaged or not already shared, because the ethical, social, and/or religious framework is quite unique.

A second type of consequence depends on the adoption of the margin of appreciation argument, which can determine the persistence of models and rules, which are not necessarily really shared among the contracting states, but are intended as profoundly connected to a certain tradition, territory or group of people.

The chapter concludes with emphasising that these interpretive strategies do not come together by themselves; they are created and 'formed' by real time-bound people with real and practical needs, policies and strategies[10] and quite often the relation between law and politics (or policies) is expressed and manifested in jurisdictions, especially in supranational ones involved in fundamental human rights cases. Because of this, the contribution of the ECHR to certain political theories or conceptions, to the diffusion of a specific legal rules or models and to the promotion of certain values and principles, is crucial.

---

10   P.G. Monateri, 'Methods in comparative law: An intellectual overview' in P.G. Monateri (ed.), *Methods of Comparative Law* (Edward Elgar, 2012) 11.

Therefore, it is important to consider jurists' historical, professional and societal background, as they use language and hermeneutic processes to assess human life and interests in a discourse, which has the purpose of being acceptable in a legal context.

The decisions of courts are relevant, but we should also consider why they have decided as they did, the influences to which judges are subjected and the various origins of such influences.[11] These influences may arise because of the wide support given by scholars to a doctrinal innovation, but they may also concern the judge's background, for example, a judge appointed from an academic position may tend to put more stress on scholarly opinion than a judge who has always practiced law.

The Margin of Appreciation as a Policy-oriented Hermeneutic Argument

It is evident that a wide or a narrow approach to the margin of appreciation argument and a remarkable self-restraint in evaluating which national provisions violate articles 8, 12 and 14 of the European Convention on Human Rights has consequences for the dissemination of juridical solutions and models on the pervasiveness of legal and normative traditions of European countries throughout Europe, as law and rules are commonly formed by imitation.

The case law of the European Court of Human Rights does not produce *stare decisis*, but it is particularly eminent and authoritative, as one of the parties is always a contracting State whose legislation or case law is being challenged as breaching fundamental rights under the Convention.

Recourse to the margin of appreciation argument, if it is successful, has the result of establishing that there is no violation of the Convention and allows contracting States a broad competence and discretion in the way national authorities and courts assess a certain policy, maintain a model, or a certain practice as part of their culture and juridical traditions.

At the same time the analysis of the cases shows that the ECHR might use the 'margin of appreciation' to concentrate or diffuse solutions that are the heritage of few or many legal traditions. The result can be qualified as the attempt to promote the diffusion or the abandonment of certain cultural, ethical and legal models through a particular kind of legal order and across different geographical levels: the ECHR and national jurisdictions and legal systems, considered both in their territorial and political dimensions and not just horizontally among municipal legal systems.

We are confronted by a pattern in which governments and Parliaments are not the main actors. In fact, even if States have subscribed to the Convention on Human

---

11   In other words, how a judge thinks and acts, as an active law maker or with a high level of interpretative restraint, is important in influencing the way in which we perceive him/her and, in general, our conception of the judiciary role.

Rights and have legislated to give it effect or passed legislation which appears to be in contravention of the Convention, they often have to go through the process of legal transplant 'suggested or decided' by the European Court of Human Rights in order to comply with the Court rulings. Besides the legislative and judicial framework of those rules there may also be a governance project with concrete and practical implications, in the sense that some choices are not neutral, because they are oriented by values, which are the expression of social, religious or ethical ways of feeling;[12] for example, in promoting or discouraging the use of gamete donation, therapeutic abortion, pre-embryo analysis, the recognition of same sex couple rights, the adoption of child into 'a-typical families' and so on, the Court promotes certain values instead of others in potential contrast, making thereby policy choices.

These policy oriented choices have practical consequences in terms of the diffusion of certain fertilisation techniques or embryo diagnostic tests, which can be used by private and public hospitals, by doctors and specialists; in terms of pharmaceutical products that can be sold or not; in terms of impact on the economic impact on certain industries and so on.

The diffusion of law, in such a hypothesis, involves the movement from a powerful centre, the Strasbourg Court, to a dependent periphery, the Member State, which occurs through the path of Court interpretation and decision making. The determining agency or formant here is the judicial one.[13]

---

12   Recently, after a flying start, it is more commonly thought that many projects, the aim of which is 'to build up a common core of European and Western law, are to be seen for what they really are: biased, non-neutral political projects of governance supported by the use of academic discipline of Comparative Law'. See Monateri (n10) 18.

13   According to the Common Core methodology, summing up Sacco's theory, Ugo Mattei and Mauro Bussani have argued that a 'list, even exhaustive, of all the reasons given for the decisions made by the courts is not the entire law. The statutes are not the entire law. Neither are the definitions of legal doctrines given by scholars. In order to know what the law is, it is necessary to analyse the entire complex relationship between what Sacco calls the "legal formants" of a system, that is, all those formative elements that make any given rule of law statutes, general propositions, particular definitions, reasons, holdings, and so on. All of these formative elements are not necessarily coherent with each other within each system. Only domestic jurists assume such coherence. To the contrary, legal formants are usually conflicting and can better be pictured in a competitive relationship with one another. For example, we must not only know how courts have acted but we must also consider the influences to which the judges are subject. Such influences may have a variety of origins. They may arise because scholars have given wide support to a doctrinal innovation, but they may also concern the judge's background. A judge appointed from an academic position will tend to put more stress on scholarly opinion than a judge who has always practiced law. The text of a statute is one of these influences even when previous judicial decisions have disregarded it, because there is always the possibility that courts will return to the letter of the statutory provision. All this, however, may still be insufficient to understand the law in a given system. Statutes or code provisions in a given system can be identical to the provisions enacted in other systems, but can be applied differently [...]. On the other hand, provisions or general definitions in two systems can differ while operative rules are the

From a methodological point of view, my analysis uses the dynamic approach of the legal formants theory, which allows us to consider law as a social activity, underlining how the judicial formant functions to give form to the law. The expression 'formant' introduced here refers to an important notion in the theoretical approach that I adopt in my reconstruction. This notion needs to be carefully defined. According to this theory a 'formant' is a group, a type of legal expert, or a community, institutionally involved in the activity of creating law.

Generally speaking, in the Western legal tradition we can consider legal professions to be legal formants, in the sense that the practical lawyer, the legal policy maker (a legislator, an appellate court judge, or an upper-level administrator) and legal scholar are all concurring actors in shaping the law, through statutes, holding opinions, writing articles, treaties, briefs, articulating general principles and strict rules.[14] Some scholars have emphasised that 'Law is not a harmonious set of elements, but a composite of different models and clashing texts reconciled by ingenious lawyer'.[15] The notion of legal formant is more than an esoteric neologism for the traditional distinction between *law, jurisprudence*, and *doctrine*, that is, between enacted law, case law and scholarly writings.[16]

In this way, ECHR decisions, including the use or misuse of the 'margin of appreciation' argument, can be conceived of as formants, because they give a

---

same [...]. A full understanding of what the legal formants are and how they relate to each other allows us to ascertain the factors that affect those solutions. This clarifies the weight that interpretative practices (grounded on scholarly writings, on legal debate aroused by previous judicial decision, etc.) have in moulding the actual outcomes'. Cfr, <http://www. jus.unitn.it/dsg/common-core/approach.html>. On legal formants theory, see R. Sacco, 'Legal formants: A dynamic approach to comparative law' (1991) 39 1 *The American Journal of Comparative Law* 1–34 and 343–402; R. Sacco and A. Gambaro (eds), *Sistemi Giuridici Comparati* in *Trattato di Diritto Comparato* (UTET (Unione Tipografico-Editrice Torinese), 1996) 4–7; R. Sacco, *Introduzione al diritto comparato* (Vth edn, UTET (Unione Tipografico-Editrice Torinese), 1992) 43; A. Watson, 'From legal transplants to legal formants' (1995) 43 3 *American Law Journal of Comparative Law* 469.

14   On the concept of Western legal tradition, see M.A. Glendon, M. Gordon and P.G. Carrozza, *Comparative Legal Traditions* (2nd edn, West Group, 1994) 6–8; P. Stein and J. Shand, *Legal Values in Western Society* (Edinburgh University Press, 1984); P. Glenn, *Legal Tradition of the World. Sustainable Diversity in Law* (Oxford University Press, 2010) 117; P.G. Monateri, 'Black Gaius. A quest for the multicultural origins of the Western legal tradition' (2000) 51 *Hastings Law Journal* 490.

15   Monateri (n10) 8.

16   'Within a given legal system, the legal rule is not uniform, not only because one rule may be given by case law, another by scholars and yet another one by statutes. Within each one of these sources there are also formants competing with each other. For example, the rule described in the headnotes of a case can be inconsistent with the actual rationale of the decision, or the definition of a code can be inconsistent with the detailed rules contained in the code itself'. The above quote explains the use of this method in the study of European and Western legal countries, see the common core project approach <www.jus.unitn.it/dsg/common-core/approach.html> accessed 15 October 2013.

shape to a 'piece of law', which is in itself the product of the interpretation of a number of documents used by professionals (in our case by ECHR judges) according to their personal or (in our case, maybe) institutional strategies. As a result, a certain legal tradition (in our case the one which has been perceived as common to the majority of those European legal systems which have signed the European Convention on Human Rights) is intended to be 'the constructing product arising from conflicting narratives, that is from competing packages of factual elements and rhetorical devices used to assemble the past in the form more apt to legitimate the present. The sense of the past and the canonical assumption of a given tradition have to be seen as the unitary result of a skilful act of crafting a variety of independent documents and texts competing for hegemony'.[17]

A. and others v Ireland, 16 December 2010

To illustrate the impact of the ECHR under the formants' theory I will focus in particular on some decisions on *in vitro* insemination and abortion, starting with *A. and others v Ireland*, 2010. This case concerned the Court's evaluation of Irish legislation that criminalises abortion, with the exception of the case of danger to the mother's life, and its relationship to Art. 8 of the Convention.[18] The main aim of Article 8 is to protect individuals against arbitrary interference by public authorities; it may also impose upon States such positive duties and obligations as are necessary to ensure the effective enforcement of the rights protected therein.[19] In this case, the Court was interested in deciding if there was a positive obligation on the State to provide for a real and practicable procedure for the applicant

---

17   Monateri (n10) 8.

18   Art. 8 ECHR guarantees the right to respect for private and family life, home and correspondence. Its scope is very broad: it extends to many areas of life and has an impact on different legal fields reaching from family law to criminal law.

19   'The object of the Article [8] is "essentially" that of protecting the individual against arbitrary interference by the public authorities. Nevertheless it does not merely compel the State to abstain from such interference: in addition to this primarily negative undertaking, there may be positive obligations inherent in an effective "respect" for family life. This means, amongst other things, that when the State determines in its domestic legal system the regime applicable to certain family ties such as those between an unmarried mother and her child, it must act in a manner calculated to allow those concerned to lead a normal family life. As envisaged by Article 8 (Art. 8), respect for family life implies in particular, in the Court's view, the existence in domestic law of legal safeguards that render possible as from the moment of birth the child's integration in his family. In this connection, the State has a choice of various means, but a law that fails to satisfy this requirement violates paragraph 1 of Article 8 (Art. 8–1) without there being any call to examine it under paragraph 2 (Art. 8–2)'. See *MarckX v Belgium* App no 6833/74 (ECHR, 13 June 1979) and *X and Y v the Netherlands* App no 8978/80 (ECHR, 26 March 1985).

(a woman affected by cancer) to establish her entitlement to a lawful abortion in Ireland, given the due respect to the interest protected under Art. 8.

It is not the intention of this chapter to analyse general principles in defining what is meant by a 'State's positive obligations' and how the Courts applied these principles to the case, which, a matter that, even if it is interesting, is beyond the scope of this chapter. I will concentrate instead on the arguments used by the Judges regarding the 'proportionality test' and the use of the 'margin of appreciation' criterion with a view to examining the balance – found in the legislation of different States – between the foetus's right to life and the mother's right to personal autonomy and self-determination.[20] The solution confronting such conflicting interests is a hermeneutic choice that would ensure a balance between them and the prevailing of one of them over the other. Whatever the outcome would be, any interpretative option would affect family and private life, personal choices of life and many aspects of private autonomy.[21]

According to the Court, there is an evident trend among European States to avoid all questions connected to scientific, religious or philosophical issues about the beginning of life, which coexists with the trend to consider the right to life of the mother and her right to personal autonomy and self-determination as superior to that of the foetus, especially during the first two–four months of pregnancy.[22] Applying the proportionality test, there are two elements that should be analysed:

a. the existence of a European consensus on allowing abortion; and
b. whether or not the Irish sanctions in cases of therapeutic abortion or well-being abortion represented a breach of Art. 8.

---

20 The doctrine of proportionality allows the Court's investigation into the reasonableness of the restriction and requires that there be a reasonable relationship between a particular objective to be achieved and the means used to achieve that objective. The different versions of the proportionality test appear to reflect various standards of review in different contexts. A strict approach is adopted by the Court where fundamental rights are at stake (such as family or private life) and consists of a four questions test: 1. Is there a pressing social need for some restriction of the Convention? 2. If so, does the particular restriction correspond to this need? 3. If so, is it a proportionate response to that need? 4. Are the reasons presented by the authorities, relevant and sufficient? For a further analysis see <http://www.coe.int/t/dghl/cooperation/lisbonnetwork/themis/echr/paper2_en.> accessed 15 June 2014. See also E. Ellis, *The Principle of Proportionality in the Laws of Europe* (Hart, 1999); M. Forowicz, *Shaping Rights in the ECHR: The Role of the European Court of Human Rights* (Oxford University Press, 2013); Y.A. Takahashy, *The Margin of Appreciation Doctrine and the Principle of Proportionality in the Jurisprudence of the ECHR* (Intersentia, 2002).

21 See P. Ronchi, '*A, B and C v. Ireland*: Europe's *Roe v. Wade* still has to wait', (2011) *Law Quarterly Review* 365–9.

22 *The Role of Consensus in the System of the European Convention on Human Rights, Dialogue between Judges*, European Court of Human Rights, Council of Europe, 2008, available at <http//echr.coe.int/Documents/Dialogue_2008_ENG.pdf> accessed 15 October 2013.

As far as point a) is concerned, there is evidence that a large consensus exists among the Council of Europe Member States in allowing abortion 'on broader grounds than accorded under Irish law', as only 'three States have more restrictive access to abortion services than Ireland namely, a prohibition on abortion regardless of the risk to woman's life'.[23]

In other decisions, in which the Court has found that a general consensus on matters concerning human rights exists, even if with some exceptions, it has usually concluded that this consensus narrows the 'margin of appreciation' of individual states. In other words, the 'margin of appreciation' increases if the consensus decreases or is not argued for.[24] The rationale is clear: the harmonising function of the Court's jurisprudence is gradually creating a common framework of reference in the application of individual human rights protection within State jurisdictions, ensuring equal protection regardless of their place of residence and without any discrimination.

However, in this case, it appears that even if such a consensus exists, such consensus does not affect the broad margin of appreciation of the State, because in the Court's opinion the fact that the applicant has the right 'to lawfully travel abroad for an abortion with access to appropriate information and medical care' is enough to justify and consider the Irish prohibition of abortion for health and well-being reasons fair and lawful, under Art. 8 of the European Convention on Human Rights, 'based as it is on the profound moral views of the Irish people as to the nature of life'.[25]

In other words, even if few countries have an abortion regime as strict as the one in the Irish legal system, and even if the consensus of the majority of the contracting States is oriented in order to broaden women's rights to abortion and the scope of the 'health and well-being reason', the Court did not recognise a breach of article 8, because, according to its decision and to the Irish defensive arguments presented to the Court, the national provisions could be considered to mirror the Irish people's moral views on the nature of life.[26] Placed in the balance,

---

23   See paragraph 235 of the decision under consideration. For the comparative analysis and method of the ECHR, reference can be made to C.L. Rozakis, 'The European judge as comparatist' (2005) 80 1 *Tulane Law Review* 272.

24   The concept will be clearer after reading the subsequent analysis on the other decisions mentioned below.

25   See paragraph 241 of the decision.

26   Actually, it has to be underlined that abortion is a controversial issue in Irish politics and five national referendums have been held on the topic in the last 30 years. In 2013, Ireland passed a new law allowing abortion under certain circumstances. On 30 July 2013, President Michael D. Higgins signed off on the *Protection of Life During Pregnancy Act 2013* without referring it to the Supreme Court after meeting his advisors, the Council of State. The new law provides for a woman's right to an abortion if her life is at risk, including from suicide. See <http://www.irishexaminer.com/breakingnews/ireland/abortion-bill-signed-into-irish-law-by-president-higgins-602117.html> accessed 15 June 2014, and 'World abortion policies 2013', United Nations 2013, accessed 3 March 2014.

here the margin of appreciation had a greater weight than the general consensus of States on a certain model or juridical solution.

This approach shifts the attention from the balance between the foetus and/ or the mother's right to life and health, to the balance between the 'State margin of appreciation' and the common consensus of contracting States, giving a ruling which is really far from harmonising legal rules and operational rules among those States.

According to my personal reconstruction of the scheme of arguments used by the Court, it is important to stress two points:

a. Irish law allows abortion for those who can travel abroad and it suffices to protect their private life under Art. 8;[27] and
b. the thesis that Irish people have profound moral views on life, birth and foetus protection above others rights affects the European consensus and overrides it, allowing a wider 'margin of appreciation' to the State in such specific case and on this particular subject matter.

Under a), the argument emphasised by the applicants was that they could not have an abortion in their country of residence, and also that having to travel abroad to have an abortion was financially expensive and raised many practical and logistic difficulties concerning, for example, insurance systems, public or private medical assistance regimes, hospital services to foreigners in the State of destination and so on. On this point the Court does not really address the issue of unjustified interference in the applicants' private life as a result of the Irish prohibition.[28] Regarding b), it can be said that as a result of this decision the Court has diminished the relevance of the European consensus through the argument of 'profound moral views', reasoning that a specific moral conception can override the European consensus.[29]

For scholarly writings see J. Herring, *Medical Law and Ethics* (4th edn, Oxford University Press, 2012) 308; K.A. Conrad, *Locked in the Family Cell: Gender, Sexuality, and Political Agency in Irish National Discourse* (University of Wisconsin Press, 2004) 79; for public opinion debate see *BBC News*, 'Woman dies after abortion request "refused" at Galway hospital' (14 November 2012); *Irish Examiner*, 'Gynaecology expert to head Savita investigation team' (17 November 2012) accessed 18 November 2012; D. Dalby, 'Religious remark confirmed in Irish abortion case', *The New York Times* (11 April 2013); J. O'Leary 'Abortion in Ireland permitted when mother's life at risk', *BBC* (18 December 2012).

27   For a broad view on Ireland's statute law and Court's case law, see J. MacLeod, 'Abortion and Ireland's Supreme Court' (14 November 2008), available at <http://www.jasonmacleod.com/?page_id=60> accessed 20 May 2013.

28   Moreover we cannot under estimate the difficulties arising from this solution in terms of parental–children relationship, having regard to the public and private interests involved. For a critique of oversimplification see R.F. Storrow, 'The pluralism problem in cross-border reproductive care' (2010) 25 (12) *Human Reproduction* 29–39.

29   For a totally different point of view, see the general rules asserted in the following official document: *The Role of Consensus in the System of the European Convention*

The decision in this case was to preserve the strict abortion regime in force at the time in Ireland, so it is characterised by the prevailing of the margin of appreciation argument. In my opinion the Court here has adopted a conservative policy, preserving a model (the Irish one), which was, according to the analysis of the Court itself and to scholarly opinions and research studies commissioned by the Council of Europe (cited by the Court in the opinion), far from the one shared among the majority of the contracting States.

Here the Court admitted that the Irish 'profound moral views' (on the foetus's right to life) – despite evidence that this is not so profound and monolithic in the Irish public debate,[30] can override the European consensus (on therapeutic abortion).

S.H. and others v Austria

First Decision of the Chamber, 1 April 2010[31]

The Chamber held that Austrian legislation, prohibiting *in vitro* fertilisation with ovum donation, violated Articles 8–14 of the Convention. In particular, the Court found that the right of a couple to conceive a child and to make use of medically assisted procreation for that end came within the ambit of Art. 8, as such a choice was clearly an expression of private and family life.

As regards Art. 14, the Chamber observed that in view of the lack of a uniform approach to this question by the Contracting States and the nature of the sensitive moral and ethical issues involved, the States enjoyed a 'wide margin of appreciation' in this field.[32] This 'wide margin of appreciation' in principle extended to both

---

on *Human Rights, Dialogue between Judges*, European Court of Human Rights, Council of Europe, 2008, available at <http//echr.coe.int/Documents/Dialogue_2008_ENG.pdf> accessed 15 October 2013.

30 See n25.

31 For a comment in Italian to this first decision, see F. Cerri, 'Corte Europea e fecondazione eterologa: mater semper certa est?' (2010) 4 *Europa e diritto private* 1219–30. In English, see E. Vayena et al. (eds), *Current Practices and Controversies in Assisted Reproduction* (World Health Organization, 2002) and in particular, M. Fathalla, '*Current Challenges in Assisted Reproduction*', 20.

32 Article 14 of the Convention states that 'the enjoyment of the rights and freedoms set forth in this Convention shall be secured without discrimination on any ground such as sex, race, colour, language, religion, political or other opinion, national or social origin, association with a national minority, property, birth or other status'. So, Article 14 must be pleaded in relation to some other substantive right in the Convention. It is not necessary to establish an actual violation of another Article; if the claim comes within the ambit of another protected right then it is possible for the applicant to succeed on discrimination alone, even if the primary violation has not been established, or the Member State's action has been found to come within one of the permissible exceptions to that right. For example,

its decision to intervene in the area and, once having intervened, to the detailed rules it laid down in order to achieve a balance between the competing public and private interests. The Chamber examined separately the different situations of: the first and second applicants;[33] and the third and fourth applicants.[34]

Starting from the latter, the third and fourth applicants needed ovum donation in order to fulfil their wish for a child. The Chamber found that concerns based on moral considerations or on social acceptability were not in themselves sufficient reasons for a complete ban on a specific form of artificial procreation in general and that only in exceptional circumstances would such a complete ban be a proportionate measure. The Chamber found that in respect of the risks of ovum donation invoked by the government, such as the risk of women being exploited – particularly those coming from economically disadvantaged backgrounds – or of a 'selection' of children, the Austrian *Artificial Procreation Act* already contained sufficient safeguards.[35] In particular, under section 4 of the Act, the use of artificial procreation techniques is reserved to specialised medical doctors who have particular knowledge and experience in this field and are themselves bound by the ethical rules of their profession. The Act also statutorily prohibited the remuneration of ovum and sperm donation. These measures are intended to

---

in the leading case *MarckX v Belgium* App no 6833/74 (ECHR, 13 June 1979), the Court concluded that the unfavourable treatment of illegitimate children under Belgian inheritance laws violated their right to a family life under Article 8, and breached the requirement under Article 14 that Convention rights should be secured without discrimination.

33   The case of the first and second applicants was a sperm donation one while the third and the fourth one was an ovum donation case. 'The first applicant suffered from fallopian-tube-related infertility and the second applicant, her husband, was infertile. It is not in dispute that, owing to their medical conditions, only in vitro fertilization with the use of sperm from a donor would allow them to fulfil their wish for a child of which at least one of the applicants is the genetic parent. However, the prohibition of heterologous artificial procreation techniques for in vitro fertilization laid down by section 3(1) of the Artificial Procreation Act, which, in the circumstances [...] rules out sperm donation excludes this possibility. At the same time section 3(2) of that Act allows sperm donation for in vivo fertilization'. *S.H. and others v Austria* App no 57813/00 (ECHR, 3 November 2011) para. 108–109.

34   In particular, 'the third applicant (woman) is completely infertile, while her husband, the fourth applicant, produces sperm fit for procreation. It is not in dispute that, owing to their medical condition, only in vitro fertilization with ova from a donor would allow them to fulfill their wish for a child of which at list one of them is the genetic parent. But the prohibition of heterologous artificial procreation techniques for in vitro fertilization laid down in section 3(1) of the Artificial Procreation Act, which does not permit ovum donation, rules out this possibility. There is no exception to this rule'. See *S.H. and others v Austria* App no 57813/00 (ECHR, 3 November 2011), para. 98.

35   See *Fortpflanzungsmedizingesetz* n275/1992, Federal Law Gazette 275/1992, modified in 2001 (*BGB*l. I n98/2001), available at <https://www.ris.bka.gv.at/Geltende Fassung.wxe?Abfrage=Bundesnormen&Gesetzesnummer=10003046&ShowPrintPreview =True> accessed 16 June 2014.

prevent potential risks of eugenic selection and their abuse and to prevent the risk of exploitation of women in vulnerable situations as ovum donors.

Having regard to the risk referred to by the government of creating relationships in which the social circumstances deviated from the biological ones, the Court observed that unusual family bonds in a broad sense, which do not follow the typical parent–child relationship based on a direct biological link, are not unknown in the legal systems of the Contracting States.

In fact, the *Artificial Procreation Act* under scrutiny had tried to find a solution by balancing the conflicting interests of human dignity, the right to procreation and the well-being of children, by providing that only homologous methods – such as using ova and sperm from the spouses or from the cohabiting couple themselves – and methods which did not involve a particularly sophisticated technique would be allowed, because they were not too far removed from natural means of conception. The aim was to avoid the forming of unusual personal relations – such as a child having more than one biological mother (a genetic mother and one carrying the child), and to avoid the risk of the exploitation of women.

All the arguments raised by the government were against artificial procreation in general and were therefore not persuasive when it came to allowing some procreation techniques while rejecting others. The risk of exploitation of female donors, to which the government referred, was not relevant in circumstances such as those in the case concerned. To combat any potential abuse in the Austrian situation, it would be sufficient to forbid remunerated ovum or sperm donation; such a prohibition already existed in Austria. Also, the argument that ovum donation led to unusual family relationships in which motherhood of a child conceived through artificial procreation was split between the genetic mother and the mother who gave birth to the child and led to emotional stress for the child was not persuasive, as today many children grew up in family situations in which they were genetically related to only one of the parents.

In respect of the latter specific concern, such as the creation of unusual relationships by splitting motherhood between a genetic mother and a biological mother, according to the Court opinion, these problems could be overcome by enacting appropriate legislation. The Chamber therefore concluded that there had been a violation of Art. 8 and Art. 14, because the limitations under the Austrian *Artificial Procreation Act* violated the right to a family life under Article 8, and breached the requirement under Article 14 that Convention rights should be secured without discrimination. In other words, in none of the above-mentioned arguments, was there space for the 'state margin of appreciation', even if the matters involved concerned moral, ethical and religious conceptions.

With regard to the situation of the first and second applicants, who needed sperm donation for *in vitro* insemination in order to fulfil their wish for a child, the Chamber observed first that this artificial procreation technique combined two techniques which, taken singly, were allowed under the *Artificial Procreation Act* (namely, *in vitro* insemination with ova and sperm of the couple on the one hand and sperm donation for *in vivo* conception on the other hand). A prohibition of the combination of these lawful techniques thus required particularly persuasive arguments.[36] Most of the arguments put forward by the government were, however, not specific to sperm donation for *in vitro* fertilisation. As regards the government's argument that non-*in vitro* artificial insemination had been in use for some time, that it was easy to handle and its prohibition would therefore have been hard to monitor, the Chamber found that a question of mere efficiency carried less weight than the particularly important interests of the private individuals involved and concluded that the difference in treatment at issue was not justified, again denying the Austrian 'margin of appreciation' and concluding that there had been a violation of Art. 8 in conjunction with Art. 14 in that respect as well.

According to my personal opinion and reconstruction of the ECHR legal reasoning, in this first decision of the case, the Court, more than in other cases, has had a political and cultural pilot role in promoting the diffusion of a model, which is circulating among many contracting States, even if not in the majority of them. Here the margin of appreciation, and with it the cultural and ethical heritage of the Austrian legal system, has been set aside in favour of the interests of private individuals to family life, to private autonomy and to be treated without any discrimination caused by their infertility or impossibility to procreate naturally. Despite this, it should be noted that this policy oriented decision to enlarge the area of the fertilisation techniques in order to preserve and guarantee the right to family life and personal autonomy in the Austrian legal system was short-lived as the Grand Chamber of the Court, after one year after the decision under consideration, reversed this first judgement.

Final Decision of the Grand Chamber, 3 November 2011[37]

In the same case, on appeal, the Grand Chamber came to a completely different conclusion, holding by 13 votes to four, that there had been no violation of Art. 8 or Art. 14 of the Convention.

---

36   The Austrian legislature, on the one hand, decided to prohibit the donation of sperm or ova for *in vitro* fertilisation, but on the other hand, to allow sperm donation for *in vivo* fertilisation, as a technique which had been tolerated for a considerable period beforehand and had become accepted by society. This choice has significance in the balancing of the respective interests and cannot be considered solely in the context of the efficient policing of the prohibitions. It shows the approach adopted by the Austrian legislature in seeking to reconcile social realities with its approach of principle in this field. In this connection the Court also observes that there is no prohibition under Austrian law on going abroad to seek treatment of infertility that uses artificial procreation techniques not allowed in Austria and that in the event of a successful treatment the Civil Code contains clear rules on paternity and maternity that respect the wishes of the parents. On these points see the joint dissenting opinion of judges Tulkens, Hirvela, Lazarova Trajkovska and Tsotsoria in *S.H. and others v Austria* App no 57813/00 (ECHR, 3 November 2011) paras 11–13.

37   In Italy, the decision has been analysed by E. Nicosia (2012) 5 *Foro It* 209–22.

The Grand Chamber underlined that some of the government arguments in defence of the prohibition of gamete donation for *in vitro* insemination could refer only to the prohibition of ovum donation, in order to prevent the exploitation of women in vulnerable situations or where there were potential health risks for ovum donors and to prevent the creation of atypical family relations because of split motherhood. It acknowledged that the prohibition of gamete donation of third persons was a controversial issue in Austrian society, raising complex questions of a social and ethical nature on which there was not yet a consensus and which had to take into account human dignity, the health of children conceived in this way and the prevention of negative repercussions or potential misuse. In addition, the Grand Chamber found that the prohibition of ovum donation for *in vitro* insemination, which relied on these grounds, was compatible with Art. 8 of the Convention taking into account as relevant the general framework against which the prohibition at issue had to be viewed.

The fact that the Austrian Legislature decided to forbid the donation of sperm or ova for *in vitro* insemination when enacting the law on artificial procreation, but at the same time to allow sperm donation for *in vivo* insemination – a technique which had been tolerated for a considerable period beforehand and had become accepted by society – was relevant in balancing the respective interests and could not be considered solely in the context of the efficient policing of the prohibitions. Rather this demonstrated the careful and cautious approach adopted by the Austrian Legislature in its attempt to reconcile social realities with its approach of principle in this field. The Grand Chamber also observed that there is no prohibition under Austrian law on going abroad to seek treatment for infertility that uses artificial procreation techniques which are not allowed in Austria and that, in the event of a successful treatment, the Civil Code contains clear rules on paternity and maternity which respect the wishes of the parents.[38]

Having regard to the above arguments, the Grand Chamber therefore concluded that, neither in respect of the prohibition of ovum donation for the purposes of artificial procreation nor in respect of the prohibition of sperm donation for *in vitro* insemination, did the Austrian Legislature exceed the margin of appreciation afforded to it. In other words, there had been no breach of Article 8 of the Convention as regards to all of the applicants.

Nevertheless the Grand Chamber observed that the Austrian Parliament had not, until that point, undertaken a thorough assessment of the rules governing artificial procreation, taking into account the dynamic developments in science and society noted above. The Chamber also pointed out that the Austrian Constitutional Court, when finding that the statute law had complied with the principle of proportionality under Art. 8 § 2 of the Convention, had added that the principle adopted by the statute law to permit homologous methods of artificial procreation as a general rule, and insemination using donor sperm as an exception, reflected the current

---

38 See, *mutatis mutandis, A, B and C v Ireland* App no 25579/05 (ECHR, 16 December 2010), para. 239.

state of medical science and the consensus in society. This, however, did not mean that these criteria would not be subject to developments, which the legislature would have to take into account in the future (as had indeed happened in Austria and Italy subsequently to these decisions).

The Grand Chamber reiterated that the Convention has always been interpreted and applied in the light of current circumstances.[39] Even if it had not found any breach of Art. 8 in this case, the Chamber expressed the view that this area, which is subject to particularly dynamic developments in science and law, should be kept under review by the Contracting States.[40] This second decision is a total reversal of the previous decision in respect of the same case and on the same facts.

In this second decision other values have prevailed on individual rights to family life, having regard to artificial, medically assisted fertilisation with gamete donation and the development of these techniques, as the Grand Chamber considered that the 'State margin of appreciation' could not be narrowed in a consistent way, because *in vitro* fertilisation directly affects human life and the foundation of society, and involves highly sensitive matter on which no European consensus had been reached.

It seems that, according to the Grand Chamber, there is no positive obligation for Contracting States under Article 8 to provide all the existing medical techniques of procreation for infertile couples and that the lack of a European consensus on the subject matter confers a wide margin of appreciation on States, allowing them to make their own policy decisions in a complex field that has far-reaching scientific, ethical and social implications.

The context in which this second decision comes out is the same as that in 2010, but the ethical and cultural background seems to be changed in comparison with the first decision. Probably, after the reactions to the first judgement by the contracting States and in the light of public opinion, the ECHR felt the need to revise the decision that was not welcome by everyone.

My personal opinion is that the Court has measured the reaction to the first decision and realised that there was not widespread consensus among the contracting States, so it reversed the outcome, thereby abandoning the above mentioned pilot role and adopting a more conservative solution, using the margin of appreciation argument.

Costa e Pavan v Italy, 28 August 2012

This case involved a couple, who were passive carriers of cystic fibrosis, complaining that the Italian prohibition of genetic exam on *in vitro* formed embryos

---

39   See *Rees v the United Kingdom* App no 9532/81 (ECHR, 17 October 1986), para. 47.

40   See *Christine Goodwin v the United Kingdom* App no 28957/95 (ECHR, 11 July 2002), para. 74, and *Stafford v the United Kingdom* App no 46296/99 (ECHR, 28 May 2002), para. 68.

violated their right to private and family life under Art. 8 ECHR. In particular, the principal applicants emphasised that, according to Italian legislation, if they want to procreate a child not affected by cystic fibrosis they could only start with a natural pregnancy and, then, subsequently, decide to have an abortion if the *in vivo* pre-birth diagnosis of the foetus showed a genetic disease.

The Court ascertained that Italian legislation recognises the right to use techniques of medical assisted insemination only in the case of sterile and barren couples, or in cases where the man is affected by a viral disease (HIV, hepatitis B or C).[41]

It was undisputed that the applicants were not in any of these circumstances, so they did not have access to a medical assisted insemination procedure under Italian law. They argued however, that those provisions were discriminatory in their situation and violated their right without any lawful reason – for example, the protection of health or public order. As far as the embryo pre-implant diagnosis was concerned, the Italian government admitted that this was absolutely prohibited in all cases and for any person. This, in the Court's opinion, had a bearing on the applicants' right to private and family life. The point that needed to be clarified was whether this interference, stated by the law, could be justified by a superior interest such as health, moral values, or other rights involved.

First of all, the Court highlighted that the applicants' complaint was not solely confined to the issue of whether the prohibition of pre-implant embryo diagnosis violated their rights under Art. 8, but also, and more importantly, extended to the issue of whether the prohibition itself was proportionate in comparison to the abortion regime. In other words, the couple was asking if it was not inconsistent to forbid a pre-implant analysis and the subsequent destruction of the embryo (if affected by cystic fibrosis), but to admit a therapeutic abortion of the foetus affected by the same disease, as the parents are both passive carriers.

To justify the public interference, the Italian government used arguments based on the protection of the health of the mother and foetus, and on the doctor's medical freedom of conscience and the risk of eugenic modifications. None of these arguments were enough for the Court to find that the interference of private and family life in the case was justified, holding that the protection of those interests was better ensured by a model – such as the Italian one – which allowed the applicants to choose therapeutic abortion if the foetus is affected by the disease, instead of a pre-embryo diagnosis (and a subsequent destruction of the affected-embryo). In fact, abortion implies more traumatic and severe consequences for the foetus and the parents (mainly the mother) than the earlier destruction of the embryo, as the latter is not implanted whereas the foetus is a more developed entity or centre of interests and rights.[42]

---

41   See Art. 4, para. 1, L n 40/2004 and the Decree of the Health Ministry, n31639, 11 April 2008.

42   See 'Preimplantation Genetic Diagnosis in Europe' edited by the Joint Research Centre of the European Commission, December 2007, EUR 22764 EN and the data coming

So, according to the Court, the Italian system on this issue is inconsistent. On the one hand, it forbids the implant of pre-selected embryos, which are not affected by the parents' disease; on the other hand, it allows the abortion of the foetus affected by the same disease, or rather the abortion of the foetus that 'yesterday' was the above-mentioned embryo, but created by *in vivo* and natural conception.[43] The Court went on to draw attention to the fact that in *S.H. and others v Austria*,[44] the Grand Chamber had stated that, having regard to artificial, medically assisted fertilisation with gamete donation and the development of these techniques, the 'State margin of appreciation' could not be narrowed in a consistent way.

It seems that, according to the Court, there is no positive obligation for Contracting States under Article 8 to provide for infertile couples all the existing medical techniques of procreation and that the lack of a European consensus on the subject matter confers a wide margin of appreciation on States, allowing them to make their own policy decisions in a complex field where there are far-reaching scientific, ethical and social implications. *In vitro* fertilisation directly affects human life and the foundation of society, and involves highly sensitive matter on which no European consensus has been reached, so there is considerable space for the exercise of a State's margin of appreciation.

In contrast, in the Italian case, considering that the question of pre-implant diagnosis which raised important moral and ethical questions, the court held that it is not enough to allow a wide 'margin of appreciation to the State'. In this way, the matter involved can be subject to the control of the ECHR,[45] and the pre-implant embryo genetic analyses can have a wider diffusion amongst the contracting States. This represents a step at a supranational level that provides scope for the use of pre-implant embryo analysis among States, with obvious consequences in terms of policies, research and economics. This would also imply the need for regulating – by law – the regime of pre-implant analysis, especially in those legal systems that have no rules at all in such matters. It is hard to predict which States are going to legislate in the next few years, but probably those who do so will take in consideration the indication of the ECHR and will imitate a pre-existing model.

As a consequence, the decision in *Costa and Pavan* required the Italian legislative to rethink the enacted model taking into account the principles affirmed by the Court, so that the new model that is eventually imported, rather than filling a vacuum, should replace a prior local law which is incompatible with the Convention.[46]

---

out from the Belgian draft, paras 25 and 34, available at <http://ec.europa.eu/dgs/jrc/index.cfm?id=5290> accessed 15 October 2013.

43   See ibid.

44   *S.H. and others v Austria* App no 57813/00 (ECHR, 31 November 2011).

45   See, *mutatis mutandis*, *S.H. and others v Austria* App no 57813/00 (ECHR, 3 November 2011), para. 97.

46   Twining (2004) (n1) 35 and Twining (2009) (n1).

Conclusion

In the Irish case *A. and others v Ireland* the Court ruling demonstrates how a broad approach to the 'margin of appreciation theory' and a related remarkable self-restraint in evaluating which national provisions violate Article 8, had consequences for the persistence of juridical solutions and models adopted by a State, which were very different from the traditions of other European countries. In this case the Court abandoned its role and function of diffusing solutions, which are the common heritage among the Convention's States.

In *S.H. and others v Austria*, the decision on appeal was a reversal of the previous one in the same case and on the same facts. There is a totally different reasoning on the 'consensus relevance' – or rather irrelevance – and, as a result, an enhanced role for the 'State margin of appreciation'.

In other words, according to the first decision the Austrian model was in breach of the ECHR. By contrast, in the final decision on appeal, the Grand Chamber adopted a wider approach to the 'margin of appreciation theory' and did not attribute any relevance to the common consensus of the signatory States, thereby refuting arguments of insemination and dissemination of juridical solutions and models through the jurisprudence of the court. In fact, in the latter ruling there is only a faint and weak indication, something like a vague aspiration, favouring the pervasiveness of the models and solutions of the other European countries, which would take into consideration the advancement of science in fertilisation techniques. So, on the one hand, the Court itself uses the 'margin of appreciation' to protect a 'non-common model' (the prohibition of *in vitro* insemination with gametes from a third person), and on the other hand, it wants the more common model (*in vivo* and *in vitro* insemination with the gametes of a third person), which is the heritage of many legal traditions, to spread through legislation rather than through its case law. It is hard to understand how it is possible for the Court to consider that the national statute law rules are consistent with the Convention, yet at the same time express a wish for the reform of such legal rules.

With *Costa and Pavan v Italy*, the Court demonstrated the need to clarify the differences between the case being considered and *S.H. and others v Austria*. In the latter, the decision concerned the compatibility of the Austrian prohibition on third party gamete donation in assisted insemination with Art. 8. In the Italian case, the Court had to verify the proportionality of the prohibition on pre-implant diagnosis – and the consequent destruction of the embryo affected by a genetic disease – with the provision that allows therapeutic abortion. According to the Court, in *Costa and Pavan v Italy*, the violation of Art. 8 arose from the disproportion of measures, which amounted to an undue interference in the couple's private and family life.

The question in *Costa* is very specific and, according to the comparative analysis carried out by the Court through the Commission documents,[47] only arose in the case of Italy and two other States of the 32 examined: Austria and Switzerland. So,

---

47   See E. Nicosia '*A.B. e C. c. Irlanda*' (2011) IV *Foro It* 184.

apart from in Austria and Italy, there is a common, even if not universal, consensus among the Contracting States on the admissibility of pre-implant genetic embryo analysis. Indeed it could be argued that considering the disproportion between the two different regimes (pre-implant diagnosis *in vitro* and abortion) and the general consensus of Contracting States on pre-implant diagnosis, there is no place for a State to claim a 'margin of appreciation'.

Legal rules and concepts are, of course, not the only or even the main objects of diffusion, as legal reasoning has a crucial role in determining or limiting and avoiding insemination and dissemination of legal models and rules. Diffusion may take place through informal interaction without involving formal adoption or enactment, because of the presence of a certain individual, who, as a judge, as a lawyer, or as a member of a consultative body, is involved in the process of law and decision making, especially at a national and transnational level. This individual has his/her nationality, education, social and cultural background and his/her 'value luggage' that can affect the outcome of the process in which she/he is involved. Looked at from this perspective, the words of a judge can help to better understand the influence of such hidden formants in the structure of legal systems:

> I am a judge. [...] My guess is that it depends to a large extent what you yourself are accustomed to. If you are a jurist educated in the Anglo-American common law tradition your first impression will be different from that of, say, a French, a Dutch or a German jurist. Perhaps you immediately think in terms of constitutional interpretation and the issues involved in judicial interpretative methodologies (or strategies, depending on your perception of the problems of interpretation).[48]

The reconstructive analysis of the four cases considered here shows the initial hypothesis: the policy oriented role of the ECHR, which uses in a broadening way or in a restrictive direction the margin of appreciation argument, depending on the political and ethical decisions, that are hidden behind the judgement. In other words the Court decides according to the political and ethical values that it feels are prevalent and predominant and that it wants to promote and diffuse.

This is more evident in the case law of the Court in recent years and in areas of law where scientific and technological progress is moving in directions that were inconceivable many years ago, because in such subject matters, ethical and political implications are of great impact.

In such areas the cultural and political pilot role of the Court, even if conditioned and limited by the case by case approach and by the context in which the decision

---

48   J. Gaakeer, 'Iudex translator: The reign of finitude' in Monateri (n10) 252. The author emphasises that 'a continental European jurist whose mental frame includes an appointed rather than an elected judiciary, and whose legal toolkit is mainly filled with codified law, may think in terms of an independent decision maker who is a bulwark against too much government interference in citizens' private lives'.

emerges, is crucial in order to diffuse or limit the circulation and imitation of common and shared abortion regimes (the Irish case), or in order to promote the use of a certain pre-implant analysis diagnosis technique (the Italian case) and the necessary functional law rules, or in order to broaden or limit in vitro fertilisation techniques (respectively, with the first and the second decision on Austria's law) promoting or discouraging the circulation of a certain model.

My personal opinion is that the Court uses the margin of appreciation argument, not only or mainly to protect and recognise the national sovereignty or a profound tradition and moral view of certain people and societies, but as an hermeneutic support to decisions taken at a political level, according to an anti-formalistic approach to interpretation and legal reasoning.

Chapter 10

The Feature of *Droit Commun* in the *Disposition Preliminaire* of the Civil Code of Quebec: A Clue to the Bijurality of the Legal System?

Biagio Andò

Introduction

Comparative legal studies have developed numerous theories – and correlatively a quite extensive vocabulary – in order to delve into the fundamental issue of the diffusion of law. Words such as 'transplantation', 'reception' and/or 'transposition' have become widespread terms in the scholarly debate, each underlying a different point of view on how the circulation of law may occur and has occurred throughout history.

Rather than proposing a new general theoretical approach to this phenomenon, this chapter discusses a specific case of diffusion, in which civil and common law traditions lie at the roots of the system – Quebec. Its bijural[1] foundations will be investigated through the concept of *droit commun*, acknowledged from the *Disposition Préliminaire*[2] of the Civil Code of Quebec (from now onwards

---

1   This writer prefers the expression 'bijurality', 'bijural systems' to that, much more frequently used, of 'mixed systems'. Among the scholars using this latter terminology, the approach followed by V.V. Palmer, *Mixed Jurisdictions Worldwide* (2nd edn, Cambridge University Press, 2012) has to be remembered. Palmer claims that some jurisdictions could be grouped in a legal family as they share basic features, such as the 'specificity of mixture' – that is, their being built upon dual foundations of common law and civil law material, and the 'structural allocation of content', being the field of private law predominantly moulded by civil law, and public law by Anglo-American law.

The underlying aim of this chapter is not that of finding convergences between Quebec and other systems sharing specific features, but the opposite one, viz. that of unearthing some of its original traits strictly related to its legal identity.

2   For the sake of simplicity, in the following pages reference will be made to the French version of the legal text and the expressions herein used, such as *Disposition Préliminaire* and *droit commun*. The English version of the *Disposition Préliminaire* reads that 'the Civil Code of Québec, in harmony with the Charter of Human Rights and Freedoms

CCQ). In particular, this concept will be explored through the perceptions and conceptualisations of Quebec legal scholars.

That a comparative law survey of a legal system cannot be reduced to its legal formant has become a common place. A fortiori this seems to be true for bijural systems, whose highly complex foundations require an in-depth examination of the crucial interactions among the socio-cultural and legal layers.

The scrutiny of *droit commun* seems to be particularly suited to that aim, due to the fact that the set of meanings framed by scholars can be thoroughly assessed only by having regard to the interplay between the socio-cultural layer of the system and the legal one. It also makes it possible to inspect the issue – deemed by this writer to be pivotal in legal studies on bijural systems – of the paths followed by the latter to drive legal change. A key role for their understanding is played by the weight of past law on the present appearance of the system, either affecting the interpretation of legal rules in force or filling the interstices of the system in cases when a rule is not expressly provided.

The widely agreed statement – even in the field of legal studies – that the present has to be understood by looking at the past is particularly meaningful for Quebec, since some attitudes developed from the legal community and dating back to the time when the legal system's foundations were laid are still at work, showing therefore a high degree of endurance. Far from just displaying a significant role on a historical footing, they often constitute a set of underlying (not always overt) assumptions on which the legal system is grounded at present. In Quebec, the process of the codification of private law – which led to the enactment of two Civil Codes in 1866 (the Lower Canada Civil Code) and in 1994 (the CCQ) – is an interesting outpost from which to assess the dialectic relationship between past and present (law). The nineteenth century European version of the concept of codification of law, grounded on the idea of a complete recasting of law, does not seem to have been engrafted in the Quebec soil.

Finally, this survey reveals as useful two general issues relevant at the level of comparative law methodology which, adapted to this case study, can be cast in these terms: is the terminology currently used in the 'diffusion of law' debate able to shed light on the ways in which common and civil law traditions have interacted, moulding the Quebec legal system? Which directions can be drawn from the Quebec case study at the more general level of the phenomenon of circulation of law?

---

and the general principles of law, governs persons, relations between persons and property. The Civil Code comprises a body of rules, which, in all matters within the letter, spirit or object of its provisions lays down the *droit commun*, expressly or by implication. In these matters, the code is the foundation of all other laws, although other laws may complement the code or make exceptions to it'.

Droit Commun in the *Disposition Préliminaire*

The introduction of *droit commun* as a main and general[3] feature in the *Disposition Préliminaire* is the result of a long process, started in 1982 with the *Projet de loi* 106, providing for the insertion of a *Disposition Préliminaire* into the Civil Code. It is expressly provided that this latter: *'régit, sauf les dispositions particulières de la loi, les personnes qui se trouvent au Québec, l'exercice de leurs droits, leurs rapports entre elles ainsi que leurs biens'*,[4] and *'est constitué d'un ensemble de règles qui, en toutes matières auxquelles se rapportent l'esprit, la lettre ou l'objet de ses dispositions, établit le droit et constitue le fondement des autre lois'*.[5] Furthermore, this provision stated that, *'en cas de silence ou d'insuffisance'* [in case of silence or deficiency] of the codal provisions, regard must be had to the *'jurisprudence constante'* [constant judge-made law], to *'doctrine reçue'* [received doctrine], to *'principes généraux du droit ainsi que parfois de la coutume et des usages'*.[6]

In 1984 some amendments were introduced to the 1982 draft version explicitly concerning private law, in which the Civil Code displays this 'foundational' role, and qualifying in a more accurate way the relation between the Civil Code and the other statutes dealing with private law matters:

> *Le code civil du Québec régit, en harmonie avec la Charte des droits et libertés de la personne, les principes généraux du droit et le droit international privé, les personnes, l'exercice des droits civiles, les rapports entre les personnes ainsi que les biens. Le code est constitué d'un ensemble de règles qui, en toutes matières auxquelles se rapportent la lettre, l'esprit ou l'objet de ses dispositions, établit, en termes exprès ou par implication, le droit privé. En ces matières, il fonde les autre lois qui peuvent elles-mêmes ajouter au code ou y déroger.*[7]

In 1986, the reference to private law was replaced eventually from *droit commun*.[8]

---

3   *Droit commun* was in fact specifically acknowledged in specific provisions under the 1866 Civil Code, such as art. 366.

4   [Governs, unless otherwise provided, persons living in Quebec, the enforcement of their rights, their relationship as well as their property].

5   [Comprises a body of rules, which in all matters within the letter, spirit or object of its provisions, lays down the law and is the foundation of all other laws].

6   [General principles of law and sometimes custom and usages].

7   [The Civil Code of Québec, in harmony with the Charter of Human Rights and Freedoms, the general principles of law and international private law, governs persons, the enforcement of civil rights, relations between persons and property. The Civil Code comprises a body of rules, which, in all matters within the letter, spirit or object of its provisions, lays down, expressly or by implication, private law. In these matters, the Civil Code is the foundation of all other laws which may complement the Code or make exceptions to it].

8   On the several draft versions of the *Disposition Préliminaire*, see A.F. Bisson, 'La Disposition Préliminaire du Code civil du Québec' (1999) 44 *McGill Law Journal* 539.

Scholars welcomed the introduction of a *Disposition Préliminaire* for its '*effet de codification*' [effect of codification of law], that is, for its being a '*disposition d'orientation du système juridique, plutôt qu'immédiatement normative*'.[9]

In the draft version of 1986, *droit commun* was defined as '*l'ensemble des principes et des règles qui s'appliquent à tous les sujets de droit à moins qu'il n'y ait des règles exorbitantes de ce droit commun prévues dans les lois ou dans les règles de common law exclusivement applicable à la couronne ou aux corporations publiques*'.[10]

The *Disposition Préliminaire* now in force reads:

> *Le code civil du Québec régit, en harmonie avec la Charte des droits et libertés de la personne et les principes généraux du droit, les personnes, les rapports entre les personnes, ainsi que les biens. Le code est constitué d'un ensemble de règles qui, en toutes matières auxquelles se rapportent la lettre, l'esprit ou l'objet de ses dispositions, établit, en termes exprès ou de façon implicite, le droit commun. En ces matières, il constitue le fondement des autres lois qui peuvent elles-mêmes ajouter au code ou y déroger.*[11]

However, no definition of *droit commun* is provided in the final version of the Civil Code currently in force.

What one may infer from a first glance at the text of the *Disposition* is that courts have the power broadly to interpret and apply the codal provisions, not being restricted to the literal approach as the only interpretative technique available in the construction of those rules.[12] It would be inconsistent with the express acknowledgement of the Civil Code as a body of law comprising '*règles qui, en toutes matières auxquelles se rapportent la lettre, l'esprit ou l'objet de*

---

9   [A provision giving guidelines, rather than one which lays down binding rules]. A. F. Bisson, 'Effet de codification et interprétation' (1986) 17 *Revue Générale de Droit* 359, 366.

10   [The set of principles and rules with a general effect not including the common law ones applying only to the Crown or to public corporation].

11   [The Civil Code of Québec, in harmony with the Charter of Human Rights and Freedoms and the general principles of law, governs persons, relations between persons, and property. The Civil Code comprises a body of rules, which, in all matters within the letter, spirit, or object of its provisions, lays down the *jus commune*, expressly or by implication. In these matters, the Civil Code is the foundation of all other laws, although other laws may complement the Code or make exceptions to it].

12   Among others see: J.L. Bergel, 'Spécificité des codes et autonomie de leur interprétation' in *Le nouveau code civil: interprétation et application. Les journées Maximilien Caron 1992* (Thémis, 1993) 3; C. Masse, 'Le recours aux travaux préparatoires dans l'interprétation du nouveau Code civil du Québec' in *Le nouveau code civil: interprétation et application, Journées Macxilien Caron* (Thémis, 1992) 149; C. Lemieux, 'Eléments d'interprétation en droit civil' (1994) 24 *Revue de droit, Université de Sherbrooke* 221.

ses dispositions, établit, en termes exprès ou de façon implicite, le droit commun'
and with its role of '*fondement des autres lois*'[13] to opt for a narrow judicial
interpretative approach to those rules. The letter of the provision is clear on one
of the major and controversial issues under the older code, that of the boundaries
within which courts are required to fulfil their task of interpretation.

More controversial issues, calling into play the substance of the *droit commun*,
cannot be solved through a literal reading of the provision: is the Civil Code just
the core or the exclusive source of *droit commun*?[14] Is *droit commun* only relevant
to private law or does it include also public law? These are questions the answers
to which require us to go beyond the level of positive law, strictly interwoven
with those historical events which have been landmarks in Quebec's legal history
and which will be considered in the fourth part of this chapter. In the next part, an
overview of the main propositions developed from legal doctrine on the concept
of *droit commun* will be examined.

The *Droit Commun* Clause in the Eyes of Quebec Doctrine

In spite of the silence of the legislature (or, more probably, because of this silence),
a significant literature exists on the issue of the meaning (and reach) of the clause
of *droit commun*.

A starting point for understanding the doctrinal debate may be taken
from Brierley's remarks in 1989.[15] His thesis is that there are several accepted
understandings of *droit commun* at work in Quebec. The first one would regard
those 'principles, variously described as universal, general or super-eminent' that
would work as implicit norms.[16] These are general arguments drawn from the
sphere of morality, religion, or so-called 'common sense', or legal maxims used
by courts to explain the patterns of reasoning followed to reach a decision. In
sum, *droit commun* includes everything that makes up the reasoning leading to the
decision that is not drawn from a legal text and reveals essential modes of thought.

---

13   See translation n11.

14   On this issue see J.E.C. Brierley, 'The renewal of Quebec's distinct legal culture:
The new Civil Code of Québec' (1992) 42 *UT LJ* 484, 500; H.P. Glenn, 'Le droit comparé
et l'interprétation du code civil du Québec' in *Le nouveau code civil* 190. In the Quebec
case law, this view is clearly expressed in *Cie Immobilière Viger v Lauréat Giguère Inc.*
[1977] 2 RCS 67.

15   J.E.C. Brierley, 'Quebec's "common laws" (Droits Communs): How many are
there?' in E. Caparros (ed.), *Mélanges L.-P. Pigeon* (Wilson and Lafleur, 1989) 111.

16   In the *Premier Rapport des commissaires pour la codification des lois du Bas-
Canada qui se rapportent aux matières civiles*, it is stated that, '*tout code de lois* [...]
*suppose nécessairement l'existence obligée de certains principes fondamentaux, sur
lesquels doit reposer et se soutenir toute législation positive*' [every code assumes of
necessity the existence of some fundamental principles, on which every legislation is based
and from which it is supported].

This *droit commun* would not change through time – hence it has to be considered 'ahistorical' – and it would be – according to Brierley – 'openly acknowledged by the civil code itself as being distinct from both its own explicit enactment and from its own historical derivation'.[17]

In a second meaning, the locution *droit commun* encompasses the law in force prior to the enactment of the Civil Code, namely the *ancien droit français*, the English law that has penetrated the realm of civil law, the Roman law. These rules or principles may be found in statutes, usages and customs and judicial decisions. Unlike the previously discussed accepted meaning, this second would have historical roots. Art. 2712 now in force would acknowledge this *droit commun*, insofar as it provides that:

> the laws in force at the time of the coming into effect of this code are abrogated in all cases: in which there is a provision herein having expressly or impliedly that effect; in which such laws are contrary to or inconsistent with any provision herein contained; in which express provision herein made upon the particular matter to which such laws relate.[18]

Understood in these two meanings, *droit commun* would not necessarily depend on an express acknowledgement in the Civil Code; it would be a 'pre-normative' notion[19] able to affect the operation of the code. The 'silent' (since it is not officially acknowledged by the legislature) operation of this concept – and of its reach within the written legal system even under the Civil Code of 1866 – is evidenced by an article dating back to the 1920s.[20] Its author, Rivard, shows that its existence is not controversial, yet it is difficult to define, precisely for '*cette expression* [...] *d'un emploi fréquent* [...] *n'a trop souvent* [...] *qu'un sens plutôt vague*'.[21] It cannot be defined in absolute, but only in relation (in opposition) to what is particular, exceptional, therefore to those laws that cannot be applied to everybody. In Rivard's view, *droit commun* has to be seen as one of the possible expressions of national law, as the law applicable when (in any case in which) any rule enacted by the legislature cannot be found. Under the old code, *droit commun* had thus a '*fonction utilitaire*' [practical function] – that of filling the gaps

---

17   Brierley (n15) 118. Yet Brierley does not specify *where* the Civil Code acknowledges *droit commun* in this meaning.

18   This *droit commun* has been acknowledged in *Lapierre v A.G. Québec* [1985] 1 RCS 241, [258]-[259] (Chouinard observes that 'what our civil law has preserved of the ancient law is not necessarily limited to what the legislator has expressly adopted and enacted').

19   That part of the *droit commun* that is not enacted is very difficult to single out: see Roderick Macdonald, 'Encoding Canadian civil law' in J.E.C. Brierley et al. (eds), *Mélanges Paul-André Crepeau* (Yvon Blais, 1997) 579, 590.

20   A. Rivard, 'La notion du "droit commun"', (1924–25) 3 *Revue du Droit* 257.

21   [This expression [...] frequently used [...] quite often has a vague meaning] ibid.

in special laws dealing with the private law field, and this was even more so, after the Confederation came to existence, for federal laws aimed at ruling private law.[22]

A third, 'legislative-bound' concept of *droit commun* that results from legislative enactments of a 'general and permanent character' concerning the regulation of the individual person and his relations with other individuals has since been unravelled. Brierley writes that, 'The code in this regard has a role that is the functional equivalent of the accumulated work of the traditional (i.e., judicially created) English common law in the shaping of private law concepts and relations'.[23] A significant example would be the Civil Code, inasmuch as it lays down the basic conceptual taxonomies of private law. The abovementioned *Disposition Préliminaire* of the new code – enacted two years after Brierley's essay – has to be understood in this third sense.[24]

These manifold understandings of *droit commun* would demonstrate its 'pluralistic' character, which however does not deny the possibility of its 'unitary' conception. It would be nothing 'more than a technique by which to acknowledge the existence of a particular set of "sources of law" [...] found to be commonly applicable in the event that no derogation to them has been made by another set of more specific norms'.[25] Through the identification of the different layers constituting the concept of *droit commun*, Brierley aims at giving a general view of Quebec law as 'open' towards outside influences.

Quite interestingly, there are no significant differences between the way Brierley frames the issue of *droit commun* in 1989 and Rivard's approach dating back to 1924. The conception of *droit commun* supported by both is that of a set of norms whose existence may lie outside written law and whose function is that of supplementing statutes.

Glenn places the expression *droit commun* in a wider conceptual framework. Whereas Rivard's and Brierley's survey is confined to the Quebec legal system, Glenn deals with the historical patterns of *droit commun* in Europe and North America.[26] His assumption is that not one single *droit commun* but several *jura communia* may exist within a given legal system at the same time or in subsequent periods, each displaying a different function. A diachronic survey of the circumstantial meanings in which *droit commun* has been used in different cultures brings to light that under Roman law it was conceived as general law, either in the

---

22   J.M. Brisson, 'Le code civil, droit commun?' in *Le nouveau code civil* 294.

23   Brierley (n15) 123.

24   For an application of *droit commun* in this third sense, *Doré v Verdun* (1997) 2 RCS 862; *Epiciers Unis Métro-Richelieu Inc. v Collin* (2004) 3 RCS 257; *Fédération des producteurs acéricoles du Québec v Regroupement pour la commercialisation des produits de l'érable* (2006) 2 RCS 591.

25   Brierley (n15) 128.

26   In this regard, see H.P. Glenn, *On Common Laws* (Oxford University Press, 2005). Part of the reasoning developed in this book is sketched in his previous article 'Persuasive authority' (1987) 32 *McGill Law Journal* 261.

form of natural law or that of *jus civile*, conceived as '*le droit qui s'applique en l'absence d'exceptions* [...] *que ce même droit formule*'.[27] This general law had a mandatory character. There was only one set of general rules, compulsory for everybody, applying to every case unless exceptions to its operation were provided.

In the medieval age, the notion of *droit commun* inherited from Roman law underwent an evolution. Being deprived of a general and mandatory character, it only applied when in a given territory other more specific laws, called by Glenn '*droits particuliers*' [particular laws], '*prioritaires* [...] *dans leur zone d'influence*',[28] might not be found. Several *iura* of a different nature thus coexisted.[29]

Glenn argues that *droit commun* not only has historical importance, but is an influential concept even at the present time, as demonstrated by the current European debate. It would not necessarily be part of State law, since the dimension of State law would be but one of its possible expressions.[30] The case of the '*droit commun de la francophonie*'[31] is taken as evidence of this assumption. This '*droit de la francophonie*' would have been carried out in Quebec by colonisers. The absence of a political power able to set a uniform and mandatory law would explain the reasons for the operation of a *droit commun* in a supplementary way. Its application, not being the result of an imposition by the political power, may be explained as the consequence of its persuasive character.[32] The 1866 Lower Canada Civil Code would not have caused the vanishing of *droit commun* which lurked behind it, not necessarily transfused into formal, positive law rules, but powerful enough to drive the application of legal rules. This conclusion is substantially shared by those who identify two aims underlying the Civil Code: on the one hand, the need for the rationalisation of the legal sources; on the other, the acknowledgement of a universalist conception consisting of an ongoing dialogue between the two 'souls' of the legal system. David Howes invokes the example of the explanation by the Reporters of Art. 1706 as paradigmatic of this conception: this provision 'declares a rule derived from Roman law, and although not found in the Code Napoleon undoubtedly expresses the law of ancient and modern France'.[33] This legislative approach corresponds to the 'dialogical', nomadic attitude of courts towards foreign authorities.[34]

---

27   [Law which generally applies when it does not provide exceptions to its operation]. See H.P. Glenn, 'La Disposition Préliminaire du Code civil du Québec, le droit commun et les principes généraux du droit' (2005) 46 *Les Cahiers de Droit* 342.

28   [Prevailing within their ambit of operation] ibid. 344.

29   Ibid. 343.

30   Ibid. 352.

31   [French speakers' *jus commune*] ibid. 344.

32   Glenn (n26).

33   D. Howes, 'La domestication de la pensée juridique québécoise' (1989), available at <http://id.erudit.org/iderudit/015058ar> 110–11 accessed 28 November 2013.

34   D. Howes, 'Dialogical jurisprudence' in W. Pue and J.B. Wright (eds), *Canadian Perspectives on Law & Society. Issues in Legal History* (Carleton University Press, 1988) 71.

This conception of *droit commun* as supplementary law would also underlie the *Disposition Préliminaire* of the CCQ in force. This would not exclude of course the possibility for the code to lay down mandatory rules; the latter, however, should not be considered as part of the *droit commun*, but rather as 'particular laws'. *Droit commun* is not wholly included within the Civil Code; it may also be found outside it. Its transnational character produces an openness of the Civil Code toward external legal sources. This openness would be, according to Glenn, be acknowledged from the same text of the *Disposition Préliminaire*, when it states that the code '*établit le droit commun en termes exprès ou implicites*'.[35] This reference to the power vested in the Civil Code to lay down also in implicit terms *droit commun*, would be evidence that '*la plus grande signification du Code civil au Québec est d'indiquer l'appartenance de ce dernier à la grande tradition civiliste et particulièrement au droit commun de la francophonie*'.[36] This conclusion has to be carefully assessed, focusing on different interpretations of the word '*établit*' and the expression '*de façon implicite*' from those followed by Glenn.

The *Dictionnaire de la langue française Le Robert* reveals that the word '*établir*' may be employed either to mean '*fonder quelque chose de manière ferme, stable*'[37] – that is, something which pre-exists, and is not created – or to mean creating something: this understanding governs the use of the word in the legal field ('*mettre en vigueur, en application, en exercice*').[38] Glenn understands '*établir*' in the former sense rather than in the one normally used in a legal context. The term '*de façon implicite*' may be understood as a reference to the possibility for courts to draw *droit commun* from a 'holistic', systematic reading of the codal provisions; it does not necessarily require them to go beyond the code and look at sources lying outside the system. Glenn's view is interesting since it is a clear sign of a 'precomprehension' of the *droit commun*, affecting the interpretation of the text of the *Disposition Préliminaire*. Glenn's approach to *droit commun* sheds light on its importance not only at a theoretical level (as to the conceptual foundations of the Quebec system), but also at an 'operational' one.

The issue of the '*responsabilité civile des municipalités*' would be a clear example of the phenomenon of the possibility of the coexistence of rules coming from the two traditions. This 'co-operation' would be clear evidence of

> *l'harmonie inhérente entre deux droits communs de caractère essentiellement*
> *facultatif et supplétif [...]. Dans un cas précis, les deux droits sont interprétés et*
> *l'application de l'un ou de l'autre ne trouble pas la légitimité continue des deux*

---

35   [Lays down the *jus commune*, expressly or by implication].

36   [The greatest importance of the Québec civil code has to be found in its civilian roots, notably in its being part of the Francophone *jus commune*] ibid. 348.

37   [To lay down something in a steady way].

38   [To introduce, to enforce]. This ambiguity may be found as to the English term 'establish'.

[...] *il y aura des moments d'influence plus ou moins forte de l'un ou de l'autre des droits, sans que l'équilibre soit rompu.*[39]

The reconciliation of common and civil law traditions made by a specific judgement, even if given from a court of the highest rank, does not bar legal change and the achievement of a different balance between the two. If the exchange of information may occur among traditions underlying different legal orders, there is an even greater possibility when two traditions concur jointly to shape the identity of a given legal system, as is the case with the Quebec legal system. Quebec's experience would be significant, as it would show that differences between the two traditions are both reconcilable and commensurable.

In this writer's opinion, Glenn's approach to the issue of the meaning of *droit commun* is fully understandable only if attention is paid to his comparative law research devoted to the concept of 'legal tradition'.[40] It is also true that his being a scholar from a Quebec experience affects his 'systemological' taxonomies; few remarks will be devoted to this issue.

His conception of tradition as a set of information – and the acknowledgement of its circulation and exchangeability among legal traditions – is presumably affected by his perception of the relationship between common and civil law within the Quebec legal context, and of their conceivability not as different closed systems, but rather as open discursive practices. The idea of 'epistemic community' as a notion encompassing those who – sharing a social identity – adhere to a tradition fits well with the reality of the Quebec legal culture: the idea of the complexity of legal traditions caused by the coexistence of multiple internal and lateral traditions; the possibility of contradictions and differences within it which do not exclude once and for all the sustainability of legal diversity; the possibility that within a given tradition a way of thinking is 'multivalent' to the extent that 'sub-traditions' are neither right nor wrong but may be right in different, multiple and even *inconsistent* ways,[41] all seem to be strongly relevant to the Quebec experience.

This concise diachronic survey from Rivard to Glenn has revealed some recurring elements in the analysis devoted to *droit commun*: an idea of 'something' – its substance is not easy to define – legally significant and pre-existing to the formal legislative acknowledgement of a supplementary nature. Yet a difference must also be remarked upon: while Rivard stresses the role of *droit commun* within

---

39   [The inherent harmony between two *jura communia* having a not mandatory and supplementary character [...] When a case comes at stake, these two set of laws can be interpreted and applied in a way which fosters the ongoing legitimacy of both [...] sometimes the influence of one will be stronger than that of the other; however, this will not unbalance their relationship] Glenn (n27) 350.

40   H. Patrick Glenn, *Legal Traditions of the World: Sustainable Diversity in Law* (4th edn, Oxford University Press, 2010).

41   Ibid. 368.

the framework of national law, Glenn's approach is manifestly transnational, advocating the 'openness' of the Quebec legal system towards external rules and principles, and claiming a strategic role on behalf of *droit commun*. The view of law as 'open' has two main effects, one more specifically related to the way in which common law has to be faced in Quebec; the other concerning the function assigned to comparative law as a practical knowledge used to deal with the complexity of the Quebec legal system. These two aspects are interwoven. As to the former, Glenn rejects the view of common law as 'foreign' in the Quebec legal system, in the grounds that it is insufficient to consider a law as foreign simply because it *'provient [...] d'un autre Etat'*.[42]

A similar position is taken by Jutras[43] and Howes.[44] In particular, Jutras carefully examines the possible options for dealing with common law sources: first, foreign sources may be dealt with *'comme si elles appartenaient formellement à l'ordre juridique québécois'*;[45] second, the implantation of a rule or institution in different soil cuts the links between the imported rule or institution and its exporter; and finally, the 'departure context' retains an influential role even if it is not binding for the interpretation.[46] Of course, that author supports the third option by virtue of the fact that it starts with the assumption that common law is not foreign.

Comparative law reveals itself to be a highly useful means of dealing with diverse legal sources. Jutras remarks that: *'le recours au droit comparé par les juges est désormais rare à l'égard de ce noyau dur civiliste'*.[47] And yet comparative law is still not understood as an autonomous branch of law relevant at a theoretical level. Glenn observes that: *'la théorie actuelle du droit comparé se trouve à l'extérieur de la pratique de droit, et nous vient de pays où le droit comparé [...] est [...] à toutes fins utiles [...] marginalisé. Ainsi, le droit comparé serait essentiellement une science taxonomique'*,[48] but as a set of conceptual tools relevant on the ground of legal practice, helping judges to handle heterogeneous legal materials in order to deal with interpretative legal issues.[49] This emphasis on practice is expressed in an essay by Tancelin, even if not linked expressly

---

42 [It comes from another state] Glenn (n14) 186.

43 D. Jutras, 'Cartographie de la mixité: la common law et la complétude du droit civil au Québec' (2009) 88 *Canadien Bar Revue* 247.

44 Howes (n34) 85, highlighting the fact that not so much the use of 'foreign' sources but rather the importation of 'foreign' techniques and methods of interpretation puts at risk Quebec legal system's integrity.

45 [As if they formally belong to the Quebec legal order].

46 Jutras (n43) 261–2.

47 [Judicial recourse to comparative law is now rare with regard to this civilian core] ibid. 270.

48 [Comparative law current theory is outside legal practice ; it comes from countries where comparative law is [...] quite useless from a practical viewpoint. Thus, comparative law has a theoretical nature] H.P. Glenn (n14) 196.

49 Ibid. 178–9.

to the role of comparative law.[50] The purpose underlying Tancelin's reasoning, dealing with the issue of '*mixité comme coexistence des "inconciliables"*' via the notion of *droit commun*,[51] looks very similar to Glenn's. Tancelin looks at two levels of law: '*l'aspect substantif de la norme juridique*',[52] moulded on civil law in that '*le droit privé québécois est organiquement semblable au droit des pays de civil law*';[53] and '*la dimension méthodologique*' [methodological dimension], which makes Quebec law '*fonctionnellement proche du droit des pays de common law*'.[54] These two levels are not mutually exclusive, but concurrent. The point of convergence would be the notion of *droit commun*, whose existence should not be found merely at the level of the '*règles de droit*', but also at the level of practice (of the law from courts). In Tancelin's discourse, the diverse threads composing the issue of *Quebec mixité* are admirably summarised as: the distinction between methodology and substantive law; the dialectic relationship between common law and civil law seen through the conceptual categories of opposition and divergence; and the view of comparative law as a set of conceptual devices used to deal with the daily needs of the system (recalling Louis Baudoin's thesis of '*droit civil québécois*' as a '*modèle vivant de droit comparé*'[55]). Borrowing Tancelin's words, '*un droit mixte serait un droit qui n'a pas subi entièrement le déclin ou l'éclipse du droit commun [...], un droit qui n'ayant pas de place dans les systèmes dogmatiques a continué d'emprunter indistinctement aux traditions nationales diverses*';[56] therefore, '*mixité [serait] une imbrication dynamique plutôt qu'une juxtaposition statique*';[57] in a sentence, '*les droits mixtes*' are '*des survivances, des copies de l'ancien droit commun, des revenants en quelque sorte*'.[58]

The view of comparative law's 'practical usefulness', based on its European origins, is not a new concept in the history of comparative law studies.[59] Even if

---

50   M. Tancelin, 'Contribution du Québec à la recherché des causes de déclin ou de l'éclipse du jus commune' 106 *Foro It* (1983), V, 207.

51   [Mixity as coexistence of 'incompatible' entities] ibid. 212–13.

52   [The substantive aspect of a legal provision].

53   [Quebec private law is structurally similar to that of civil law countries].

54   [Under a functional point of view close to common law legal systems] ibid. 209–10.

55   [Living model of comparative law] L. Baudoin, *Le Droit Civil de la Province de Québec: Modèle Vivant de Droit Comparé* (Wilson and Lafleur, 1953).

56   [A mixed legal system has not experienced the decline or the eclipse of jus commune [...], since these legal systems do not have a clear-cut place within the comparative law traditional taxonomies, they continue to borrow rules and principles from different legal traditions].

57   [Mixity [would be] a dynamic imbrication rather than the result of a static juxtaposition].

58   [Mixed legal systems [...] survivals, copies of the old jus commune, something which resurfaces throughout time] ibid. 214.

59   As is clearly expounded by M. Ancel, *Utilità e metodi del diritto comparato. Elementi d'introduzione generale allo studio comparato dei diritti* (Jovene, 1974) 9–10.

at first sight these approaches look similar, there is a clear cleavage. For French scholars of the late nineteenth century, comparative law was a practical tool intended to ameliorate State law by borrowing normative solutions from abroad, thereby enhancing closure of the system by improving national institutions. Glenn understands this practice of comparative law as a way of fostering the openness of the Quebec legal system.

The approach followed by the aforementioned Quebec authors has its roots in the late nineteenth century, as Howes explains.[60] He sheds light on the figure of Judge Taschereau and on his attitude, favourable to 'polijurality',[61] the 'tendency to look at other legal traditions' (or cultures) as presenting 'alternatives for us' instead of 'alternatives to us'.[62] Taschereau's judgments would be marked by a 'principled eclecticism', that is, the belief in the existence of a 'universal law' which transcends the boundaries between common and civil law and calls for a dialogue between these two traditions.

The position of Taschereau should not be considered as 'anglophilic'; rather, it has to be qualified as 'antipositivistic'.[63] His attitude towards written law would be 'inspired by his commitment to a particular, rational view of law, which placed it beyond definitive enactment or stipulation and rather in an on-going, imperfect process of enquiry'. Not for him the notion of the Civil Code as an 'intellectual why-stopper'.[64] Taschereau embodies the trends at work in a period during which the Supreme Court pursued the policy of the uniformisation of Canadian private law.[65] Taschereau's position was followed by another judge of the Supreme Court of Canada from the end of 1960s to 1980, Louis-Philippe Pigeon,[66] in confirmation of an attitude which has persisted through time.[67] These figures would be the expression of a '*culture orale*' [oral culture], which promoted dialogue between the Anglophone

---

60 D. Howes, 'From polijurality to monojurality: The transformation of Quebec law, 1875–1929' (1987) 32 *McGill Law Journal* 523.

61 I refer to Howes (n60) An example of Taschereau's polijurality may be found in his opinion in *The Glengoil Steamship v Pikington* (1897) 38 RCS 146, in which to deal with the issue of lack of stowage in a contract of charter, he made reference to Scottish, Louisiana, French and Italian cases.

62 Howes (n60) 525.

63 For an example of this attitude, see G. Parker, 'Canadian legal culture' in L.A. Knafla (ed.), *Law & Justice in a New Land. Essays in Western Canadian Legal History* (Carswell, 1986) 20, referring to a case in which Taschereau, instead of deciding on the basis of the Canadian Criminal Code, applied a common law crime.

64 Howes (n60) 535.

65 See P.G. Jobin, 'La circulation de modèles juridiques français au Québec. Quand? Comment? Pourquoi?' in B. Moore and G. Bras Miranda (eds), *Mélanges Popovici- Les couleurs du droit* (Thémis, 2010) 599, who considers as a significant example of this trend *Drysdale v Dugas* [1897] 26 R.C.S. 20.

66 On Pigeon's position, see Brierley (n15).

67 This process cannot be depicted as a consistent evolution, constituted by an approach that has been completely left aside in favour of another one.

and Francophone communities.[68] The code affirms its own authority as the main source in the private law area more than one decade after its enactment, in the mid-1980s of the nineteenth century. This phenomenon has been called '*la découverte tardive de l'hégémonie du code*',[69] which entailed an '*ère nouvelle qui allait être celle de l'hégémonie de la loi*'.[70] This 'positivism' would sweep away an 'eclectic' approach within the Quebec legal community.[71] Howes' writing, far from being a historical survey of past judicial trends, points to his strong degree of consonance with them and to the ongoing 'eclectic' attitude of Quebec jurists, continuing even to the present. His harsh portrait of Judge Mignault makes this clear,[72] as do his claims for the 'purity' of the Quebec legal system, rooted in a real strategy.[73]

This link between the eclecticism of Quebec legal culture and the openness of the system is also to be considered as Pierre Legrand's background, expounded in the chapter: 'The same and the different'.[74] The core idea of this chapter is that comparative law scholars have to maintain an attitude of 'non-indifference to difference' and to resist the 'stunningly insistent subjugation of the other to the self [...] falling for the treacherous seduction of semblance'.[75] That author opposes the conceivability of common and civil law as separate entities, their identity being perceivable only in relation to the 'other':

---

68   On the meaning of the categories of '*culture orale*' and '*culture écrite*' and on the transition to the former to the latter through the Lower Canada Civil Code, see the seminal essay by Howes (n33).

69   [Late discovery of the hegemony of the code]. This expression is taken from A. Morel, 'L'émergence du nouvel ordre juridique instauré par le Code civil du Bas Canada (1866–1890)' in *Le nouveau code civil* 60.

70   [A new era, notably that of the hegemony of law] ibid. 63.

71   Eclecticism reappears in Glenn's pages (n14) 180 as a keyword to understand the openness of the Quebec legal system to external influences: '*La "mixité" du droit québécois se trouvait non pas tellement dans la diversité de ses sources originales* [...] *mais dans son ouverture continue envers des sources étrangères du droit. L'étatisation locale du droit n'était pas complète; la "mixité" consiste dans cette ouverture possible envers d'autres sources*' [Quebec law mixity is not the result of the diversity of its original sources [...] but of its ongoing openness towards foreign legal sources. The local nationalisation of law was not complete; mixity consists in the possibility of the legal system to open itself towards other sources].

72   A flattering portrait of Mignault is given by J.G. Castel, 'Le juge Mignault défenseur de l'intégrité du droit civil Québécois' (1975) 53 *Canadian Bar Review* 544, who stresses his role in preserving Quebec private law.

73   According to Howes (n60) 550, this 'strategy' was articulated in four points: 1) 'deflect [...] attention from the past and focus [...] on the future'; 2) emphasize the 'bastardy of other traditions' as opposed to the 'purity' of Quebec; 3) 'demonstrate a divergence in the common and civil law solutions to a problem wherever possible'; 4) 'emphasize the hierarchy of sources'.

74   In P. Legrand and R. Munday (eds), *Comparative Legal Studies: Traditions and Transitions* (Cambridge University Press, 2003) 240 ff.

75   Ibid. 310.

The qualifiers "civil law" and "common law" do not refer in an exclusive way to one or the other of the western legal traditions. [...] one will find traces of a legal or rhetorical or anthropological or sociological or political economy said to be "civil law" more easily in jurisdictions having received Roman law and that one will find traces of a legal or rhetorical or anthropological or sociological or political economy said to be "common law" more easily in jurisdictions not having received Roman law [...] "Civil-law" and "common-law" do not exist a priori as kinds of essences, but only a posteriori in multiple incarnations. I believe in inescapable hybridity [...] I have, therefore, never propounded a theory of "civil law" or "common law" [...] I cannot relate to the idea of a specifically "civil law" or "common law" identity. [76]

What he advocates is, thus, 'a focus on the law as it is situated, as it is located'.[77] Their being 'irrevocably irreconcilable' is emphasised while at the same time it is acknowledged that in the legal context to which the author belongs they are simultaneously present. Both traditions have to be considered domestic, that is, in the sense of not being 'foreign' to the Quebec legal system, and thus also have to be considered as expression and reflection of the local society. In this way, they may be considered to mirror the society. The author defies the view of common and civil law as 'systems', as 'structured entities'.

The respective positions of Glenn, Howes and Legrand all seem to converge on the assumption that the identity of Quebec would be threatened by the simple borrowing of rules coming from outside, since afterwards these rules have to be implemented. This idea of law has not been the only one supported in Quebec. Another viewpoint has been clearly underlined by Judge Mignault and may be summarised by his statement that '*une cloison étanche et infranchissable sépare les deux grand systèmes juridiques* [...] *Il n'y a pas immixtion ou absorption de l'un au profit ou au détriment de l'autre*'.[78] Mignault's approach clearly derives from four of his writings.[79]

He emphasises the importance of '*droit civil*' not only as a historical event, but as a phenomenon with significance for the future; he emphasises what puts it at risk, that is, a judge-made law moulded on English law patterns, which disregards legal rules expressly provided by texts and has recourse for their application

---

76 Ibid. 243–4.

77 Ibid. 310.

78 [An insurmountable bulkhead divides these two legal systems [...] there is no mixing or absorption of one system to the benefit or detriment of the other] P.B. Mignault, 'Les rapports entre le droit civi e et la "common law" au Canada, spécialement dans la province de Québec' (1932–33) 11 *Revue du Droit* 201, 206.

79 'L'avenir de notre droit civil' (1922–23) 1 *Revue du Droit* 56; 'Les rapports entre le droit civile et la "common law" au Canada'; 'The authority of decided cases' (1925) 3 *Canadian Bar Review* 1; 'Le ccde civil de la Province de Quebec et son intérpretation' (1935–36) 1 *University of Toronto Law Journal* 104.

to foreign authorities instead of French ones; he views common and civil law traditions as '*deux grands systèmes jurisprudentiels*' among which '*[I]l n'y a pas immixtion ou absorption de l'un au profit ou au détriment de l'autre*'.[80] He conceives of common law as 'an unwritten law while the civil law is a written one';[81] he views Lower Canada as more inspired by the '*ancient droit coutumier français*' [old French customary law] than the *Code Napoléon*; he understands 'le droit civil' as '*un système logique. Toutes les conséquences normales d'une règle de droit sont comprises dans la règle elle-même. Cela autorise le procédé de raisonnement connu sous le nom de déduction*';[82] moreover he conceives of the Civil Code not as an ordinary statute, the meaning of which has to be unearthed through interpretative techniques other than the literal, but as one that is able to give to its provisions a broad scope.

Taschereau and Mignault are the figures who, within the judicial circle, represent in the clearest way the two poles of the Quebec legal culture: on the one hand, an idea of law as a phenomenon relevant at an 'oral' level, for written law cannot contain all that is legally significant within its realm (Taschereau); on the other hand, the conception of law as necessarily written down (Mignault). The written form – entailing '*la textualisation des sources*'[83] as well as '*celle des techniques et méthodes d'interprétation de ces sources*'[84] – triggers a process of rationalisation of the law leaving aside an 'inclusive' attitude in favour of an 'exclusive' one.[85] Mignault would represent a 'closing' attitude in the Quebec legal system which has taken a variety of forms, identified in '*l'intégrité, la résistance, le ressentiment, et la complétude*'[86] and resurfacing in different periods. The attitude embodied by Mignault has been explained as the result of the end of the dialogue between common law and civil law jurists, due to the fact that this relationship changed in substance, becoming 'one-way', that is, the unidirectional influence of the English legal community on the French one, and leading to the '*involution du nationalisme canadien-français*'.[87] The actual difference between Taschereau and

---

80   [See translation at n78] Mignault (n78) 211.

81   Mignault (n79) 1.

82   ['Civil law' as 'a rational system. Every effect flowing from the application of a legal rule has to be found within the provision. This mechanism is called deduction] Mignault (n79) 129.

83   [The definition of legal sources in legal texts].

84   [Legal rules providing the techniques and methods of interpretation of these sources].

85   Howes (n34) 105.

86   [The integrity, the resistance, the resentment, the completeness] D. Jutras, '*Cartographie de la mixité*' 249. For this approach see M. Cantin Cumyn, 'Les innovations du Code civil du Québec, un premier bilan' (2005) 46 *Cahiers de Droit* 463, 469: '*l'objectif de la codification d'affermissement de la tradition civiliste québécoise s'exprime d'abord dans la Disposition Préliminaire*' [the aim – underlying codification – of strengthening Quebec civilian tradition is first expressed through the Preliminary Provision].

87   [The involution of the French-Canadian nationalism] Howes (n34) 118.

Mignault is that the latter narrows the existence of *droit commun* down to written law: from the multiplicity of meanings vested in the concept of *droit commun* to one only. The Civil Code is the *droit commun*. This view is clearly based on a conception of the law as the by-product of the Nation State.

Back to the Past: In Search of the Historical Roots of *Droit Commun*

It may be argued that the 'eclectic' discourse of Quebec scholars on *droit commun* has been affected by the ways in which the concept of law developed in the territory of Quebec under French and later, British, domination. Is this 'eclectic' attitude, consisting of an expression of legal self-determination vis-à-vis civil and common law traditions, the result of the autonomy enjoyed by the Quebec community even under the French and British powers? Some turning points in Quebec legal history will be briefly remembered and assessed.[88]

Quebec law under French domination had, at the beginning of French settlement, a 'private' character: political, judicial and administrative power was not exercised by public bodies, but by private persons following authorisation from the French Crown. The French Crown had sovereignty over Quebec, but in an 'indirect' way. This statement seems to be supported by two events: the cession of Quebec from the French Crown in 1627 to a private subject, the *Compagnie de Cent Associés*[89] and the cession of Quebec in 1664 to the *Compagnie des Indes Occidentales*. These events probably explain why the above-quoted scholars conceived of law not necessarily as a manifestation of State will. These few words are, of course, not able to provide full evidence of the above cautiously sketched hypothesis. An ad hoc historical survey would be necessary, which is not possible here.[90] If it were considered plausible, its logical consequence would be that the perception of law as a 'pre-statal' phenomenon would have been a trait peculiar to the Francophone community.[91]

Another turning point in Quebec legal history under French domination seems to have occurred in 1663, when the Superior Council of Quebec was created. The Council was directed to judge '*selon les lois et ordonnances de notre royaume* [...]

---

88 On Quebec legal history, the landmark work of R. Lemieux, *Les origines du droit franco-canadien* (Théoret, 1901) has to be acknowledged.

89 Lemieux (n88) 256, remarks that following this cession '*[d]u régime royal, le Canada passa au régime commercial*' [*Canada dismissed the royal regime and adopted the commercial regime*] (my emphasis).

90 Howes (n34) 106, remarks that this kind of survey would be really difficult for the '*existence de lacunes majeures dans l'histoire du droit québécois*' [existence of major gaps in Quebec legal history].

91 According to Mignault (n78) 201, '*la Province de Québec* [...] *est fille* [...] *de la France de l'ancien règime*' [the province of Quebec [...] is an offspring [...] of the old regime France].

en la forme et manière qui se pratique et se garde dans le ressort de notre cour de parlement de Paris'.[92] The institution of the Council created an ambit of Quebec institutional autonomy from France relevant on the ground of what nowadays is considered public law. At that time, besides the *Coutumes de Paris*, the *Lois* and *Ordonnances*, which, prior to 1663, modified and supplemented the Custom, were considered as sources of law. Why should 1663 be considered as such a turning point? Because from that time onwards the status of *Ordonnances* issued in France as legal sources was controversial in Quebec. According to some scholars,[93] not all the *Ordonnances* issued in France were deemed to be law in Canada, but only those that had been registered in Quebec. The *Ordonnances* enacted in France were not therefore law in Canada per se, the new law needing a formal act of adoption from the Superior Council to be acknowledged as a legal source in Quebec. This need for registration may be understood as a form of control of their suitability for the colony.[94] The *Ordonnances* enacted prior to 1663 were not registered since they were, as Walton puts it, 'to a large extent declaratory' in that: '[t]hey codify the old law'.[95] What does Walton mean by 'old law'? He presumably refers to the law in force when the French community moved from France to Canada, that is, mostly the *Coutume de Paris*, as interpreted with the aid of the old French commentators on that *Coutume* and on the *Droit Coutumier* in general.

The character of Quebec private law as an expression of the Francophone culture was not even challenged under the British Empire. The watershed of this era is represented by the Quebec Act, enacted in 1774: according to the historical reconstruction by Lemieux,[96] neither before nor after this Act were the Francophone foundations of private law touched, due to the fact that Quebec was ceded from France to England, and not conquered by the latter.

As for the Quebec Act, s8 is the most important for all the discourses revolving around the historical origins of Quebec bijurality. It provided that 'in all matters of controversy, relative to property and civil rights, resort shall be had to the Laws of Canada, as the rule for the decision of the same'. Moreover, the Act provided at s9 that 'nothing in this Act contained shall extend, or be construed to extend, to

---

92   [According to laws and ordinances of our kingdom [...] as enforced in our court in Paris]. Quotation taken from Lemieux (n88) 265.

93   The historical events summarised may be interpreted in different, if not opposite ways. In the text, the interpretation aimed at grounding a margin of autonomy to Quebec following the institution of the Superior Council is supported by F.P. Walton, *The Scope and Interpretation of the Civil Code of Lower Canada* (Butterworths, 1980) 36–7. A different approach is followed by J.A. Dickinson, *Law in New France* (University of Manitoba Canadian legal history project, Working Paper series, 1992).

94   This rule has been unambiguously stated by the Privy Council in *Symes v Cuvillier* (1880) 5 AC138.

95   Walton (n81) 37, who singles out the legal sources governing Quebec under the French regime as: 1) *Coutumes de Paris*; 2) *Arrêts du Conseil du Roi*; 3) ordinances of administrative authorities in Canada; 4) judgments of the courts.

96   Lemieux (n88) 363–72.

any lands that have been granted by his Majesty, or shall hereafter be granted by His Majesty, His Heirs and Successors, to be held in free and common Socage'. The Quebec Act thus does not contain an overall discipline of the areas of the legal system: apart from the case of 'property and civil rights', it states that English laws rule the field of criminal law. The other legal areas were not even mentioned.

The letter of ss8–9 does not support the view of the Act as the foundation for the bijurality of the system.[97] However, this interpretation kept a strong hold on Quebec authors, who deemed that the private law field fell within the realm of French law, understanding the expression 'Laws of Canada' as a synonym of 'French civil law',[98] and public law within that of the English law. A plausible reason for this interpretative trend is that it mirrors the perception and the approach of the Francophone part of the Quebec legal community to the theme of the legal foundations of the system.[99] Among Quebec legal historians, this Act would be the result of the victorious struggles of the French-Canadian component of Quebec society, successful in reversing English attempts to abolish the previous Quebec legislation in order fully to submit the territory to English law.[100] The reading of

---

97   This meant that in the field of property a coexistence in different parts of Quebec territory of two distinct bodies cf law – French and English – occurred. The reasons for the introduction of English forms of property is explained by J.E.C. Brierley, 'The co-existence of legal systems in Quebec: "Free and common socage" in Canada's *"pays de droit civil"'* (1979) 20 *Cahiers de Droit* 277

98   See Lemieux (n88) 381: *'Dans toute affaire en litige, concernant leur propriétés et leurs droits de citoyens, ils ont recours aux lois et coutumes du Canada, c'est-à-dire que les Canadiens auront le béréfice des lois françaises en matières civiles'* [when a legal issue concerning their property or their civil rights has to be decided, they make recourse to Canadian laws and customs, that is, Canadian people will enjoy the opportunity of using French laws in civil matters].

99   See the above summarised explanation by Robert Yalden, *'Unité et différence*: The structure of legal thought in late nineteenth-century Quebec' (1988) 46 (2) *University of Toronto Faculty Law Review* 365, 383 ff. According to the latter author, the moulding of public law on Anglo-Canadian patterns was not opposed within Quebec's legal circles since they were expression of a non-activist conception of the State, which was largely agreed in Quebec. The interesting element in Yalden's account of the bijurality is the fact that the English shape of the public law does not seem the mere result of colonisation, but instead is mainly the result of a Quebecois attitude of disregard toward public law as the field in which the State displays its activity, rooted in liberal thought. This interpretative approach emerges in some (old and recent) judgments. The expression 'laws of Canada' has been interpreted as referring to *'droit civil'* in *Laurentide Motels Ltd. v Beauport (Ville)* (1989) RCS 705, and as referring to the *'ancien droit français'* in *Canada (Attorney – General) v Quebec (Attorney -General)* (1921) 1 AC 413.

100   Lemieux (n88) 360, remembers that some fringes of the English government were aware of the risk of a sudden and radical change in the Quebec laws, and therefore claimed for the application of the public law maxim *'de laisser subsister les lois du peuple conquis jusqu'à ce que le vainqueur en ait proclamé de nouvelles'* [leave unchanged the law of conquered population till new laws are enforced], especially for the peculiar situation

the Quebec Act as a statute providing for the division of spheres of influence might be considered as an attempt by the Francophone culture to protect private law from the risk of penetration by elements foreign to it.[101]

Conclusion

The *droit commun* clause has been seen as a magnifying glass for perceptions of the ways in which the common and civil law traditions have coexisted and interacted. According to some authors, the inherent flexibility and immateriality of the concept of *droit commun*, its uncanny essence, convey a view of these traditions not as 'closed structures', but rather as discursive practices. A summarising statement of this view of *droit commun* may be found in the conclusions drawn by Glenn in his aforementioned essay '*La Disposition Préliminaire du Code civil du Québec*':

> *Il est de la nature d'un droit commun* [...] *de ne pas avoir de frontières, géographiques ou conceptuelles, précises. Les droits communs flottent, ce qui est indiqué aussi par leur caractère non obligatoire et supplétif. Ils existent donc à l'intérieur de juridictions précises, mais aussi au-delà de celles-ci.*[102]

The reasoning of the aforementioned authors around the concept of *droit commun* has shed light on how the cohabitation of the two traditions is deemed to be possible. The latter have not been conceived of as different entities, but rather as both expressing the *droit commun*, which is at the roots of the system. This has significant repercussions for the role ascribed to one of the basic distinctions

---

of Quebec, '*une ancienne colonie française, établie depuis longtemps, et possédant un code de lois bien connues*' [an old French colony, established since long time, ruled from a code of well-known laws]. Lemieux deals with the issue if the Treaty of Paris of 1763 and implies that English laws related to the private law field have to be automatically applied to Quebec territory. He argues that this did not occur since Quebec was not conquered, but ceded.

101   Proof of what has been said in the text is that s9 has, in spite of its letter, been interpreted not in the sense that it had recognised the operation of the English laws, but that forms of tenure different from those marking the French seigneurial system were possible, albeit falling under the Laws of Canada (moulded on French civil law). The possibility of the interpretative approach splitting the model of tenure from the English rules of property will be once and for all excluded from the Constitutional Act of 1791, providing expressly the application of English law to lands granted in socage. This solution will be later confirmed by the British 1825 Act, which also admitted the possibility for the local laws to adapt the Laws of England to the local circumstances.

102   [The main character of *jus commune* [...] is that of not having clear-cut boundaries, geographic or conceptual. *Jura communia* float because of their non-mandatory and supplementary character. They exist within given jurisdictions, but also beyond them] Glenn (n24) 352.

of the civil law tradition – that is, the distinction between private and public law that scholars use as a significant criterion when dealing with bijurality in order to assess the different patterns of influence displayed by civil law and common law traditions on those complex systems.[103] The notion of *droit commun* blurs those clear-cut boundaries.

Furthermore, the same idea of 'reception' as a notion generally used to explain how the law of a system may be affected by legal sources external to it, cannot hold in cases like Quebec because the premise on which this is grounded – a law which is 'foreign' and becomes 'law' in a system other than that in which it was born – does not seem adequately to describe the ways in which the interaction between the two legal traditions have been perceived to have occurred in Quebec by the majority of the authors considered above. Even the word 'diffusion' – although having a much broader scope than 'reception' in that it encompasses manifold patterns of the spread of law not limited to a linear transfer of formal rules but extending also to some immaterial legal layers, such as 'mentality', unspoken assumptions and so on – does not describe adequately the widespread perception within Quebec that the aforementioned interaction is an internal process; the scheme 'outside-inside' (or within and without), which seems to this writer to be at the basis of many patterns of 'diffusion' drawn by scholars, is not applicable to it. These traditions are not conceived as mutually foreign in the Quebec legal context. The legal system is considered 'open'; the notion of *droit commun* is seen as supplementary law, not binding and not exclusive, unlike law as the by-product of the State. This formulation underlies Glenn's writings. The other side of the coin of *droit commun*'s supplementary character is its persuasiveness. The acknowledgement of *droit commun* as a notion giving salience to the unwritten law – that is, the law that is embodied neither in the Civil Code nor in other statutes – would be the expression of the force that was at work even before its formal acknowledgement by the legislature in 1991 with the CCQ.

The sharp cleavage between common and civil law – grounded on the idea of difference – is overcome in favour of the 'sustainability of difference' and of an eclectic approach which refuses the binary attitude well expressed by the expression 'either … or'. The conception of these traditions as discursive practices and not as structured entities makes it possible to defeat the premise of their clear-cut difference and their possibility of being assembled – and inevitably transformed – from the Quebec legal context. This conception of the above-recalled traditions does not seem the result of the dominance of a common law cultural approach. Rather than being explicable either in terms of imposition or the slavish attitude of the receiving towards the received, this eclectic approach seemingly consists in the choice made among external theories and doctrines according to their consistency or proximity with Quebec's indigenous identity. This conception of law as not necessarily involving a structured set of authoritatively posited, explicit norms seems to correspond with a widespread attitude in European legal culture in

---

103 Palmer (n1).

advance of the codification of law,[104] which was eventually overcome by the latter. One possible explanation for the similarity between old Europe and Quebec would be that this European cultural background took root along with the settlement of a French community. What seems interesting is that this eclectic approach is still current. One should ask why this has occurred. Is it the same *rationale* that allegedly inspired jurists such as Taschereau, or is it a different one? This question needs further discussion and development and will have to be the subject of a future project.

---

104 G. Gorla, *Diritto comparato e diritto comune europeo* (Giuffré, 1981: in particular, see *Il ricorso alla legge di un 'luogo vicino' nell'ambito del diritto comune europeo*, and *Unificazione 'legislativa' ed unificazione 'giurisprudenziale'*, chaps 21–2).

Chapter 11

Law in Changing Circumstances: Evolution of Liability for Succession Debts in Poland

Elwira Macierzyńska-Franaszczyk*

Introduction

The complex nature of the law of succession reflects various arguments of an historical, ideological, political, economic, social and legal nature. The provisions of the law of succession are deeply rooted in the nature of national private law systems. The law of succession is a synthesis of other parts of the national private law system and results to some extent from regulations of other parts of private law. Despite this, there are significant similarities between succession law provisions among European civil law systems. The law of succession responds to universal and Europe-wide problems. Its purpose is to determine who is to continue or succeed to the legal personality of the deceased, and to determine the legal and economic consequences of this *mortis causa* transition. Different legal institutes[1] have been developed in various national systems to solve similar problems. The fact that according to the Roman law tradition successors are liable for succession debts sets the framework for, and determines the contours of, the provisions on the liability for succession debts in civil law systems. These provisions determine the proprietary and financial consequences of a succession and reduce the economic risks associated with the untimely death of creditors and debtors. The shape and function of such provisions are, however, designated by the political and economic priorities of national legislatures. These factors determine the character and specificity of the system of liability for succession debts.

---

* This contribution is part of the project financed by the Polish National Science Center awarded on the basis of Decision No. DEC-2011/01/N/HS5/04009.

1 I use the term 'institutes' as understood to mean separate legal instruments that build and particularise the system of succession law among various legal orders. As to the relationship between the terms 'institutes' and 'institutions' in general, see R. Foqué and A. Verbeke, 'Towards an open and flexible imperative inheritance law' in C. Castelein, R. Foqué and A. Verbeke, 'Imperative Inheritance Law in a Late-modern Society: Five Perspectives' (2009) 26 *European Family Law Series* 203.

The evolution of the Polish rules on the law of succession in the twentieth century reveals how significantly various legal and extra-legal factors influenced the shape of the Polish system of liability for succession debts.

Historical Outline

The first codification of the Polish law of succession arose in the turbulent period of the first half of the twentieth century, and can be understood in the context of the nineteenth-century European codifications which influenced it, among which were the German *Bürgerliches Gesetzbuch* (*BGB*), the French *Code Civil* (FR *CC*) and the Austrian *Allgemeines Bürgerlisches Gesetzbuch* (*ABGB*). Since these codes were already applicable in different areas of modern-day Poland, they provided an obvious starting point and defined the contours for codification when Poland unified in 1918.

The mix of different influences can be explained by historical fact. From the second half of the eighteenth century (1772) onwards, Poland was gradually partitioned and annexed to the Russian Empire, the Kingdom of Prussia and Habsburg Austria. The territorial divisions were altered in 1807 by the French Emperor Napoleon who created the Duchy of Warsaw. The annexed regions or districts of the divided state were subjected to five different legal systems. The territory of Western Poland, incorporated into the Prussian confederation – later to be transformed into the German Reich, was governed by the *BGB*. The Austrian *ABGB* was applied in the south. The French *Code Napoléon*[2] was in force in the Duchy of Warsaw. In the Eastern part of Poland annexed by Russia, certain parts of the Russian Code of Laws (*Svod Zakonov*, Vol. X, part I) were applied. In addition, a small southern part of Poland was governed by Hungarian customary law.[3] After the First World War, when the Polish Republic was finally restored (1918), the newly reborn state did not have a uniform civil law code. There was also no willingness to extend any of the applicable Western codifications to the united territory.[4] The need to create an autonomous, unified legal system arose as one of the fundamental conditions of the resurrection of the Nation State of Poland.[5]

---

2   From 1825 it was partially replaced by The Civil Code of the Kingdom of Poland (*Kodeks cywilny Królestwa Polskiego*).

3   For a more detailed discussion see A. Rudziński, 'Sovietisation of civil law in Poland' (1956) 15 *American Slavic and East European Review* 216.

4   The Codification Commission initially considered the idea of extending one of the then applicable Western systems to the whole unified territory. The idea was finally abandoned, since these laws were often seen as the law of the oppressors. See further on the concept of adopting the *Code Napoléon, BGB* or *ABGB*, Z. Nagórski, 'Codification of civil law in Poland (1918–1939)' *Studies in Polish and Comparative Law* (1st edn, Stevens and Sons, 1945) 54.

5   Nagórski (n5) 46.

Twist and Turns of the First Codification

The lengthy process of harmonisation and codification of Polish civil law was launched by a settlement of the Codification Commission in 1919.[6] The new codification of the law of succession was initially considered as a priority.[7] The first draft of the succession liability rules was published by Henryk Konic as early as 1924.[8] The proposed rules were explicitly modelled on the district laws applied in Poland (in particular the *BGB*, the *ABGB*, the *Code Napoléon*) and the Swiss Civil Code (*ZGB*).[9] However, the lack of a single political vision in the Polish government regarding further reforms of property and succession law slowed down the legislative activity in this area.[10] This meant that the project never became the subject of broad legislative debate.

The provisions on liability for succession debts were finally subjected to discussion during the Third Congress of Polish Lawyers in 1936.[11] Two different concepts regarding limitation of liability for succession debts by Stefan Wróblewski and Kazimierz Przybyłowski were presented to the public.[12]

The idea of codification was only revived again in 1945, after the end of the Second World War. The duality of concepts proposed in 1936 reappeared in the

---

6 Act of 3 June 1919, *Journal of Laws* (1919) 44/315. The broad work of the Codification Commission in the area of the law of succession is discussed in: L. Górnicki, *Prawo cywilne w pracach Komisji Kodyfikacyjnej Rzeczypospolitej Polskiej w latach 1919–1939* (1st edn, Kolonia Limited, 2000) 269; see also J. Gwiazdomorski, *Prawo spadkowe* (1st edn, Państwowe Wydawnictwo Naukowe, 1959) 16–17.

7 The law of succession was the subject of deliberation at the Sixth Congress of Polish Lawyers and Economists in 1920 in Warsaw – see: (1920) 27 *Gazeta Sądowa Warszawska* 223.

8 The draft was partially published by H. Konic, 'Projekt ustawy o prawie spadkowem w ogólności' (1924) 49 *Gazeta Sądowa Warszawska* 34–45.

9 The author referred to legal institutes and provisions adopted by German, French, Austrian, Russian and Swiss legislation. See: Konic (n9); Górnicki (n7) 272ff.

10 Górnicki (n7) 270.

11 See: 'Report on the discussion of the private law section of Codification Commission' submitted by the rapporteurs of the plenary of the III Congress of Polish Lawyers in 1936 in Katowice (1936) 49 *Gazeta Sądowa Warszawska* 682ff; K. Przybyłowski, '*Ukształtowanie zasad dotyczących odpowiedzialności za długi spadkowe w polskim prawie cywilnym*' (1969) XIII–XIV *Studia Cywilistyczne* 240; Górnicki (n7) 310.

12 The concept of limited liability for succession debts resulting from a lack of any successor statement presented by Stanisław Wróblewski and supported by Maurycy Allerhand, met with a strong criticism. The opposing concept, proposed by Kazimierz Przybyłowski, providing that in the event of no successor statement there should be unlimited liability, gained greater support. See: *Protokół z posiedzenia podkomisji postępowania niespornego z dnia 3 stycznia 1935 r.; Referat z posiedzenia podkomisji prawa spadkowego z dnia 18 października 1938 r.* – both dedicated to the discussion on the draft of Article 35 proposed by Wróblewski. See also Górnicki (n7) 301ff.

post-war codification proposals.[13] The law of succession was finally codified in the Succession Decree of 1946 that came into force on 1 January 1947.[14] The Decree of 1946 was criticised as being a compilation of major continental European Codes, instead of an autonomous and original work. Critics pointed out the inadequacy of the legislative patterns employed when compared with the state of the Polish economy, society, customs and laws. Undoubtedly the Polish codification arose under the influence of four commonly accepted legislative systems, formally autonomous but interacting one with another.[15] The codification proposals were strongly supported by comparative analysis, which covered among other issues, the model of devolution of inheritance, the scope of succession debts and duties, the scope of entities bearing liability, and the institutes modifying the general rules of liability and limiting the scope of liability.[16] Recourse to existing major European codifications, like the German *BGB*, French *Code Napoléon* and Austrian *ABGB*, was common in the codification process, and this was reflected in its results.[17] This consequence was natural since all these Codes had replaced or supplemented previous Polish law during the time of partition and were, in the transition period, still in force in different districts of Poland. In addition, the Swiss *ZGB* provided a source of model provisions. The Polish legislature modelled the provisions of the new Decree on European codifications, but did not import their rules.

Succession Decree of 1946: Codification or Compilation?

The Polish legislature followed the Western systems as to the main civil law approach and principles of the law of succession. The Western models were, however, not merely transposed into the Decree. There are various examples from the general structure of the system of liability for succession debts, as well as of separate legal institutes, which demonstrate that the Western systems

---

13　Jan Gwiazdomorski supported the principle of unlimited liability restricted by acceptance *cum beneficio inventarii* (succession with the benefit of an inventory). Kazimierz Przybyłowski, in contrast to his previous proposals, presented the concept of the limited liability for succession debts. See: Przybyłowski (n12) 241; Górnicki (n7) 310ff; J. Gwiazdomorski, *Prawo spadkowe w zarysie* (4th edn, Państwowe Wydawnictwo Naukowe, 1985) 19ff.

14　The provisions of substantive law were covered by the Succession Decree of 8 October 1946 (*Journal of Laws* (1946) 60/328) and the Decree of 8 October 1946 – Provisions introducing the Law of Succession (*Journal of Laws* (1946) 60/329).

15　See: *Report* (n12) 683. Also: Przybyłowski (n14) 239.

16　*Report* (n12) 682ff.

17　The Polish legislature disregarded provisions of Russian law and followed the Western pattern, which were more reminiscent of the Polish Acts of 1818 and 1825. The critics of the Russian Code emphasised the outdated nature of the Russian provisions, its dependency on religious views and discrepancies between *Svod Zakonov* and the newly codified Polish law of obligations. See: Nagórski (n5) 47 and 53ff; *Report* (n12) 682.

served as a source of inspiration for the Polish legislature in the new codification tempered by appropriate modifications in line with contemporary economic and social needs.

The primary objective of the Decree was the adoption of the Roman concept of universal succession. Despite the fact that the concept was followed by all of the systems referenced, only the French and the Austrian codes clearly mentioned that debts are transferred to the successors, while the German and Swiss codes mentioned in general that the succession is transferred, without specifying whether the transfer refers to active or passive components of inheritance.[18] The Polish legislature avoided this apparent imprecision by stating in Article 1 of the Decree that the inheritance consists of all rights and obligations of the deceased and in Article 4 that the succession consists in transferring the inheritance as a whole to successors. The principle of universal succession was clearly indicated by the Polish legislature as a mechanism justifying the successor's liability for succession debts.

Pursuant to Article 3 § 1 and Article 32 of the Decree, successors become liable at the moment of the deceased's death, according to the doctrine *le mort saisit le vif*[19] which is similar to that followed by the German and French systems, but not by Austrian law, where the inheritance is regarded as *hereditas iacens*,[20] from the moment of deceased death up to the moment of a formal statement of acceptance by the successor.

Some differences existed between the referenced systems concerning the liability of co-successors. The German and Austrian Codes followed the path of joint and several liability of co-successors, which lasts until the partitioning of the inheritance. After the partitioning of the inheritance successors were liable in proportion to their inherited shares. Under French law, co-successors were liable proportionally to their shares in the succession from the opening of the succession.[21] The Decree, similarly to the French Code, rejected joint and several liability and provided that co-successors were liable proportionally to their shares in the succession.[22]

The essential difference among the European codifications lay in the limitation of liability for succession debts. The German, Austrian and French systems adopted the general principle of unlimited liability, contrary to Russian law, where the liability was in principle limited.[23] The Polish legislature adopted

---

18 For discussion on the idea of universal succession in the German system – see L. Michalski, *BGB-Erbrecht* (4th edn, C.F. Müller 2010) 2; K.-H. Muscheler, *Universalsukzession und Vonselbsterwerb: die Rechtstechnischen Grundlagen des deutschen Erbrechts* (1st edn, Mohr Siebeck, 2002) 11ff.

19 Literally: 'the dead seize the living'.

20 The Latin term denoting 'the vacant inheritance' not taken up by the successors.

21 See Article 1220 French *CC*, § 820 *ABGB*.

22 Article 51 of the Decree.

23 See § 1967 *BGB*, Article 873 and 1259 French *CC*, Article 1259 *Svod Zakonov*.

the prevailing principle of unlimited liability. Despite the uniform principle of unlimited liability, the actual level of liability profoundly differed in the various legal orders. Each system created an original mosaic of legal instruments restricting or modifying the unlimited liability. The aim of these instruments is to balance the degree of protection against the economic effects of succession between creditors and debtors of the succession, and the personal creditors of successors.[24] Their composition reflects the social, political and economic objectives of the national legislature.

Pursuant to French and Austrian law, the successor was allowed to limit the liability of succession debts at the moment of acceptance of the succession, by acceptance *cum beneficio inventarii*.[25] However, the consequences of the acceptance *cum beneficio inventarii* differed in Austrian and French law. Under French law, the successor who accepted the succession with the benefit of an inventory was only liable for debts up to the value of, and only of, the assets of the inherited estate.[26] According to Austrian law, the liability was limited up to the value of the inherited estate, but burdened the entire estate of the successor, unless the two estates, that is, that of the successor prior to the succession and the inherited estate, were separated.[27] The acceptance *cum beneficio inventarii* was not recognised in the German legal order, where successors were allowed to reject or to accept the succession, and the inventory was used for securing the inheritance, not for limiting liability.[28] In Germany the basic institute for limiting liability for succession debts was the public convocation procedure (convocation of creditors).[29] The convocation was recognised in the German and Austrian legal orders.[30] All of the referenced systems provided for other subsequent instruments to protect successors against the economic results of an over-indebted succession. The German legislature limited the liability of successors through the specific mechanism of prescription for claims brought later than five years after the devolution of the succession.[31] The German and French law-makers allowed the

24   The German *BGB* offered the most complicated but also most restrictive instruments for protecting successors. The Austrian and French law provided various instruments that served to balance the level of protection of creditors and debtors.

25   The Latin term for 'the benefit of inventory'.

26   See Article 802 French *CC*. See C. Demolombe, *O spadkach. Tom II* (1st edn, E Wende i Spółka, 1900) 75.

27   E. Till, *Wykład austryackiego prawa spadkowego. Tom VI* (1st edn, Księgarnia H Altenberga, 1904) 390ff.

28   F. Bossowski, F. Zoll and J. Wasilkowski, *Encyklopedja Podręczna Prawa Prywatnego* (1931) 2201; S. Szer, *Prawo spadkowe* (1st edn, Państwowe Wydawnictwo Naukowe, 1951) 125.

29   The successor who accepted a succession was allowed to request creditors of the inheritance to notify their claims. Successors were allowed to refuse claims of creditors excluded in the convocation procedure if the inherited assets were completely exhausted.

30   See § 1970 *BGB*.

31   See § 1974 *BGB*.

successor to escape from liability by transferring the inheritance to creditors,[32] but the conditions of these institutes were different in each of the systems. The German legislature was the only one that provided for insolvency proceedings.[33] The French, Austrian and Swiss legislatures proposed the liquidation system instead of the highly complicated and costly insolvency procedure.

Contrary to French, Austrian and German law, the Polish Decree provided a simplified system of liability for succession debts. In accordance with leading Western codifications the Polish legislature adopted the principle of unlimited and personal liability for succession debts. However, following the French, in preference to the Austrian model, the Decree entitled the successor to accept the succession *cum beneficio inventarii*.[34] Nevertheless, similarly to Austrian law, the result of *beneficio inventarii* was the limitation of the successor's personal liability up to the value of the inherited assets.[35] In contradistinction to the *ABGB*, the Decree did not allow for a reversion from acceptance *cum beneficio inventarii* to a straightforward acceptance. The Polish doctrine considered that this rule, similarly to German views, would interfere with the principle of unconditional acceptance of inheritance.

Both qualitative and quantitative analyses, carried out for purposes of this chapter, indicate that the Polish system of liability for succession debts was significantly simplified in comparison to other Western codifications. In the Polish Decree there were only 10 provisions regulating the whole system of liability for succession debts.[36] The Polish legislature did not adopt the convocation procedure, which provided a basic protection to successors and creditors in the German and Austrian order.[37] Nor were the institutes of formal separate administration of the inheritance, surrendering inheritance to creditors, or the insolvency procedure reflected in the Polish Decree.

The original instrument of the Polish system was the liquidation of the deceased's estate under the supervision of the Court, preceded by a separation of estates. The specific instrument dedicated to the protection of creditors was the separation of the inherited assets from the successor's estate (*separatio bonorum*). The separation of estates was also allowed under Austrian and French law.[38] However, the conditions for and effects of separation differed significantly in the Austrian, French and Polish legal orders.

---

32 See § 1992 *BGB*, Article 802 FR *CC*.

33 See § 1975 *BGB*.

34 See L.N. Brown, 'Inheritance and the Communist legal order' (1963) *Soviet Studies* 306.

35 Article 49 § 2 of the Decree.

36 The German legislature devoted 64 provisions for liability for succession debts, the Austrian 27 provisions and the French 36 provisions.

37 For general discussion of legal instruments modifying the unlimited liability for succession debts in Western provinces see A. Ohanowicz, 'Prawo spadkowe województw zachodnich' Zoll and Wasilkowski (n29) 2164ff. See also: Szer (n29) 125.

38 Cf. Article 878 French *CC*.

The Decree was undoubtedly inspired by the common nineteenth century means used to alleviate the challenges of a capitalist economy. Certain selected legal rules and institutes of the Western European codes were creatively transplanted into the Polish system of liability for succession debts. The Polish legislature, albeit inspired by leading European codes, created a markedly reduced system of liability. The Decree rejected the casuistic method of regulation particular to the *BGB*, as well as outdated rules found in the Austrian and French codes. Moreover, it jettisoned the complexity of provisions securing a balance between protection of successors and creditors.

The simplification of the system of liability was justified by the less affluent state of Polish society. In fact, the economic reality showed that even those instruments limiting liability which were used in the Decree were of little practical importance due to the economic condition of the country. Despite the fact that the Decree protected creditors more strongly than successors, such a narrowly regulated system of liability would not be sufficient for emerging capitalist reality. A glance at this set of provisions from today's perspective gives the impression that the legislature was uncertain as to the priorities and assumptions that should underlie the Decree. Although the Succession Decree provided for a unified system of liability, based on the capitalist-oriented Western models, it intuitively adapted them to the post-war economic and social conditions of the young liberal state.

New Economic Reality

The Polish law of succession entered the next phase of codification in the middle of the twentieth century. The aim of the transformation launched in 1948 was an approximation of the Eastern European legal systems to a new political, economic, cultural and legal model.[39]

The new approach reversed the way in which the existing codification was perceived and evaluated. The Decree was considered to be incompatible with values of the new economic system. The inadequacy of the existing law became an argument for the development of a new Civil Code.[40] The idea of 'social engineering through law' became alarmingly real.[41] It was stated that the assumptions of the new instruments of the law of succession should be based on an analysis of the degree of reconstruction of the socio-economic system, an assessment of the degree to which the institutes of the law of succession might foster the capitalist system, and define the range of instruments necessary to limit the operation of

---

39   A. Rudziński, 'Sovietisation of civil law in Poland' (1956) 15 *American Slavic and East European Review* 235.

40   Cf. Gwiazdomorski (n7) 23ff.

41   P. Cserne, 'Drafting civil codes in Central and Eastern Europe. A case study on the role of legal scholarship in law-making' (2011) *Pro Publico Bono* online 4.

the law of succession.[42] The law of succession was perceived as a pillar of the capitalist system[43] that hampered the creation of the new economic order.

The change of reference patterns resulted primarily in the idea to substitute the principle of limited liability for succession debts for the Polish system of liability.[44] It was, however, realised that the principle of limited liability, which protects successors not creditors, would backfire, since the largest creditors were mainly state entities disposing of public property. The idea was therefore abandoned and the proposal of limited liability for succession debts was quickly assessed as pointless, as well as unjustified in the new socio-economic circumstances.[45] In the rationale supporting the project of the new civil code it was pointed out that in the new economic order the indebtedness of natural persons above the value of their assets was the exception rather than the rule, with the result that complicated rules of liability for succession debts were redundant and should be repealed.[46] This reveals the extent to which the law of succession was influenced by economic policy at the time, the ideological programme of which consisted in the liquidation of capitalist private property and consequently denying the very existence of the law of succession.[47]

After being in force for 18 years the Decree of 1946 was replaced by the new Civil Code of 1964,[48] with effect from 1 January 1965. The system of liability reflected the rather minor importance of the law of succession for the legal system. Ideological and socio-economic assumptions resulted in further simplification of the system of liability for succession debts.[49] The Civil Code of 1964 abandoned the institutes of the separation of estate and the liquidation of the inheritance. According to the Polish legislature both instruments generally lost their practical meaning under the new legal order.

The new concept of liability for succession debts was constructively criticised by academics and lawyers.[50] Despite the high quality of legislative sophistication, the system of liability reflected the assumption of the limited scope of private property, the subsequent limitation of inherited assets and the protection of public creditors. The Code provided for a dual system of liability and a specific set of

---

42   See: J. Gwiazdomorski, 'Dziedziczenie ustawowe w projekcie Kodeksu cywilnego PRL' *Materiały Dyskusyjne do Projektu Kodeksu Cywilnego Polskiej Rzeczypospolitej Ludowej, Materiały Sesji Naukowej 8–10 grudnia 1954 r.* (1955) 222–4; also: S. Szer, 'Z zagadnień kodyfikacji prawa spadkowego (Uwagi ogólne)' (1951) 5–6 *PiP* 920ff.

43   Gwiazdomorski (n14) 13.

44   Comp. Brown (n35) 311.

45   Przybyłowski (n12) 246.

46   Przybyłowski (n12) 241.

47   K. Marks and F. Engels, *Manifest Komunistyczny* (20th edn, Książka i Wiedza, 1953) 59.

48   (1964) 16/93 *Journal of Laws*.

49   Przybyłowski (n12) 244; J. Gwiazdomorski, 'Prawo spadkowe w kodeksie cywilnym PRL' (1965) 5–6 *PiP* 722.

50   Gwiazdomorski (ibid.) 722, 725; J. Stanisław Piątowski, *System prawa cywilnego. Prawo spadkowe. t. IV* (Zakład Narodowy im. Ossolińskich, 1986) 33.

provisions regulated the liability for debts arising from agricultural farms (Article 1081 CC).[51]

The protection of the successor was reduced to the right to waive the succession or accept it with the *beneficium inventarii*. If the successor let the time allotted for making an inventory elapse, he was regarded as accepting the succession straightforwardly and therefore liable for all its debts without limits (implied unlimited liability).[52] The acceptance *cum beneficio inventarii* became the single instrument for limiting the liability of successor for the inherited debts. Besides removing the traditional individual instruments protecting successors or creditors, the Polish legislature adopted additional rules to protect the creditors of the succession. The joint and several liability of co-successors until the partitioning of the succession (Article 1034 CC), as well as the restricted impact of a defective inventory of the estate (Article 1031 § 2 CC), or improper repayment of succession debts by a successor accepting succession *cum beneficio inventarii* (Article 1032 CC) significantly undermined the economic security of successors.

The system of liability for succession debts reflected the assumption of the progressive reduction of private property. The set of reduced provisions contrasted strongly with the more comprehensive systems of liability for succession debts followed by Western economies. This was, nevertheless, a system generally based on the Decree and thus influences by legal instruments taken from leading European Codifications. It was stated that the Civil Code was still a synthesis of elements derived from French, Austrian and German legislation, which were 'creatively developed' and 'melted into a new and original legal work'.[53]

The Picture Today and Future Perspectives

The reduced system of the liability for succession debts has generally been left unchanged since 1965. The process of transition from a socialist to market economy, launched in 1989, reveals a deepening inadequacy of the applicable rules of liability for succession debts to meet the changing circumstances. The availability of credit for natural persons combined with a lack of accumulated private assets increases the risk of inheriting an over-indebted succession. The existing system of liability for succession debts does not provide the successor with legal instruments that ensure a limitation of liability even if the succession is accepted with the benefit of an inventory. The entire system of liability perfectly

---

51   This was a consequence of distinct rules of inheriting agricultural farms, which served to protect agricultural farms against partitioning caused by division of inheritance.

52   There are exceptions to the implied simple acceptance. Pursuant to Article 1015 para. 2 CC if the heir is a person who does not have full capacity for legal acts or a person with respect to whom there are grounds for full legal incapacitation, or a legal person whose failure to declare causes the acceptance under benefit of inventory.

53   L. Górnicki, *System prawa prywatnego. T. I* (2007) 120ff.

reflects the statement, originating from German *doctrine* that 'the liability for succession debts is like a mousetrap'.[54]

The idea of reforming the provisions of liability was presented in the 'Green Book – the Optimal Vision of the Civil Code', published in 2006. The Polish legislature surprisingly positively, but hastily, assessed the quality of the system of liability for succession debts and listed only sample postulates *de lege ferenda*.[55] Among the proposals mentioned by the Polish national legislature, were the regulation of the convocation procedure and the maintenance of joint and several liability of co-heirs after the division of the estate.

To date the applicable law still reflects the economic foundations of the socialist system and clearly favours the principle of the protection of creditors. The selective re-codification of 2009 brought about a new instrument, the absolute legacy (*zapis windykacyjny*, Articles 981¹–981⁶ and 1034¹–1034³ CC). According to Article 1034³ CC the legatee is liable for succession debts, always limited, up to the value of the legacy. The reform has resulted in the creation of a parallel system of liability for succession debts which on the one hand is much more favourable to legatees, but on the other hand has aggravated the position of successors.

In May 2013, the Polish Codification Commission launched a re-codification proposal. The draft proposal amends the provision of Article 1015 § 2 CC and provides for the implied limited liability for succession debts. Additionally, an entirely new instrument, the inventory list of the inheritance, which is a private document drawn up by successors involving a notary public and serving to determine the composition of the inheritance assets (*wykaz inwentarza*), has been proposed.

The Codification Commission is still continuing work on the new codification. It is impossible to predict the final form that the provisions of liability for succession debts will take. Nevertheless, the entire statements and draft signal the removal of the key risks resulting from inheriting debts exceeding assets. In achieving that aim, the system will probably become much more complex as the result of the introduction of instruments allowing for the factual realisation of limited liability, such as a convocation procedure, a hierarchy of debts, the separation of assets, or a liquidation procedure.

European Perspective

The ongoing Europeanisation of private law seems to provide two avenues of development: the unification of the law of succession in the form of a single

---

54   R. Meyer-Pritzl and J von Staudinger, *Kommentar zum Bürgerlichen Gesetzbuch mit Einführungsgesetz und Nebengesetzen. Teil Y. Erbrecht*, available at <www. beck-online.beck.de> (2012) 116, accessed 20 June 2013.

55   Z. Radwański, *Zielona Księga. Optymalna wizja Kodeksu cywilnego w Rzeczypospolitej Polskiej, Komisja Kodyfikacyjna Prawa Cywilnego działająca przy Ministrze Sprawiedliwości* (1st edn, Oficyna Wydawnicza MS, 2006) 147.

Act applicable across Europe, or merely interaction between the European legal environment and the codification of the national law of succession. Although substantive provisions of the law of succession are left to the exclusive competences of the national legislature, national drafts might follow EU codification standards.[56]

The European legislature has not made the harmonisation of the substantive provisions of the law of succession a priority. It is also unlikely that any hypothetical European Civil Code will cover the law of succession. To date, the legislative work conducted at European level has focused on some selected problems of private international law, such as the European Testament or European Certificate of Succession.[57]

The idea of harmonising the substantive law on succession is not unrealistic. The persistent emphasis on the failure of the harmonisation process to properly approximate the substantive law ignores the fact that similar doubts were presented towards the earlier studies on the Europeanisation of family law. The research of the Commission of European Family Law[58] reveals that it is possible to find a common denominator for provisions that are deeply rooted in profoundly different cultures.[59] Common values, principles and legal constructions can also be found within the area of the law of succession.

The development of the Polish law of succession in the twentieth century did not proceed in isolation from the European legal environment. Rather there was a perceptible diffusion of rules and concepts that were then conditioned by the geographic, political and economic context of Poland. As these conditions have changed so too has the law. Today contemporary changes to the Polish law of succession occur in the European environment. It remains unknown how these universal determinants will influence the future evolution and diffusion of the national legal orders in Europe.

---

56   M. Pazdan Radwański (n56) 183.

57   Regulation (EU) No 650/2012 of 4 July 2012 of the European Parliament and of the Council on jurisdiction, applicable law, recognition and enforcement of decisions and acceptance and enforcement of authentic instruments in matters of succession and on the creation of a European Certificate of Succession (2012) OJ C 201/107.

58   See: <http://ceflonline.net/>.

59   See, for example, K. Boele-Woelki and D. Martiny, The Commission on European Family Law (CEFL) and its principles of European family law regarding parental responsibilities, ERA Forum (2007) 8 125–143. See also: K. Boele-Woelki, B. Braat and I. Curry-Sumner (eds), *European Family Law in Action: Volume I – Grounds for Divorce* (Intersentia, 2003); *European Family Law in Action Volume II – Maintenance between Former Spouses* (Intersentia, 2003); *European Family Law in Action Volume III – Parental Responsibilities*; *European Family Law in Action Volume IV – Property Relations between Spouses* (Intersentia, 2009).

Chapter 12

Albanian Civil Law and the Influence of Foreign Laws

Juliana Latifi

Introduction

While Albanian civil law is young,[1] it has had time to undergo fundamental transformations in three different time periods. Each codification of Albanian civil law from 1928 up to now has been a reflection of the country's social and economic situation at the time. As part of these transformations, foreign laws have had, and continue to have, a considerable influence on Albanian civil law, thus begging the question of the manner and degree to which foreign law has in fact influenced Albanian law. First of all, one needs to note that this influence has differed: Albanian civil law has shifted from the civil law family tradition to socialist law, only to return again to the civil law tradition – but without completely losing the signs of socialist law.

Since 1928, Albanian civil legislation has passed through four distinct stages:

- the Civil Code of the Albanian Kingdom which was approved in 1928 and entered into force on 1 April 1929;
- Albanian civil legislation of the period between 1945 and 1981;
- the Civil Code of the Socialist People's Republic of Albania which was approved in 1981 and entered into force on 1 January 1982; and
- the current Civil Code of the Republic of Albania, which entered into force on 1 November 1994.

This chapter will describe the historical evolution of Albania civil law and also consider the influence of foreign law in the development of its patterning and the continuing significance this has had and still has in locating Albania within the broader legal map of the world. It will be evident that the evolution of the Albanian civil legislation was not a smooth one: the repeal of one law leaving its place for another one. This was dictated by a radical and violent overthrow whereby a social system was replaced by another – based on the doctrine of the communist state, and without maintaining the prior heritage created over

---

1   The Albanian Civil Code entered in force almost one century later than French Civil Code (1804) and Italian Civil Code (1865).

the years. It is important, therefore, to emphasise that the legal inheritance from the pre-war period, including the Civil Code of the Albanian Kingdom, the jurisprudence and the limited legal doctrine of the time, was regarded as 'hostile' and contrary to 'communist morality'. Consequently everything from this period was considered 'archival' and could not be used even for research purposes. The legislation of this period was completely annulled and replaced by the 'new legislation' of the state of the dictatorship of the proletariat.[2] The extreme actions of the communist state of the time knew no limits: in 1966, even the Ministry of Justice was abolished.[3]

Today Albania aspires to be part of the EU. This aspiration has been reflected, for example, in the signing of the 2006 EU-Albania Stabilisation and Association Agreement.[4] In light of this state of affairs, the need to make amendments to the Civil Code has become crucial in order to respond to new economic and social developments in Albania and also to approximate Albania's legislation to the EU's *acquis*, based on Article 70(1) of the above-mentioned Stabilisation and Association Agreement which states:

> [T]he Parties recognise the importance of the approximation of Albania's existing legislation to that of the Community and of its effective implementation. Albania shall endeavor to ensure that its existing laws and future legislation shall be gradually made compatible with the Community *acquis*. Albania shall ensure that existing and future legislation shall be properly implemented and enforced.

Civil Code of the Albanian Kingdom and the Influence of Foreign Law

After a five-century period under the Ottoman Empire, during which the Islamic traditions of *Sharia* and *Mexhele*[5] constituted the basic law in the country, and after the long conflicts before and following the first World War, the Albanian state, which was created on 28 November 1912, began, for the first time, to regulate private-law relations through a Civil Code that was quite advanced for the time. The Civil Code of the Albanian Kingdom of 1928 entered into force on

---

2   J.H. Merryman, *The Civil Law Tradition* (2nd edn, Stanford University Press, 1985) 4–5.

3   The Ministry of Justice was abolished in 1966 and was then re-established in 1990 with the proclamation of democracy in Albania.

4   Ligji *'Për ratifikimin e Marrëveshjes së Stabilizim-Asocimit ndërmjet Republikës së Shqipërisë dhe Komuniteteve Europiane e Shteteve të tyre Anëtare'* Law No. 9590, signed 27 July 2006 OJ [2006] No. 87 (hereinafter Stabilization and Association Agreement).

5   *Sharia* was the Islamic law while *Mexhele* was the Turkish Civil Code during the Ottoman Empire.

1 April 1929,[6] at the start of the consolidation of the Albanian state.[7] This code was considered to be a 'great achievement' because of its values and importance that marked the beginning of the development of capitalist relations in Albania.[8]

The 1928 Civil Code – sometimes called the Civil Code of Zog[9] (hereinafter referred to as the ZCC), was influenced by the French model (Civil Code of Napoleon). It constituted a novelty in the circumstances of the Albanian state and society of the time. Foreign laws[10] – not only French and Italian (primarily) but also German and Swiss laws, to some extent, inspired Albanian legislation to provide for the equality of all citizens, the emancipation of land ownership, and the freedom to engage in economic activities. The acceptance of foreign law in the ZCC was not as much an 'issue of quality' as it was an 'issue of power'[11] because foreign civil codes and some laws, especially the French and Italian models, which had the most influence upon the Albanian Civil Code, were laws belonging to the thinking and norms of movements such as the Italian Renaissance and the French Revolution, which had had a profound influence upon modern western civilisation.

The entry into force of the ZCC also meant that Albanian civil law now belonged to the Roman-German family,[12] thereby detaching it permanently from

---

6   The Albanian territory from the fifteenth century to the beginning of the twentieth century was a Province of the Ottoman Empire. Albania could not have its own civil legislation as all civil relationships were regulated by Islamic tradition and legislation (*Sharia*, *Mexhele* and the Land Code). During this period cannon law was practiced simultaneously with Islamic law.

7   The beginning of the existence of Albania, a small country situated in the western part of Balkan Peninsula, as an internationally recognised state occurred after its admission to the League of Nations, on 17 December 1920 and pursuant the Decision of 9 November 1921 of the Conference of the Ambassadors in Paris, which confirmed the independence of the Albanian State, which has been self-proclaimed by the Albanians on 29 November 1912. The state borders were also defined in 1913 by the Conference of Ambassadors of the Principal Allied and Associated Powers (Great Britain, Germany, Russia, Austro-Hungarian Empire, France and Italy). On this see also, A. Puto, *Shqipëria Politike 1912–1939* (1st edn, Dudaj, 2009) 469–70.

8   A. Luarasi et al., *Historia e shtetit dhe e së drejtës në Shqipëri* (5th edn, Luarasi University Press, 2007) 398–404.

9   Ahmet Zogu was the King of Albania during the period from 1928 to 1939.

10   *Tabelë konkordimi mid's Kodit Civil Shqiptar dhe Kodeve të hueja* [Table of the concordance of the Albanian Civil Code and Foreign Civil Codes] (Edition of Civil Code 1929, Papirus edn, 2010); See Puto (n7) 470.

11   K. Zweigert and H. Kötz, *An Introduction to Comparative Law. General Principles. Vol. I.* (2nd edn, trans. M. Semini Tutulani, SHBLU (Publishing House of the University Library) 1994), 136.

12   C.J.J.M. Stolker was involved in the project for the drafting the new Albania Civil Code from the Council of Europe in conjunction with the Italian lawyer, Prof. Gianmaria Ajani and the French law professor Georges Wiederkehr (who was the head of the team). In his article, C.J.J.M. Stolker, 'Drafting a new civil code for Albania. Some personal experiences contrasted with the World Bank's initial lessons' (1997) Leiden University

Ottoman law. The jurists of the time, who had a western education, based the design of the ZCC on the following main legal acts:[13]

- the French Civil Code (1804) (hereinafter FCC);
- the Italian Civil Code (1865) (hereinafter ICC);
- the Preliminary Provisions of the Italian Civil Code (1865);
- the German Civil Code (1900) (*Bürgerliches Gesetzbuch*) (hereinafter referred to as the BGB) (1990);
- the Italian Nationality Law (1912);
- the Swiss Civil Code (1912);
- the Joint Italian-French project 'On Obligations' (*Des obligations/Delle Obbligazioni*) (1928).

General Concepts and Institutes of Law in the ZCC

The 1928 Civil Code contained a total of 2,047 articles, the majority of which were based on the French and Italian codes, but at the same time the influence of the German and Swiss legislation was also obvious. One of the ZCC's special features was that in its fourth and final book, it enacted into law the Italian-French project 'On Obligations'.

Therefore, the structure and content of the Code was clearly based on more than one model.

The first book, entitled *Persons and Family*, was a combination of French, Italian, German and Swiss legislation – specifically, the civil codes of the period. The book begins with provisions relating to the civil rights enjoyed by every Albanian citizen, followed by rules and regulations governing the right to be granted, or to be deprived of, Albanian citizenship – here, under the influence of the French model. This part was followed by provisions on civil-status acts, again, along the lines of the French model, in which the family was considered to be one of the achievements of the French revolution.[14]

Internationale Juristenvereinigung Osnabrück 1997, available at <https://openaccess.leidenuniv.nl/handle/1887/1302> accessed 2 April 2013, he wrote:

> [T]he first Code, adopted in 1928, was a draft prepared by a Commission of five members, which was strongly patterned on the French (1804 *Code Civil*) and Italian (1865 *Codice Civile*) models.

13   G.F. Ajani, 'Codification of civil law in Albania' in G. Ginsburgs, D.D. Barry and W.B. Simons (eds), *The Revival of Private Law in Central and Eastern Europe* (Martinus Nijhoff Publishers, 1996) 518, he wrote:

> Examination of the 1928 *Kodi Civil* shows that it was broadly patterned on French Civil Code and the 1865 Italian Civil Code. Elements were also drawn from the Italian-French draft on Obligation. [...] Less important influences, limited to isolated provisions, echo the Swiss Civil Code and Code of Obligation.

14   See Zweigert and Kötz (n11) 125.

Under the influence of the German and Swiss models, the ZCC regulated legal persons. In terms of regulating this part of the law, the Albanian Code was quite advanced for the time (although Albania was still a feudal country). The goal of the Code was to facilitate the capitalist development of the country, legalising for the first time the creation of commercial legal persons. Furthermore, it also allowed for the establishment of associations that had no commercial purposes as legal persons, and it acknowledged associations of a political nature (Art. 424, ZCC).

Like the Italian Civil Code, the second book of the ZCC was entitled 'Inheritance'. Here, the ZCC regulated the institute of inheritance in a separate book – unlike the French Civil Code, in which inheritance was perceived as a separate institution, under the title *Des différentes manières dont on acquiert la propriété*. Most of the provisions of this second book were based on the Italian Civil Code but also influenced by the French Civil Code. In fact, the second book may be considered one of the major achievements of the ZCC. It marked for the first time in the Albanian legal landscape that inheritance issues were regulated under the influence of a progressive philosophy: the right to inheritance should be enjoyed by every individual, a concept borrowed from the FCC, including by children born outside wedlock, and the right to inheritance was provided not only to men but also to women, an approach with was regarded as being quite advanced for the time.[15] Also, for the first time in Albanian legislation, wills were deemed to be the expression of the free will of the testator and the regulation of wills in this book was of major importance.

The third book of the ZCC was entitled *Objects, Ownership, and Its Modifications*. Comparing this structure to that of the Italian Civil Code, the third part of which was entitled just *Della proprietà*, or to the French Civil Code, the second part of which was entitled *Des différentes manières dont on acquiert la propriété*, one can see that all of the articles in this book were based on the provisions of both the Italian Code and the French Code.[16] On the right to ownership, the ZCC presented the principle that, 'Ownership shall be the right to enjoy and dispose of a property, without any other limitations besides those regulated in law or by regulation'.[17] The concept of ownership was, therefore, based on *corpus* and *animus*.[18] However, possession of movable property was

---

15   Puto (n7) 470.

16   Zweigert and Kotz (n11) 143. This book (Part 8 – The reception of the Code Civil) highlighted the fact that:

> [T]here was a noticeable French influence on Italian jurists. It is not strange that, starting from the nineteenth century and thereafter, Italian jurists based Italian law exclusively on the French law and especially in the framework of private law for which the Civil Code of Napoleon adopted in 1804 represented a source of inspiration for Italian jurisprudence.

17   Art. 794, ZCC.

18   Ownership consists of a physical element, the *corpus* (physical performance acts on the object) and a psychological element, the *animus domini* (affirmation of the intention to be owner). On this see also, F. Terré and P. Simler, *Droit Civil. Les biens* (7th edn, Dalloz, 2006) 148–9; M. Fromont, *Grands system de droit étranger* (5th edn, Dalloz, 2005) 60.

equated with the right to maintain ownership of the property (*en fait de meubles possession vaut titre*).[19]

The fourth book of the ZCC also concerned property and was entitled *Methods of Acquisition and Transference of Ownership and Other Rights to Objects*, and was inspired by the Italian–French project *On Obligations* (1928).[20] This book was preceded by a general provision that stated, 'Ownership shall be acquired through conquest. Ownership and other rights to properties shall be acquired and transferred through inheritance and conventions. It may also be acquired through prescription'.[21] In the fourth book, the ZCC regulated different kinds of contracts, including an intertwining of those contracts which were considered as traditional contracts, such as: contracts of sale, exchange, donation, *emphyteusis*, rent, permanent royalties, use of borrowings, loans and guarantees, with new contracts which reflected the development of capitalist relations at the time, such as: labour contracts, entrepreneurship contracts and contracts of association, prescription, transaction, gambling, deposits and others. The fourth book also included the registration or notation of property in public registers. Through property transcription, this Civil Code (which was the first and only one in the history of the Albanian state since the declaration of independence from the Turkish Empire on 28 November 1912, until 29 November 1944, National Liberation Day) marked the initiation of a new era. In doing so the ZCC followed the line of the major civil codes[22] of the time, in which property was considered sacrosanct and enjoyed absolute protection. The ZCC also contained a list of the limitations in the regulation of the rights to real property, as found in the French and Italian codes.[23]

The entry into force of the ZCC of 1928 was accompanied by the Law Provisions on the Application of the Civil Code. An important feature of this law was the adoption of a rule that repealed Ottoman law once and for all:

> *Mexhele*, the Land Code, as well as all other provisions of *Sharia* and the ecclesiastical provisions belonging to the family law and other civil laws, all laws and regulations in general running afoul of the new Civil Code, shall be repealed. (Art. 61, ZCC)

However, the new Civil Code would not last long. Despite the values the ZCC presented, having been based on the contemporary legislation of the time, the

---

19   B. Benussi, *Sendet, Pronësia dhe modifikimet e saj. Libri i tretë i K.C.Z.* (1st edn, Ministry of Justice, 1931) 86.

20   This project was aimed at unifying the obligations' laws in Italy and in France. It introduced the joint work of an Italian–French commission that was chaired by two distinguished jurists of the time, Édouard Lambert, a legal scholar from Lyon (1866–1947) and Vittorio Scialoja (1856–1933), an Italian politician who was Minister of Justice in 1909 and Minister of Foreign Affairs in 1919.

21   Art. 1067, ZCC.

22   French Civil Code, German Civil Code, Italian Civil Code and Swiss Civil Code.

23   See Fromont (n18) 60.

changes that took place in Albania following the Second World War and the establishment of the so-called 'power of the people' would lead to its repeal in 1945.[24]

Albanian Civil Legislation During the Period 1945–1981

The next period in Albania's legal history was clearly influenced by the socialist law of the Soviet Union. The Italian, French, German and Swiss laws and the jurisprudence that had been the basis of much of Albania's civil legislation in the previous period were now seen as part of the legal and cultural baggage of capitalist states. As such, they were certainly not suitable as sources of legislation in Albania's new socialist society. That said, Soviet socialist law was based on the *Pandectist* system and, as a result, Albania's socialist law preserved a certain German influence, albeit an indirect one.[25]

According to Carel Stolker:

> Albanian's civil legislation of the time was inspired by the Marxist-Leninist doctrine. Technically, it contained elements of the Soviet model, but it also followed a German pattern which was also reflected in Soviet codifications. After World War II, and before 1981, Albanian civil legislation was enacted in the form of separate statutes.[26]

Once the Civil Code of 1928 was repealed, legislators followed by issuing legislation adapted to the new forms of social and economic relations that were appearing in the new socialist society. Beginning in the 1950s, a number of new laws regarding civil-law relations were adopted, including: 'Law No. 2022 of 2 April 1955 'On the General Part of the Civil Code of the People's Republic of Albania'; Decree No. 2359 of 15 November 1956 'On Legal Transaction and Obligations'; Decree No. 1892 of 5 July 1954 'On Inheritance'; and Decree No. 2083 of 6 July 1955 'On Ownership'.[27]

---

24 In accordance with Law No. 61 of 17 May 1945 ['On the Repeal of Legal Provisions Promulgated During the Foreign Occupation and on the Validity of the Legal Provisions in Force Before 7 April 1939', all of the old legislation was to be repealed and replaced by the new legal order based on the new democratic nature, an expression of the winning of the National Liberation War] (author tr.).

25 This itself was one of the systems of civil law family according to which the civil code is structured into five parts: General Part, Law of Obligation, Law of Real Rights, Family Law and Inheritance Law. This system is applied in the German, Swiss and Portuguese Civil Codes.

26 Stolker (n12) 31.

27 G. Hamza, 'Continuity and discontinuity of private/civil law in Eastern Europe after World War II' (2006) Vol. 12 Issue 1/2006 *Fundamina Journal*, available at <http://uir. unisa.ac.za/bitstream/handle/10500/3666/hamza congress CC.pdf> accessed 3 April 2013:

> [T]he countries of this region may be divided basically into three major groups according to their own legal traditions. Group "A" comprises countries

In the jurisprudence of the time, the creation of the legal norms established
by the above-mentioned acts, were considered to be based on a defined system,
according to which:

> We have a systematic regulation of the norms of our civil law, which in general
> is fair and appropriate for the relations regulated by our civil law, which [...]
> are mainly property relations, based on the system of the socialist economy and
> socialist ownership [...].[28]

Thus, the civil-law system in the jurisprudence of the time was conceived of in the
following way:

- The general part of the law included subjects of the law (physical and legal
  persons), objects (properties) of civil-law relations, legal transactions,
  representation and prescription.
- Ownership law included ownership in all its forms, socialist state
  ownership, cooperative socialist ownership, social ownership, personal
  and private ownership, as well as the institutes of possession and burden on
  immovable properties.
- Legal transactions and the law of obligations were included in a separate
  law. It did not divide the law into obligations and contracts,[29] in which the
  latter were considered as special obligations and their number was limited,
  embracing the principle of *numerus clausus* (Art. 33(2), Decree 'On Legal
  Transactions and Obligations').
- Copyright law, was regulated for the first time by Decree No. 4389,
  dated 7.05.1968 'On copyright' and Decree 4548, dated 3.10.1969, 'On
  inventions and rationalizations'. Both decrees envisaged the intellectual
  and industrial rights in a moral and material way.[30]

---

like the former Union of Soviet Socialist Republics (USSR), the former
Czechoslovakia, at present the Czech Republic and Slovakia (after the demise of
Czechoslovakia on 1 January 1993), Poland and Hungary which are characterized
by [the] adoption of socialist civil codes. Group "B" is characterized – like
Bulgaria and Albania (until the promulgation of the Civil Code in 1981) – by
having adopted special laws relating for instance to the law of property, the law
of obligations, the law of succession, [et cetera]. Group "C" (e.g., Romania)
is characterized by conserving its former "bourgeois" (i.e. non-socialist)
Civil Code.

28   A. Nathanaili, *E drejta civile e Republikës Popullore të Shqipërisë* Vol. I (5th edn,
Revista-Dispenca, 1974) 29.

29   A. Sallabanda, *E drejta e detyrimeve* (5th edn, SHBLU (Publishing House of the
University Library) 1987) 27.

30   Copyright law and the law of inventions, under the influence of Soviet legal
doctrine were considered as part of the specific civil law. On this see D.M. Genkin et al.,
E drejta civile sovjetike (Sovetskoe grazhdanskoe pravo) (2nd edn, Ministry of Justice of

- Family law was regulated by Law No. 4020 (Family Code) dated 23.06.1965. This code was very important because for the first time all types of family relations (marriage, divorce, adoption, tutorship, etc.) were specifically regulated by law.
- Inheritance was regulated by Decree No. 1892, dated 5.07.1954 'On Inheritance', which envisaged the statutory regime and testate succession. The right of heirs was up to the third degree (sisters and brothers of deceased). The law acknowledged only a will made by a notarial act (Art. 41).

In this model, Albanian civil law followed the *Pandectist* system, using special laws to regulate the following: general principles of civil law; the law of obligations; real rights; family law, and inheritance law.[31] These special laws, which were drafted in accordance with the Soviet model,[32] marked the initiation of the inclusion of Albanian civil law within the family of socialist law.

The laws of the time were considered a 'legal superstructure' built upon the new forms of economic relations appearing in Albania in the process of establishing a socialist society.[33] Nevertheless, despite the changes taking place in Albania at the time, private property did not completely disappear and it was still recognised as one form of ownership. However, this was short-lived, as the massive nationalisations and expropriations that were then undertaken led to the gradual disappearance of private property and the rise of new concepts such as state ownership of everything and the individual right to personal property only. These new concepts were reflected in the legislation that followed in 1981 that would regulate civil-law relations for a period of almost 12 years.

Albania People Republic tr, 1951, MDRPSH (Ministry of Justice of the People's Republic of Albania) 1956) 233.

31   This opinion has been clearly explained by Hamza (n27), available at <http://uir. unisa.ac.za/bitstream/handle/10500/3666/hamza congress CC.pdf>, he wrote:

In the countries of Central and Eastern Europe, the legal traditions that are in substance based either directly on Roman law or on *Pandectist* legal traditions have to be taken into consideration.

32   I. Elezi, *Mendimi juridik Shqiptar* (1st edn, Albin, 1999) 80, he wrote:

[For the purpose of establishing the system of law and legislation in general, the Soviet law and legislation had been used as models. The theory in all the sectors of the rule of law was a development of these bases. Albanian legal thought in that period was mainly oriented towards the Soviet one and it supported the socialist system] (author tr.).

33   Art. 1(2), Civil Code of 1981 provided: [[T]he civil law shall be based on the socialist social order established in the Constitution of the People's Republic of Albania], while Art. 2(2) of the same law provided that: [Civil rights may not be exercised in opposition to the duties of the socialist establishment or socialist cohabitation rules] (author tr.).

The Civil Code of 1981

The fact that Albanian civil law belonged to the family of socialist law became clear with the Civil Code of 1981, adopted by Law No. 6340 of 26 June 1981 on the Civil Code of the Socialist People's Republic of Albania,[34] which entered into force on 1 January 1982.

According to Professor Gianmaria Ajani:

> The second Civil Code of Albania adopted in 1981 was inspired by Marxist-Leninist Doctrine. Technically, it contained elements of the Soviet model, but it also followed a German (that is to say *Pandectist*) scheme which we find in Soviet codification as well.[35]

The communist ideology was embodied in the content, duties, foundations and principles of civil legislation, in which:

> The Civil legislation of the Socialist People's Republic of Albania shall express the will of the working class and other working masses, organized in the proletariat dictatorship state. Juridical-civil relations shall be based on the socialist ownership of production tools and the socialist economy system. (Art. 1(3), Civil Code)[36]

The principle of the Constitution of 1976 that definitively denied the right of the individual to private property and under which the state owned everything,[37] resulted in the loss of the underlying foundations of civil-law relations, primarily property relations, because the individual was stripped of the right to property. Confirmation of this can be found in Art.7 of this Civil Code which provided: 'The regulation of civil-law relations shall be carried out under the condition [...] that private property has disappeared'.

The institute of ownership was divided henceforth into two types: state ownership and individual ownership. According to the principles established in the articles of this institute, 'State property shall belong to all the people and shall be the highest form of socialist property. The state shall be the sole owner of all state property' (Art. 70(1) and (2), Civil Code). The Code did not recognise other real rights at all. They were non-existent for the legislator at that time.

The Civil Code of 1981 was framed in a very simple way and contained only 354 articles. It could be said that its contents were too sparse compared to the

---

34 *Kodi Civil i Republikës Popullore Socialiste të Shqipërisë*, No. 6340 signed 26 June 1981, *Kodet e Republikës Popullore Socialiste të Shqipërisë* [1982] (hereinafter the Civil Code of 1981).

35 Ajani (n13) 518.

36 Ajani (n13) 51.

37 See Terré and Simler (n18) 98.

Soviet legislation or to that of other socialist states.[38] The loss of the property foundations that underpinned the civil-law relations of individuals defined the fate of the Code, which contained a limited number of legal provisions in which the main institutes of the civil law were minimised or left unregulated. Professor Gianmaria Ajani wrote:

> Moreover, the self-sufficient Albanian regime, run by Party leaders for many decades, isolated the country from international trade and the world market. [...] The unique isolation of Albania from world economy, in sum, did not permit the 1981 Civil Code to adapt to changing circumstances and, therefore, the Code, in fact, outlived the legal culture that created it.[39]

Or, in the words of Professor Stolker:

> The 1981 Civil Code was unsatisfactory in certain important respects, it is inferior to other socialist codes because it lacks even those fundamental rules on private or individual activity that were found in most other socialist legislation.[40]

Inheritance, for example, was not acknowledged as a separate institute but was regulated as a type of acquisition of ownership, because the individual had very limited rights to devise and inherit. The limited number of legal heirs up to the third degree, which ended with siblings or the children of siblings, as well as grandparents, showed the limitations that had been placed on this institute. In the event that there were none of the above-mentioned family members, the property of a deceased went to the state (Arts 106 and 107, Civil Code). Similarly, institutes such as legacies and burdens,[41] found in the legislation of all Western countries, were not regulated in the provisions on inheritance relations. The principle that an inheritance is opened when the person leaving the inheritance dies and that it is regulated in conformity with the law of the time when it is opened was also seriously infringed in the final and transitory provisions of the 1981 Code.[42] Article 352(1) provided that, 'The provisions on the acquisition of ownership through inheritance shall be implemented also for inheritances opened prior to the entry into force of this Code'. In drafting this this rule, the legislator gave the new law (CC, 1981) retroactive power for

---

38   Elezi (n32) 133.
39   Ajani (n13) 519.
40   Stolker (n12).
41   A testator may charge the heir or the heirs appointed by will to perform an action beneficial to the society or to perform any other action, without conferring any benefit on the person charged with this action (hence the term: burden).
42   N. Biçoku, *E drejta e Trashëgimisë e Republikës së Shqipërisë* (4th edn, Onufri, 1997) 28–32.

legal relationships that originated under the previous juridical regime, contrary to traditional legal doctrine of civil law (also observed previously in Albanian) that the heritage relations were governed only by the law in force at the time of death of the deceased.

The same phenomenon occurred in the regulation of the institute of obligations and contracts. There was no distinction made between obligations and contracts.[43] The definition of the contract in the code's provisions was of a very special nature, thus; 'Citizens shall sign contracts for the fulfillment of their material and cultural needs as well as for the use, enjoyment, and provision of their individual properties' (Art. 142(3), Civil Code). The Code established the principle of *numerus clausus*, the so-called principle of the limitation of permitted contracts.[44] Furthermore, a considerable number of important civil contracts that were in use in the private market were not recognised or regulated by the 1981 Civil Code at all, as a consequence of the fact that private property had been disallowed. These included contracts such as: *emphyteusis*, entrepreneurship, banking, franchising, royalties, insurance and others. Despite these features, which were the result of the communist regime of the time, the Code respected the rules of codification in so far as:

1. Numerous forms of socio-economic relations were regulated by laws, and, specifically, civil-law relations.
2. The Code included within its provisions the principles of the Constitution of 1976. It enforced the Constitution in the hierarchy of legal acts.
3. It was in harmony with other laws operating within the framework of civil-law relations.

Also, as with many conventional continental codes, the Civil Code of 1981 was divided in two parts: general and specific. The institutes of the general part included: civil-law relations and legal transactions, subjects of civil-law relations, representation, and prescription (under the Soviet model).

The following institutes were included in the specific part: ownership (inheritance was not a separate institute but was incorporated in this part because as indicated above, it was considered a method of acquiring ownership), and obligations, including contracts. However, the general and specific parts were, in fact, intertwined. The principles provided in the general part regulated other institutes found in the specific part – not unlike the BGB.

In general terms this was the pattern of the 1981 Civil Code in structure and content. The Civil Code of 1981 was in force for a period of almost 12 years. The changes that occurred in Albania in the 1990s, however, made its continued existence impossible.

---

43 Sallabanda (n29).

44 M. Semini, 'Të rejat që solli Kodi i ri Civil lidhur me kontratat dhe interpretimin e tyre' (1995) No. 3 *Revista Drejtësia* 33.

The Civil Code of 1994

The shifting of regimes and the entry of Albania's economy into the free market after the 1990s called for the adoption of a new civil code that would have to fill a very large legislative gap, regulating the new forms of relations that had started to appear, as well as paving the way to sanction them in an economy on the road to capitalist reforms.

The drafting of the new 1994 Civil Code was preceded by the adoption of two very important laws that provided the foundation for acknowledging and sanctioning private property.[45] Law No. 7512 of 10 August 1991 'On sanctioning and protecting private property and free initiative, private independent activities and privatization', provided that, 'all sectors of the economy [were] free to be privatized and [could be used] for the exercise of private activity' (Art. 3).[46] Under this framework, every natural or legal person would enjoy the right to privatisation thereby creating a category of subjects based on this law and called the 'new owners' of former state property.

Further, the regulation of civil-law relations would be carried out through the adoption, *inter alia*, of Law No. 7698 of 15 April 1993 'On restitution and compensation of property to the former owners'. After 50 years, the state acknowledged the right of ownership of former owners or their heirs with respect to 'nationalized, expropriated, or confiscated properties, under legal and subordinate legal acts, as well as court decisions, issued after 29 November 1944 or wrongfully seized by the state, in any other way' (Art. 1).[47] The adoption of this law not only marked an important moment for Albania, but it also put an end to the injustices previously perpetrated by the state. The above-mentioned laws paved the way for the restoration and recognition of private property, a reality that remains present in Albania today.

Albania's Civil Code of 1994, adopted by Law No. 7850 of 29 July 1994, entered into force on 1 November 1994 (hereinafter sometimes referred to as the ACC). The Code was adopted pursuant to Law No. 7491 of 29 April 1991 on

---

45   Ajani (n13) 520 wrote:
    In recent years all post-socialist countries have adopted (and continuously amended) regulations on privatization, on the leasing of capital goods and on negotiable securities. These regulations need today to be coordinated within the general framework of the civil code.

46   Ligji *'Për sanksionimin dhe mbrojtjen e pronës private dhe nismës së lirë, të veprimtarive private të pavarur dhe privatizimit'* with subsequent amendments, No. 7512, signed 10 August 1991. [1991] OJ No. 6 (hereinafter Law [On sanctioning and protecting private property and free initiative, private independent activities and privatization]).

47   Ligji *'Për kthimin dhe kompensimin e pronave ish-pronarëve'*, No. 7698, signed 15 April 1993. [1993] OJ No. 5. This law was later abrogated and replaced by another: Ligji *'Për kthimin dhe kompesimin e pronës'* No. 9235, signed 29 July 2004. [2004] OJ No. 61 (hereinafter Law [On restitution and compensation of property]). In the second law the principles of the original law essentially remained in force.

the Major Constitutional Provisions, as amended, including its important human-rights amendment, Law No. 7692 of 31 March 1993, on the Fundamental Rights and Freedoms of the Individuals.

Nearly 19 years have passed since the entry into force of the Civil Code. Obvious traces of the former socialist law continue to cause problems up to this day, especially because of certain unclear provisions. With the signing and entry into force of the Stabilisation and Association Agreement, Albania now has to ensure that its legislation is in accordance with that of the EU's *acquis*.[48] Albania's civil legislation, and especially the 1994 Civil Code, represents important elements of this approximation process.

General Conception

The 1994 Civil code has a general part (called the first part of the code) that is followed by the other parts of the Civil Code.[49] The Code is not divided into general and special parts.

The Civil Code is composed of five parts:

- Part 1: General part, regulating physical and legal persons, representation, legal transactions and the validity thereof, prescription and the forfeiture of rights.
- Part 2: Objects and ownership (definitions of property, ownership, co-ownership; usufruct, usage and habitation rights, servitude, remedies for ownership, beneficial possession).
- Part 3: Inheritance (general provisions, inheritance by law, inheritance by will).
- Part 4: Obligations (general provisions, execution and liquidation of obligations, obligations resulting from causing damage (torts), non-obligatory payment, unjust enrichment).
- Part 5: Contracts (contracts in general, special types of contracts).

The Albanian Civil Code follows the linguistic style of the French Civil Code in that each of its chapters starts by defining the meaning or content of the institute of law it regulates.

Institutes of the Civil Code

Institutes of the general part
The general part of the Civil Code is organised in four titles that refer to the four institutes of civil law: (1) subjects of the law; (2) representation; (3) legal transactions; (4) prescription of actions and the forfeiture of rights.

---

48   Art. 70, Stabilisation and Association Agreement (n4).
49   R. Gjata, *E Drejta Civile* (1st edn, AlbPAPER 2006) 15–16.

In this part of the Civil Code, it could be said that the institutes regulated, specifically subjects of the law, representation and legal transactions, are the same as the regulations contained in the Albanian legislation of 1954–81.[50] Thus, it would appear that the notion of legal transactions is based on the Soviet model,[51] which was also present in Decree No. 2359 of 15 November 1956 'On Legal Transaction and Obligations', according to which, 'A legal transaction is the legal expression of the will of a natural person or legal entity that aims to create, change, or extinguish civil rights and obligations'.[52] However, the notion of a legal transaction is very broad, and it can cover not only normal types of contracts, including those agreements that serve to carry out a transfer of ownership, but also wills (testaments) or acts of representation.

The institute of representation is defined as a unilateral legal transaction, which implies that representation rights are regulated by law, a power of attorney or the courts (Art. 64, ACC). In this framework, the Albanian civil law uses the German rule, according to which only a power of attorney duly prepared before a notary, in accordance with the law, by the person being represented and delivered to the representative is valid against third parties.[53]

The new elements are provided in the fourth institute entitled 'Prescription of Actions and the Forfeiture of Rights'. This institute is referred to in the fifth title, entitled *Della prescrizione e della decadenza* of the seventh book of the Italian Civil Code (hereinafter ICC), also entitled: 'Protection of Rights' (original *Della tutela dei diritti*). Indeed, the content of this institute in the Albanian Civil Code is the same as the content of the institute in the Italian Civil Code. Thus, the general term of prescription, as provided by Article 112 of the ACC has the same definition of prescription in the Italian Civil Code: 'The right of action which is not exercised within the term defined by law, extinguishes'. The period of prescription is also the same as the prescription period provided in Article 2964 of the Italian Civil Code under the title *Della prescrizione ordinaria*, that is, 10 years (Art. 114, ACC). The causes for suspension and interruption of prescription are also nearly the same (Art. 129–133, ACC; Art. 2941–2945, ICC).

The influence of the Italian Civil Code is also fairly obvious in another part of this institute that is entitled the 'Forfeiture of Rights' (*Della Decadenza*). Both Codes provided that: 'When a right must be exercised within a specified period under the penalty of forfeiture, the provisions that regulate the interruption of the

---

50   *E drejta civile ruse. (Rossiia grazhdanskoe pravo)* (Office of the General Prosecuting Attorney Shkodër, edn 1948) 29–32. The general part of the Civil Code has not fully detached itself from the old structure, which was based on the former Soviet law, the Civil Code of the Russian Socialist Federative Soviet Republic. This book was translated from Russian into Albanian in 1948. The author/s, year of publishing and publisher is unknown. There is only one copy which is held in the National Library.

51   Genkin et al. (n30) 252.

52   Art. 79, ACC.

53   Fromont (n18) 39; see also, Arts 164–81, German Civil Code.

prescription do not apply. Also, the suspension causes do not apply, except for the exceptional cases, when the law itself permits the suspension of the restricted term' (Art. 137, ACC and Art. 2964, ICC).

The institute of ownership

When regulating the institute of ownership, the Civil Code of 1994 sanctions only one kind of property in concept and type, but allows many kinds of owners, among which there is no basic difference from the legal point of view. State property is no longer recognised as a special type, but the state is acknowledged as being one of the subjects that can own property. In the regulation of this institute, the Code follows the line of the Italian legislation.[54]

The second part of the code is entitled 'Objects and Ownership'. Despite the fact that it is structured differently, this part of the code includes the same institutes as the third part of the Italian Civil Code, entitled *Della proprietà*. The definition given by Article 141 of the ACC is broader than the one found in the analogous article of the ICC, Article 810.[55] Article 141 provides that, 'An object is anything that may constitute an object of ownership or of any other right *in rem*'. Under the influence of Albanian legal tradition, there is a specific element of the Code that regulates co-ownership, which is acknowledged to exist among the members of farming families. This kind of co-ownership was inherited from the above-mentioned Decree on Ownership, which was part of customary law[56] and is regulated by the current Civil Code as a form of property belonging in general to the members of the family (farmland).

With reference to possession, the Civil Code borrowed a rule from the Italian Civil Code (Art. 1153, ICC), according to which, 'A person who, on the basis of a legal action for the transfer of ownership, acquires movable property against payment in good faith becomes the owner of said property even if the first party was not the owner', however, the [person acquiring the property], even in good faith, does not become the owner of the property when the said property was stolen. The same regulation is found also in the Albanian Civil Code (Art. 166, ACC).[57]

With respect to the transfer of ownership over immovable property and in accordance with the Albanian legal tradition, an ownership right is transferred at the moment of the signing of a contract or the moment of the fulfilment of a legal action. Thus, the Albanian legislation accepts the system of contract signing as a general rule (Article 164, ACC), because the signing of a contract and the fulfilment of a valid legal action makes the purchaser or acquirer of immovable property immediately the owner of the property. Consequently, the registration or

---

54   F. Galgano, *Diritto Privato* (7th edn, A. Brati tr, Luarasi Press, 2006) 132–96.

55   Art. 810, ICC says: *Sono beni le cose che possono formare oggetto di diritti* [An object is anything that may constitute an object of ownership] (author tr.).

56   A. Nathanaili, *E drejta e pronësisë në Republikën e Shqipërisë* (5th edn, Revista-Dispenca, 1974) 126.

57   Galgano (n54) 190.

transcription of a legal action is not evidence of the validity (of the contract). The failure to register a contract in the register of immovable property does not render the contract for the transfer of the immovable property invalid, but it makes it impossible for the buyer to transfer [the property] to third parties.[58]

The institute of inheritance
Inheritance is regulated in the third part of the Civil Code and is conceived of as a separate institute. It is regulated in almost the same manner as the 1954 Decree 'On Inheritance', but at the same time the specific provisions are also influenced by Italian, French and German Civil Codes. The provisions regulating this part provide for a system of acquisition by inheritance in which, after the opening of an inheritance proceeding, the heir also acquires *ipso iure* the possession of the inherited property without the need to seize it.[59] A will (testament) is considered the main method of acquiring property through inheritance, but its forms are limited. The Civil Code acknowledges only two types of wills: holographic wills and wills by legal instrument. It also acknowledges 'special wills' made under special conditions such as: in places without a notary public; by those on active military service; in hospitals; and on an Albanian ship that is sailing or has stopped in a foreign port.

It does not acknowledge forced heirs/*disposable portion*,[60] and implements the rule of the hereditary reserve (*réserve héréditaire*). For this category, the Albania Civil Code provides that: 'A testator cannot exclude from legal succession his minor children or other minor heirs who inherit by substitution or his other heirs unable to work if they are called to inherit'.[61]

The innovation presented in this part is that, under the influence of the German Civil Code,[62] the range of legal heirs has increased up to the fifth degree.[63] Article 365 of the ACC provides that, when a deceased has no living descendants, parents, other ancestors, siblings, or descendants of said siblings, the property of the

---

58   *Vendimi Unifikues i Gjykatës së Lartë të Republikës së Shqipërisë* No. 1, signed 6 January 2009. [2009] OJ No.171 (hereinafter the [Unifying Decision of the High Court of Albania, No. 1 of 6 January 2009]).

59   Art. 331, ACC; Biçoku (n42) 58.

60   Forced inheritance/disposable portion. Forced heirs are descendants of the deceased, so called because under the regime of forced inheritance, they are entitled to a certain portion of their parent's estate, called the legal portion, forced portion, legitime, or legitimate portion. For the remaining portion, a testator may freely dispose of which is not subject to the legitime conditions.
See also, Galgano (n54) 994.

61   Art. 379, ACC.

62   § 1929 (1), More distant degrees, BGB, says: 'Heirs on intestacy of the fifth degree and of the more distant degrees are the more distant forebears of the deceased and their descendants' (N. Mussett tr.), available at <http://gesetze-im-internet.de/englisch_bgb/englisch_bgb.html#p6415> accessed 3 April 2011.

63   The previous Civil Code 1981 regulated the legal heirs up to the third degree (sisters and brothers of a deceased).

deceased shall pass to his or her next of kin, without distinguishing between the line of his or her father and mother, but in no case further than the sixth degree.[64] The current Civil Code also re-establishes the concept of legacy and burden in inheritance relations, but the number of provisions regulating these two institutes is limited, compared with those that are provided by the Italian and also the French Civil Codes. Under Albanian law, a legacy is explained as follows: 'A testator may charge the heir or the heirs appointed by will, to transfer to one or more legal heirs a property interest from the estate, without making them heirs.[65] A burden is defined as meaning: 'A testator may charge the heir or the heirs appointed by will to perform an action beneficial to the society or any other action, without giving any right to the person charged with this action'.[66]

Obligations
The fourth part of the Civil Code of 1994 is entitled 'Obligations'. While it does not follow any particular model, there are elements of both the former Soviet law and a number of Western codes, in particular those of France, Italy, Germany and Dutch.[67]

The notion of an obligation is detached from the notion of a contract, and here the Albanian Code follows the same line as that of the German Civil Code. The ACC's definition of an obligation is the same as that of the former Soviet law,[68] that is, a legal relation through which a person (the debtor) is obliged to give something or to perform or not perform a certain action for the benefit of another person (the creditor), who also has the right to demand being given something or for an action to be performed or not.[69]

Regarding the consideration of 'Torts' in Article 608, the ACC borrows the general responsibility clause from French law[70] and the double requirements

---

64   In cases where there is no legal heir, the state takes the deceased's property.

65   Art. 384, ACC.

66   Art. 386, ACC.

67   Genkin et al. (n30) 409–20.

68   Art. 107, Civil Code of the RSFSR; Genkin ibid. 412.

69   Art. 419, ACC; with some minor changes we find the same concept of obligations currently in the Civil Code of the Russian Federation. Art. 307,

   [The concept of an obligation and the grounds for it to arise, RFCC, says:

   1. By force of an obligation, one person (the debtor) shall be obliged to perform in favour of another person (the creditor) a certain action, such as: to transfer the property, to perform a job, to pay the money, etc., or to abstain from a certain action, while the creditor shall have the right to claim that the debtor discharge his obligation.

   2. Obligations shall arise from an agreement, from the infliction of damage, or on the other grounds indicated in the present Code] (no official translation), available at <www.russian-civil-code.com/> accessed 2 April 2013.

70   Art.1382, FCC, says:

   [Whatever any action of man which causes damage to another, obliges the one by whose fault it occurred to compensate it] (G. Rouhette and A. Rouhette-

of illegality and fault from the German law, also found in the Italian model.[71] Following the concept of moral damages found in the BGB,[72] such damages can be awarded in cases envisaged by law (Art. 617(1) ACC), when it is found that a person is responsible for damaging another's personality by publishing inaccurate, incomplete, or deceptive information. According to Article 608(1) of the ACC, moral damages are recoverable: 'A person who, illegally and with fault, causes damage to another person [...] is obliged to compensate the damage caused'.

Under the influence of the Dutch Civil Code (DCC),[73] Articles 613 to 624 of the Albania Civil Code cover: 'personal liability'; 'presumed liability'; and 'liability based on the exercise of a dangerous activity'. Thus, the Albania Civil Code along the same lines as Dutch Civil Code provides:

- damage caused by minors less than 14 years old and by persons who are totally incapable of acting are not liable for the damage caused (Art. 613 ACC; § 6:169 DCC);
- an employer is liable for the acts of employees who are in his service during the exercise of duties charged to them by him (Art. 618 ACC; § 6:170 DCC);
- representative's liability, if the representative's activity in the exercise of the powers assigned to him, brings a wrongful liability towards a third person, the represented is also liable towards this person (Art. 620 ACC; § 6:172 DCC).
- liability resulting from use of animals, when the owner of an animal or one who uses it is liable for the damage caused by the animal (Art. 621 ACC; § 6:179 DCC);
- liability from the exercise of a dangerous activity, when the person who performs activities that are dangerous by their nature or by the nature of the means (things) used and causes damage to other persons (Art. 623 ACC; § 6:174 DCC);
- liability concerning the environment, when the person who wrongfully damages the environment, by deteriorating, changing or harming it, completely or partially (Art. 624 ACC; § 6:175 DCC).

In all these cases the person is obliged to compensate for the damage caused, except when he proves that all the necessary and suitable precautions were taken to avoid the damage. Moreover, the concept of the payment of compensation for the damage is made up of actual damage as well as loss of profit.[74]

Berton tr.), available at <http://195.83.177.9/upl/pdf/code_22.pdf> accessed 3 April 2013.

71   Art. 2034, ICC; Galgano (n54) 437–40.
72   Fromont (n18) 46.
73   Ibid. 72.
74   Art. 640, ACC.

Some provisions of these laws have or are likely to have to change in order to approximate Albania's domestic legislation with that of the EU *acquis* in accordance with the above-mentioned Stabilisation and Association Agreement. In particular two directives are relevant:

- Directive 2000/35/EC of the European Parliament and the Council of 29 June 2000 'On combating late payment in commercial transactions'. This directive is aimed at providing adequate protection for lenders for the purpose of harmonising the rules for late payment with the general provisions for the fulfilment of other obligations.
- Directive 85/374/EEC of the Council of 25 July 1985 'On the approximation of law, rules and administrative provisions of the Member States connected to the liability arising out of the defective products',[75] as amended by Directive 199/34/EC.

Contracts

The Civil Code of 1994 establishes the principle of contractual freedom, avoiding the principle of *numerus clausus*, the so-called principle of permitted contracts, leaving open the possibility that other similar contracts or separate types of contracts may be entered into, provided that they comply with the general principles and do not run foul of the law.[76] The regulation of the institute of contract in the ACC is a combination of the Italian and German laws. The implementation of the rules related to legal actions is characteristic of this part, as well as the rules of obligations in general. In the ACC, the notion of a contract is also conditioned by its definition as a legal action through which one or several parties create, change, or cancel a legal relation (Art. 659, ACC). Under the influence of the Italian law (Art. 1325, ICC), Article 663, ACC, entitled 'Requisites of Contracts', provides that: 'The requisites of a contract are: the agreement of the party that has undertaken the obligation, a motive for the obligation, an object that forms the content of the contract, and the form as prescribed by law'. Following the line of the Italian legislation, in particular Article 1346, ICC, the Albanian Civil Code further defines, 'The object of a contract must be possible, lawful and determined or determinable' (Art. 678, ACC). Also along the Italian line and specifically Article 1343, ICC, Article 677, ACC, states, 'In a contract, the motive is unlawful when it is contrary to mandatory rules or to public policy, or when the contract becomes a means to avoid the fulfilment of a norm'.

---

75   Council Directive (ECC) 86/653/ of 18 December 1986 'On coordination of the law of Member States connected to self-employed commercial agents' [1986] OJ 382/17.

76   M. Semini Tutulani, *E drejta detyrimeve dhe kontratave. Pjesa e Përgjithëshme* (Afërdita, 1998) 35–7.

Concerning the interpretation of contracts,[77] the ACC follows the line of civil law tradition by following the rule that the literal interpretation of the words in a contract is not important, but that what is important is the spirit of the contract, evaluating the behaviour of the contracting parties in general before and after the conclusion of the contract.[78]

The Code is in line with the BGB with respect to the drafting of contracts.[79] Compliance between the offer and acceptance is required. The offer binds the proposer for a reasonable time until the response of the other party (Art. 665, ACC). Under the German model, discussions on drafting a contract should follow the good-faith principle.[80] In the event that one of the contracting parties possesses professional knowledge and the other party has full confidence in him, the first party must provide the other with information and instructions in good faith (Art. 675, ACC). The cancelation of a contract with reciprocal obligations is in line with Italian law. In the event that one of the contracting parties does not fulfil its obligations, the other party may either require the fulfilment of the obligation or the cancellation of the contract, in addition to payment for damages (Art. 698, ACC).[81]

Special contracts are also regulated in this part, which is characterised by the fact that 'major types of contracts (such as forwarding, transportation and carriage of goods, commercial representation) have been affected in recent years by EC legislative activity'.[82] Because of such activity, the part regarding special contracts has started to be amended, as was also determined by the adoption of Law No. 9901 of 14 April 2008 'On Entrepreneurs and Commercial Companies'. The amendments are aimed at improving the legal framework regarding commercial issues.[83] Together these changes and others are directed at promoting the approximation of Albanian civil legislation with Council Directive (ECC) 86/653/ of 18 December 1986 'On coordination of the law of Member States connected to self-employed commercial agents'.[84]

---

77   Art. 681, ACC, says:
   [When interpreting a contract, the common and real intent of the parties must be sought and not limited to the literal meaning of the words including their overall understanding before and after the conclusion of the contract] (author tr.).
78   Semini Tutulani (n76) 39–42.
79   §145, On the binding effect of an offer, BGB, says:
   [Any person who offers to another to enter into a contract is bound by the offer, unless he has excluded being bound by it]. See also, Fromont (n18) 39.
80   §242, Performance in good faith, says:
   [An obligor has a duty to perform according to the requirements of good faith, taking customary practice into consideration].
81   Galgano (n54) 391.
82   Ajani (n13) 525.
83   Final Report on Proposed Changes to the Civil Code. EURALIUS Mission, European Union 2010.
84   Council Directive (ECC) 86/653/ of 18 December 1986 'On coordination of the law of Member States connected to self-employed commercial agents' [1986] *OJL* 382/17.

Conclusion

The description of the characteristics of the Albanian Civil Law clearly shows that it belongs to the Civil Law family. The influence of foreign laws has been and is today considerably in its development. This influence has varied over time, thus Albanian civil law has shifted from the law of the civil law family tradition to socialist law, only to return again to the civil law tradition – but without completely losing the signs of socialist law.

Currently, the Albanian Civil Code of 1994 confirms it is difficult to predict the importance of the change occurring in legal systems and especially how countries that used to belong to the Romano-German law family will reintegrate again into this family. This difficulty originates also from the fact that an experience that has lasted for several decades cannot immediately disappear.[85] Even today the Albanian Civil Code of 1994, which preceded the new processes that took place after the 1990s, has started to be amended so as to comply fully with the integration processes that Albanian is engaged in to achieve approximation with the *acquis* of the EU in the framework of the Stabilization and Association Agreement. Only by being adjusted in accordance with the necessities of the time can it cope adequately with these integration processes and be at the same level with the other codes of the civil-law family, affirming its worth as a member of that family.

---

85   R. David and C. Jauffret-Spinos, *Les grands systèmes de droit contemporain* (10th edn, Dalloz, 1992) 20.

Chapter 13

'Svěřenský fond' (Trust Fund): A Daring New Legal Transplant in Czech Law

Kateřina Ronovská

Introduction

In the last 20 years discussions over the need of revision in the area of private law have resulted not only in 'formulatory' changes, but also paradigmatic ones in the Czech Republic. This process recently culminated in the adoption of the New Civil Code (hereinafter 'New Czech CC'), a Business Corporations Act and an International Private Law Act to become effective 1 January 2014. The new legislation predominantly follows from elements in pre-Second World War Czechoslovak law, in force until 1948, when the Communist regime took over power, while it also makes use of the experience and models of other European countries. However, the aim and purpose of this 'revival' process is more than a change in wording. Rather, it seeks to enshrine private law in a form which is standard in Europe and which corresponds with the needs of modern society.

Probably one of the most significant conceptual changes resulting from this reform is the reinforcement of the autonomy of the individual's will. It also gives an owner greater autonomy when disposing of his estate both *inter vivos* and *mortis causa*. One of the most daring (and controversial) innovations, introduced by the New Czech CC, has been the creation and regulation of the '*svěřenský fond*' ('trust fund') – a *trust-like* institute inspired by the concept of *Fiducie* in the law of Quebec.

The new Czech regulation of the trust fund has recently attracted a great deal of attention.[1] In continental European law it is a construct that has to ensure, functionally, the existence of institutes that are comparable to the Anglo-American trust. Until now Czech law has had relatively little experience of the trust concept and trust-like institutions although it did acknowledge various versions of fiduciary administration (tacit assignment, security transfer of rights, deposit and so on).

Elsewhere in Europe it is also possible to notice the emergence in the last few years of discussions on the use of instruments comparable to the *trust*, or *trust-like* instruments, which can be created for different purposes. At the same time, however, it is still quite uncommon for national legislators to make legislative

---

1   Czech Civil Code, 2012, ss. 1448–1474.

changes introducing such institutes into their national legal systems.[2] A possible reason may be that in principle, the *trust* is, and still remains, a *common law* instrument that is difficult to transfer to traditional legal orders based on *civil law.*

Current developments in Europe, however, are heading towards the convergence of legal cultures, which is necessarily associated with the modification of some traditional approaches. Consequently, *civil law* has been opening up to concepts that had previously been impossible for a long time. It has also been losing the strength of conceptual foundations, which were, on the one hand, criticised as too restrictive, and, on the other, appreciated as elegant beams of a well-balanced structure. However, it seems that differences between the traditions of *civil law* and *common law* may not be as entrenched as is often implied.

Conception of the Trust Fund and Administration of the Property of Others – A Quebec Inspiration

With certain variations, the New Czech Civil Code adopted the regulation of *fiducie* from the Civil Code of Quebec (1994).[3] Apart from the regulation of Quebecian *fiducie* itself, the CCQ also inspired Czech legislators to adopt the general regulation of the administration of the property of others.[4] There were various reasons for doing so, yet the attention to, and the choice of, the Quebec model was due to the fact that it is a mixed jurisdiction combining elements of *common law* and the *civil law* (notably from the French Civil Code). In this context, it is important to remember that although the Czech regulation has adopted the CCQ wording, it has not adopted its conceptual background. However, together with the administration of the property of others in general, the trust fund is located (according to the Quebec example) among substantive (absolute) rights.

Identically to the concept of *fiducie* in the Quebec Civil Code, the Czech legal regulation also conceives the trust fund as consisting of autonomous assets established when certain property is earmarked in order to serve a certain purpose. The property in the trust fund represents a separate and independent possession. The law expressly stipulates that the trust fund property is neither in the possession of the trustee, nor in the possession of the settlor, nor in the possession of the person intended as the trust fund's beneficiary. This Quebecoise solution of possession without ownership is unknown to Czech law founded as it is on the Romantic and later Austrian conception.[5]

---

2   The Czech 'trust fund' is not the only exception. A special trust-like instrument was, for instance, also introduced by the Hungarian CC in 2014. Also, discussions are currently under way about such a possibility in Slovakia.

3   Civil Code of Quebec, 1994, s. 1260 – 1298.

4   Civil Code of Quebec, 1994, s. 1299–1370.

5   B. Havel and V. Pihera, *National Report for the Czech Republic*, International Conference Trust, Fiducie, Treuhand in Europe and Trusteeship in the Czech Republic,

Section 1448 of the New Czech Civil Code states that:

A trust results from an act whereby a person, the settlor, transfers property from his patrimony to another patrimony constituted by him which he appropriates to a particular purpose under the contract or a testamentary disposition and which a trustee undertakes, by his acceptance, to hold and administer [...] The formation of a trust gives rise to a separate and independent ownership of the transferred property and the trustee is obliged to hold the property and administer it.

The similarities of this language to that of the Quebec Civil Code are striking, in so far as Section 1260 CCQ provides: 'A trust results from an act whereby a person, the settlor, transfers property from his patrimony to another patrimony constituted by him which he appropriates to a particular purpose under the contract or a testamentary disposition and which a trustee undertakes, by his acceptance, to hold and administer'.

Nevertheless it seems impossible to rely upon the Quebecoise doctrinal interpretation of judgments, given the legal interpretative differences that exist between the New Czech CC and the Quebec Civil Code, particularly in terms of the conception of ownership. While the Quebec Civil Code has been influenced mainly by the French law, the New Czech CC draws mainly on Austrian law (ABGB) as its main source of inspiration which was in effect until 1950. For the purposes of further reflection, it should be noted that while the official wording of the CCQ uses the concept of *fiducie*, its English version works with the concept of *trust*, although these two institutions are not entirely identical.[6] The New Czech CC 'transplanted' from the CCQ not only the trust fund but also the general regulation of the administration of the property of others.[7]

The main feature of such asset administration is the autonomous position of the administrator (trustee) during administration and the discretionary nature of the activity. The administrator is authorised, and at the same time obliged, to decide on the disposal of trust assets at his own discretion. In this particular regard the administration of the property of others does not differ from the classic mandate contract.

The provisions for the administration of the property of others do not establish any new substantive rights, although at first sight they might appear to do so with their systematic inclusion in Part 3 of the New Czech CC.

Prague, January, 2013 published in B. Havel and V. Pihera, *Trust a srovnatelné instituty v Evropě* (Trust and Comparable Institutes in Europe) (Nakladatelství Eva Rozkotová, 2014).

6 Ibid.

7 The introduction of this regulation produced a large number of questions, the examination of which goes far beyond the scope of this chapter. There are, however, no major doubts on the applicability or scope of the regulation concerning the administration of the property of others via trust funds.

General Characteristics of the Trust Fund

The '*svěřenský fond*' (trust fund) is created as a possible legal form for the substantive-legal administration of the property of others when the founder (settlor) commits certain specified assets for a particular purpose from his general assets and a trust administrator (trustee) undertakes to manage these specified assets in his own name on behalf of the fund in favour of the beneficiary. Even if, unlike a foundation or an endowment fund, the trust fund is not endowed with its own legal subjectivity (legal personality), the separate and independent ownership of the specified assets emerges through the establishment of a trust fund. Such assets are not under the ownership of the founder/settlor (the person who establishes the fund), the trust administrator/trustee or the person who should benefit (the beneficiary). Instead this is a case of 'ownership without a master', an unknown concept in Czech law, built on Roman and Austrian foundations, even though our law recognises or has recognised various forms of divided or feudal ownership. The legislators have introduced into Czech law a tool that is based on a concept of common law, albeit adapted for the mixed jurisdiction of Quebec. It is a classic example of a legal transplant, augmented here by the fact that the body of Czech law has never known such an institution.

The trust fund may be established for a private purpose on behalf of a certain or determinable person – the beneficiary, to whom or for whose benefit performance should be granted from the trust fund. But (unlike the usual regulation of the trust in common law countries) also for the purpose of pursuing any other private or community objectives, not primarily directed at benefitting a specific person, including the trust fund established for the purpose of supporting the commemoration of a deceased person. As in the common law, a trust fund can be also set up as 'charitable trust fund' with the aim of contributing to the public good in different spheres of culture, education, religion or science. The main purpose of a charitable fund cannot consist in engaging in entrepreneurial activities or any other ways of achieving profit.

A trust fund formally carries its own name – 'designation', which must testify to its purpose and contain the words 'trust fund'. A trust fund comes into being at the moment when the trust administrator takes over administration of the assets. Every trust fund has to have formal documents – unilateral acts, for which the law sets out an obligatory minimal content and form. In these the settlor should expresses his intention as to how the trust fund will be managed by the administrator (trustee) and all other important questions. The requirement of the existence of the trust documents in the form of a notarial deed excludes the possibility that informal arrangements could be claimed to have the status of a trust fund. This significantly narrows the applicability of this institute in the Czech law.

Any natural person can be a trust administrator (trustee). A legal person can be a trustee only if the law allows this. To date, authorisation for trust funds has been limited to investment companies.[8] The trustee is called upon to hold and manage

---

8   Czech Act on Investment Companies and Investment funds (2013).

the independent assets: he is responsible for the full administration of the assets in the trust fund (therefore, not only the administration of the maintenance of the fund but also how it is used).

The position of the founder is significant, not only for the creation of the trust fund, but also for its duration; he has the option to reserve the right to determine the beneficiaries even after the creation of the fund, the right to remove or appoint the trustee, and the right to supervise the trust fund's administration, and so forth. The settlor and beneficiary may also act as a trustee but the trust fund must have another independent trustee who is neither the settlor nor the beneficiary. The trustee is obliged to perform his or her duties with due diligence (defined in Czech company law), which relies upon certain knowledge. Therefore the trustee must demonstrate the necessary skills for the specific fiduciary administration. Furthermore a trustee acting with due diligence should perceive any imminent conflict of interest and notify the beneficiary without delay. The conflict may arise as a result of the existence of certain assets rights which are beneficial to the trustee and which could be exercised in relation to the beneficiary or the trust fund itself.

Over and above these rights, the New Czech CC gives the settlor, beneficiary or any other person who demonstrates a legitimate interest, the right to challenge the trustee's acts and any property transfers from the trust to a third party which contravene the trust's rules.

The trust fund is terminated upon the expiry of the period for which it was established and/or upon accomplishing the goals for which it was established. The dissolution of the trust fund may also occur as a result of court decision.[9]

The Trust Fund in the Context of Other Instruments Introduced in the New Czech Civil Code

It could be said that whereas trusts are functionally utilised in the world of *common law*, *civil law* jurisdictions have traditionally used the institution of the foundation (a legal person with full legal capacity) and other trust-like institutions (French *Fiducie*, German *Treuhand*, Czech trust fund etc.). Similarly, from the historical perspective Continental Europe has reacted to the institution of the trust as a distinct conception of property law in such a way that it cannot be inferred that parallels to the trust are intended. It is obvious that both conceptions relate to the general conception of fiduciary – but each in its own way.

From 1 January 2014, the New Czech CC offers, in addition to the trust fund, a selection of other instruments for the purposes of asset administration. In the area of fiduciary assets in addition to currently existing forms – foundations and endowment funds, a new option for the administration of funds is available in the form of affiliated funds. This choice is unprecedented, not only in terms of (historical) Czech law, but also in comparison to many other European countries.

9　Czech Civil Code, 2012, s. 1469.

The fact that the trust fund concept and affiliated funds have entered Czech law has meant a certain shift in the foundations of Czech law from the traditional formal legal approach to a more functional approach, despite those instruments being 'foreign' to Czech law.

From this functional perspective, under Czech law the closest institutions to the trust fund are foundations and endowment funds. Unlike the corporation, the foundation and endowment fund are created also through earmarking assets intended for a particular purpose. In this respect they are functionally comparable to the trust funds since they allow one, depending on the owner's intention, to administer the property in a specific way and reserve it for a defined purpose. Unlike the trust fund, however, the foundation and endowment fund are legal persons (with separate legal personality). Additionally a trust fund is not recorded in any public register, whereas the very existence of the foundation and endowment fund is dependent on being recorded in a public register.

There are also differences in the process of founding and creating a trust fund. Whereas a foundation and an endowment fund are always founded by a unilateral legal act by the founder (or founders) and created by an entry in a public register, a trust fund, created *inter vivos* has a contractual (mostly bilateral) basis and is created at the moment when the trust's administrator accepts responsibility for its administration.[10] Unlike a foundation and an endowment fund a trust fund can also be created for investment purposes to make a profit to be distributed among the founders, employees, shareholders and other persons. Consequently the relation between the founder, administrator/trustee and beneficiary are governed by the rules for the administration of the property of others, which do not apply to an endowment fund, since this fund (as a legal person) is the owner of the assets committed by the founder.

A foundation and an endowment fund reflect the will of the founder as an established legal person, the basis of which consists of a set of assets dedicated towards the fulfilment of its intended purpose. The idea behind a trust fund is mainly the fulfilment of the trust's purpose and (unlike a foundation) it need not have a permanent or a profitable character. Unlike a foundation, it is not assumed that a trust fund or an endowment fund will have a permanent existence; they can be set up for a certain period or to fulfil a one-off or short-term goal. On the other hand, it is also possible to set up a trust fund and an endowment fund for an unspecified period.

The New Czech CC also offers property owners the additional possibility of establishing a '*přidružený fond*' (an 'affiliated' fund).[11] The legal provisions of the affiliated fund are also new to the Czech legal environment. Based on the explanatory memorandum to the new Czech CC, the provisions on affiliated

---

10   Retaining the requirement of the existence of the contract excludes the possibility of creating an *inter vivos* trust fund by means of unilateral actions, which is the standard in *common law* countries.

11   Czech Civil Code, 2012, s. 349.

funds aim to reflect precisely the concept of 'dependent' foundations. To create an affiliated fund, the foundation can be entrusted by way of a written contract with the administration of assets which are eligible to be assets of the foundation, to use these assets in line with the purpose of the foundation. The stated purpose must, of course, be related to the foundation's mission and cannot consist of support for political parties and movements. The owner of the assets remains the founder; he is the person who entrusts the assets to the administration of the foundation. On the basis of this fact, he is also the only person who supervises the affiliated fund. Due to the need to distinguish between the assets of the affiliated fund and the administering foundation, the latter is required to register assets in the affiliated fund separately from its own assets. If the foundation is dissolved, the liquidator will be required to dispose of the affiliated fund in such a way as to ensure the continuation of its purpose.

The sparse regulation has so far given rise to certain ambiguities in terms of the character of the trust fund. At the moment it looks as if the regulation of the trust fund and the law governing foundations end up in close proximity, where the borders and functional distinction between them may not be altogether clear.

The New Czech CC also contains provisions regarding other separated assets which should be mentioned here. The most important is the regulation of trust fund succession (Sections 1512 to 1524). This reintroduces the traditional institute of *fideicommissionary substitution* into the Czech law, that is, the testator's bequest by virtue of which the first heir instituted is entrusted with the obligation to preserve and transmit to a second heir the whole or part of the inheritance. The inherited property belonging to the trust fund represents a separate part of the assets of the so-called first heir whose right to dispose of these assets may be limited (since these assets must be transmitted to someone else pursuant to the will of the deceased).

Nevertheless, in contrast to the trust fund, the first heir, regardless of the limitations of their rights, is always in the position of the owner. In this case, the function of the administrator of the property of others is absent; the first heir always holds the inheritance for themselves, at least by virtue of the rights of the first heir as beneficiary. Compared to the trust fund, the essential difference lies in the restricted purpose of the trust fund succession, which is exclusively to maintain the integrity of the patrimony and to transfer it to the specified person; there is no other separate purpose of trust fund succession. In this respect, the regime of acting *ultra vires* is different: whereas the first heir always acts as the owner and third persons are protected, the trustee does not act as the owner. For this reason, when the trustee exceeds the scope of his/her authority, there are other avenues of redress, for example in criminal law.

In the New Czech CC, the trust fund is conceived of as a special structure in terms of the obligations involved and the substantive law. The trust fund is established and the trustee acquires the rights associated with his or her function originally on the basis of the separate act of earmarking certain assets as trust funds and the trustee's acceptance of the office. This situation must be distinguished from cases of mere representation, including indirect representation. Any form of representation is excluded in this case, since the trustee does not act on behalf of the trust fund (which is not a person) or on behalf of any other third party. Regardless of the fact that the trustee may take office on the basis of a contract with the settlor, their position cannot be confused with the position of an assignor or principal. The trustee is not in an assignment relationship with any party, but performs his or her function 'for the trust fund', nor can the trust fund be compared to the effects of a contract concluded for the benefit of the third party either. In this respect, the trust fund demonstrates a certain property-law character, which justifies why it is systematically classified among the regulation of absolute rights.

Conclusion

There are therefore, a number of forms of asset administration provided for by the New Czech CC which an owner of assets can choose from in order to achieve his intended purpose, some of which may be better suited to his purposes than others. It is entirely up to the settler/founder whether he decides to establish a legal entity (foundation, endowment fund, or some form of business corporation), or makes use of some form without separate legal personality (such as a trust fund, affiliated fund, asset administration on the basis of a contract of mandate or so on).

The new Czech CC aims to introduce the institution of the trust fund as a Continental-European version of a 'trust-like' institution. In contrast to its Quebec template and to trusts in the Anglo-American legal systems it is interpreted relatively conservatively. In the case of trust funds the law requires a mandatory document in the form of a notarial deed and does not permit their gradual or implied establishment (as in the case of the constructive trust), which to a certain extent blurs the distinction between endowment funds and trust funds. The basic distinguishing criterion is, however, the lack of a legal personality in the case of a trust fund, that is, the status-nature of the endowment fund and the obligational-substantive legal nature of the trust fund. Whereas the owner of the assets of an endowment fund is the endowment fund itself, the trust fund is not the owner of the assets committed to it.

The trust fund exhibits a surprising number of features shared not only with the foundation and foundation fund (with legal personality), but also with the affiliated fund. This is probably due to the fact that it is a manifestation of fiduciary obligation in the sense that the administrator is entrusted with the property of another by a legal act, whereby the owner makes a contractual disposition of his own property. The conceptual and most important difference lies primarily in who owns the assets in these funds: whether it is the original owner (as in the case of an affiliated fund), the fund itself (as in the case of an endowment fund) or nobody (as in the case of a trust fund).

In the case of the trust fund, the settlor does not express the intention to establish a legal person (otherwise they would establish a foundation, a foundation fund or another legal person such as a corporation). On the contrary the settlor obviously expressed the intention to establish a trust fund, and it would be inconsistent with legal certainty if their intention was subsequently re-characterised in the direction not originally intended. Yet it remains true that the trust fund certainly is, in terms of its function, an instrument functionally competing with legal persons.

The New Czech Civil Code offers owners of property a broad range of possibilities of how to manage their assets. A number of different aspects will play an important role when deciding on which possibility to choose. In particular, consideration may be given to the purpose, the proposed circle of beneficiaries, the method of achieving the intended purpose, any limits on trading in and disposing of property, and differences in the way in which individual types of foundation are dissolved. The disadvantage of trust funds in comparison with endowment funds is that they are to a certain extent a foreign element in the continental European legal environment. The chosen concept is new, untried and also unusual, which makes it difficult for many to grasp.

Beyond the private-law legal framework, public law is also crucially important in the field of asset administration. An especially important role is played by the conception of trust funds in fiscal law. Even though the final form of the related tax regulations is still the subject of legal-political debate, today it is already clear that trust funds will be considered taxable subjects (similar to legal persons), a characteristic which may make them less attractive or may contribute to uncertainty as to how they differ from other institutions discussed above. The current legal picture in the Czech legal system where a trust-like form has been introduced illustrates how difficult it is for the continental legal environment to cope with institutes coming from 'the other world'. Only time and legal practice will show how this daring legal transplant will 'fit' with the rest of the Czech legal system.[12]

---

12 For more detailed information on trust fund in the Czech Republic see (in Czech language) Vlastimil Pihera, 'Nejpodivnější zvíře v lese – poznámky ke svěřenskému fondu' *Obchodně právní revue* No. 10/2012 (C.H. Beck, Prague) 12; Kateřina Ronovská, 'Nadace (a trusty) v kontinentální Evropě – pohled funkcionální' *Obchodně právní revue* No. 7–8/2012 (C.H, Beck, Prague) 278; V. Pihera, 'Trust. Vybrané aspekty' *Obchodně právní revue* No.7/2009 (C.H Beck, Prague) 196.

Chapter 14

Diffusing Bad Ideas:
What the Migration of the Separation of
Powers Means for Comparative Law

Eoin Carolan*

The Separation of Powers

As an idea which was ostensibly derived from the domestic constitutional practice of a single state but which has subsequently been adopted as a core constitutional value in many jurisdictions, Montesquieu's separation of powers model should be 'a poster-child' for the transplantation of constitutional innovations. Widely celebrated and globally diffused, the concept of a tripartite separation of powers is generally regarded as one of the most important constitutional insights of the Enlightenment era.

It has been cited as an influence on the development of the constitutional structures of multiple states, varying from the eighteenth century's radical new American republic to those states that more recently obtained independence in the post-colonial era[1] or aftermath of the Cold War.[2] Indeed, the theory's ubiquity is such that it even has political and normative resonance in states that do not traditionally adhere to a tripartite model of government. It was instructive, for example, that the UK's creation of a Supreme Court and reform of the role of the Lord Chancellor were discussed in separation of powers terms,[3] even though the separation of powers has not traditionally been regarded as part of the United Kingdom's constitutional system.[4] That the theory could be cited as a legitimate institutional norm in such a

---

* This chapter was first presented at the WG Hart Workshop on Comparative Aspects on Constitutions: Theory and Practice in June 2010. I am grateful to all participants in the workshop for their helpful comments and suggestions, with the usual disclaimer that the errors are all mine.

1 See, for example, Article 6, *Bunreacht na heireann* (The Constitution of Ireland).

2 For an analysis of how this has subsequently developed, see P. Kopecky, 'Power to the executive! The changing executive-legislative relations in Eastern Europe' (2004) 10 *Journal of Legislative Studies* 142.

3 See, for example, R. Masterman, 'A Supreme Court for the United Kingdom: One step forward, two steps back' (2004) *Public Law* 48; K. Malleson, 'Modernising the Constitution: Completing the unfinished business' (2004) 24 *Legal Studies* 119.

4 Robson, for example, dismissed it as a 'rickety chariot'. W. Robson, *Justice and Administrative Law* (2nd edn, Stevens, 1947) 14.

historically alien context underscores its broad applicability and apparent efficacy as a constitutional transplant.

However, the popularity of the separation of powers has often obscured the fact that the tripartite model suffers from several fundamental flaws. While the contention that the separation of powers is a 'bad idea' may be a controversial one, it is instructive to note that the theory has been subjected to sustained and consistent criticism for several decades.[5] Geoffrey Marshall, for example, famously dismissed the theory many years ago as 'infected with so much imprecision and inconsistency that it may be counted as little more than a jumbled portmanteau of arguments for policies which ought to be supported or rejected on other grounds'.[6] More recently, Bruce Ackerman has commented that:

> [I]t is past time to rethink Montesquieu's holy trinity. Despite its canonical status, it is blinding us to the world-wide rise of new institutional forms that cannot be neatly categorised as legislative, judicial or executive. Although the traditional tripartite formula fails to capture their distinctive modes of operation, these new and functionally independent units are playing an increasingly important role in modern government. A "new separation of powers" is emerging in the twenty-first century. To grasp its distinctive features will require us to develop a conceptual framework containing five or six boxes – or maybe more.[7]

Criticisms of the separation of powers are, accordingly, not new: for that reason, it is not proposed to address this preliminary assumption at any great length in this piece. It is useful, however, briefly to identify the theory's key weaknesses as they necessarily inform any assessment of what the diffusion of the model tells us about comparative constitutional law.

Historically Inaccurate

The tripartite model was ostensibly presented by Montesquieu as an overview of the workings of the English constitutional system. However, it has been persuasively argued that Montesquieu's description of England's institutional structures – his trivialising of the judicial power for example – was inaccurate.[8]

---

5   See, for example, M.J.C. Vile, *Constitutionalism and the Separation of Powers* (Oxford University Press, 1967); G. Marshall, *Constitutional Theory* (Clarendon, 1971); E. Carolan, *The New Separation of Powers* (Oxford University Press, 2009).

6   Marshall (n5) 124.

7   B. Ackerman, 'Goodbye Montesquieu' (2010) in S. Rose-Ackerman and P. Lindseth (eds), *Comparative Administrative Law* (Edward Elgar, 2010) 129.

8   L. Claus, 'Montesquieu's mistakes and the true meaning of separation' (2005) 25 *Oxford Journal of Legal Studies* 419. It is unclear whether this was based on a misunderstanding by Montesquieu of the system which then operated in England or whether, on the other hand, he consciously depicted an idealised version of the English system.

Impractical

The classical version of this model prescribes a tripartite separation of functions between legislative, executive and judicial branches. In practice, this is impossible to achieve. If government is to operate effectively, institutions cannot be absolutely sealed off from each other in this fashion. Madison noted the 'impossibility and inexpediency of avoiding any mixture of these departments'.[9] The result of this inherent impracticality is that contemporary constitutional structure tends not to pursue the purest version of the theory.

Indeterminate

The theory is hopelessly indeterminate. It requires the functions of government to be allocated amongst the three branches, but provides little or no guidance as to how this allocation should occur.

Under the formalist version of the theory, powers and functions are classified as legislative, executive or judicial and allocated accordingly. However, this approach simply begs the different question of the basis for such classifications. There are many functions and powers of government which are, in the abstract, impossible to conclusively identify as legislative, executive or judicial. As Stevens J. observed:

> [T]he exercise of legislative, executive and judicial powers cannot be categorically distributed among three mutually exclusive branches of government [because] governmental power cannot always be readily characterised with only one of those three labels. On the contrary [...] a particular function, like a chameleon, will often take on the aspect of the office to which it is assigned.[10]

The functionalist understanding of the theory accepts this difficulty but, once again, simply replaces one imprecise set of criteria with another. Functionalists seek to ensure that the allocation of powers or functions preserves the inter-institutional balance necessary to provide an appropriate level of checks and balances. But how is such balance to be measured? How is it determined?

> Just as the formalist theory necessarily (and misguidedly) assumes the ability to accurately define and distinguish the three functions of the state, so the functionalist approach similarly rests on the system's chimerical capacity to define, adopt and consistently employ the essentially indefinable notion of institutional balance.[11]

---

9 J. Madison, Book 47 of *The Federalist Papers* (2nd edn, University of Chicago Press, 1990) 155.

10 *Bowsher v Synar* 478 US 714, 749 (1986).

11 Carolan (n5) 26.

Ineffective

As a model of institutional arrangement, such indeterminacy is particularly problematic. The purpose of a constitutional model of institutional structure is to assist in the organisation and operation of government. The separation of powers is, however, incapable of providing such assistance. The theory can only be usefully invoked by those charged with making decisions on matters of institutional structure after some external values have been imported into it, be they some extrinsic (and often surreptitiously adopted) theory of government or the decision maker's own personal views. By itself, the model functions only in the abstract. This calls into question its entire value as a constitutional principle. As Barber has observed, '[a] utopian constitutional theory [is] a waste of time'.[12]

Anachronistic

The utility of the separation of powers theory has been further undermined by the way in which conceptions of government and of the state have changed since the eighteenth century. Government for Montesquieu was a limited rule-based activity, operated by the state's central organs. By contrast, contemporary governance is both interventionist and decentralised in character, with power and influence exercised through an array of instruments and agencies. It is unrealistic and artificial in the extreme to suggest that the complex and multi-faceted nature of modern government can be adequately described – much less regulated – by a simple three-fold categorisation of government functions.

Misleading

The criticisms outlined above indicate that the model of a tripartite separation of powers has limited, if any, value as a constitutional principle of institutional organisation. In spite of this, the model continues to be cited as a fundamental tenet of many domestic constitutional systems. The ongoing employment of the theory raises additional difficulties. One is that the theory tends to mislead rather than inform, obscuring the real basis upon which decisions about questions of institutional structure are taken. Secondly, the presence and persistence of the theory can discourage or prevent the development of alternative systems of institutional arrangement. For example, accountability in a separation of powers system is usually secured by the notional accountability of a decision maker to one of the three branches of government. In reality, however, such accountability mechanisms – such as the accountability of a minister to Parliament for the decisions of administrative bodies, or the accountability of the executive to the legislature for the execution of legislative instructions under the non-delegation

---

12 N. Barber, 'Prelude to the separation of powers' (2001) 60 *Cambridge Law Journal* 59, 62–3.

doctrine – do not reflect the way in power is truly exercised in modern government. The use of such nominal safeguards provides a veneer of accountability, thereby inhibiting the development of alternative mechanisms which would provide much greater protection for the values which the separation of powers system is supposed to protect.

It is clear from this brief recital of the difficulties associated with the separation of powers that it is, in its bare tripartite form, deeply flawed. Persistent academic criticism of the model across several jurisdictions has not affected either its usage or migration across many constitutional systems. This raises questions for our understanding of comparative constitutionalism. What does the successful migration of the separation of powers theory tell us about comparative constitutional law? Why is one of the most frequently transplanted constitutional theories a model that was descriptively inaccurate when first elaborated and prescriptively inadequate whenever it is operated? Is the diffusion of this bad idea an isolated case or an illustration of a potentially broader problem? The purpose of this piece is to conduct a broad examination of these issues. Drawing on work done in other fields on the diffusion of ideas, it aims to provide some preliminary views on the possible responses to these questions.

The Diffusion of Ideas

Diffusion research combines scholarship in areas such as sociology, anthropology, psychology, marketing and communication studies to examine the process by which ideas and innovations spread. One of the core findings of this research is that good ideas do not necessarily diffuse. The reality, in fact, is that the majority of innovations fail. Studies suggest that, depending on the parameters of the particular market at issue, only between 1 per cent and 30 per cent of the many thousands of new products introduced each year succeed.[13] Some of these products may have inherent flaws but others amongst them are likely to present an opportunity for genuinely beneficial innovations. For those in the latter category, however, there is no guarantee of success.

> Most technologists believe that advantageous innovations will sell themselves, that the obvious benefits of a new idea will be widely realized by potential adopters, and that the innovation will diffuse rapidly. Seldom is this the case.[14]

Rogers uses the example of the British Navy's efforts to control scurvy to illustrate his point. In 1601, an experiment with lemon juice by a Captain James Lancaster strongly indicated that lemons had a beneficial impact on the control of scurvy on

---

13   R. McMath, *What Were They Thinking – Marketing Lessons I've Learned From Over 80,000 New-Product Innovations and Idiocies* (Random House, 1998) 3.

14   E. Rogers, *Diffusion of Innovations* (5th edn, Free Press, 2003) 7.

ships. Sailors who were allocated lemon juice survived while 40 per cent of those who were not given lemon juice died of scurvy. Nevertheless, it was almost 200 years before the Navy adopted this practice and over 250 years later before the Merchant Navy followed suit.

This indicates that evidence that a practice or product is beneficial will not, of itself, ensure that it will be widely adopted. On the contrary, diffusion researchers regard the migration of ideas as a complex social process. Much of the work in this field focuses on the social mechanics of diffusion. While this research also has interesting implications for comparative constitutionalism,[15] this piece concentrates on the extent to which the design and characteristics of an idea can influence how it spreads. The diffusion scholarship indicates that: 'innovation attributes are significant factors in the diffusion of innovations'.[16] In particular, it has been demonstrated that certain characteristics of innovations consistently affect the speed and extent of their diffusion:

> The characteristics of an innovation, as perceived by the members of social system, determine its rate of adoption. Five attributes of innovation are: (1) relative advantage, (2) compatibility, (3) complexity, (4) trialiability, and (5) observability.[17]

Unlike product innovations, the latter two criteria are generally not applied to the study of idea-only innovations. In the constitutional context, for example, it is difficult to conceive of how a trial of a constitutional innovation could be conducted on a limited basis. Similarly, the results of a constitutional innovation cannot easily be subjected to consistent observation or assessment. Isolated illustrations of the principle in operation may provide some degree of observability, but such examples cannot form the basis for reliable findings. They may be wrongly attributed to other factors, or they may represent an atypical but high profile example of the

---

15   It raises, for example, questions in relation to the role of networks in the spread of constitutional ideas and, in particular, in relation to the influence of particular agents and/or network structures such as scholarly publications, academic conferences, judicial conferences or exchanges, inter-court communications, international charities and/or organisations with an interest in post-conflict reconstruction, and so on.

16   J.L. Perry and K.L. Kraemer, 'Innovation attributes, policy intervention, and the diffusion of computer applications among local governments' (1978) 9 *Policy Sciences* 179, 196. See also, for example, F.C. Fliegel and J.E. Kivlin, 'Attributes of innovations as factors in diffusion' (1966) 72 (3) *American Journal of Sociology* 235.

17   Rogers (n14) 35. The attributes of innovations have been categorised in other ways by other scholars. For example, Perry and Kraemer (n16) identify the key attributes of innovation as 'task complexity, pervasiveness, communicability, specificity of evaluation, departure from current technologies, and cost'. In general, however, there is a degree of commonality about the substantive content of these categories, if not about the way in which they are described and sub-divided. See, for example, Perry and Kraemer (n16) 186.

relevant principle in action. Constitutional structures are too complex to allow the impact of one principle to be readily observed.

For that reason, the analysis here is confined to an examination of how the first three characteristics are said to affect the diffusion of ideas, as well as the extent, if any, to which the migration of the separation of powers corroborates the analysis of this diffusion research.

Relative Advantage

It is obvious that ideas are more likely to diffuse if they are regarded as more advantageous than the other options available. The key point here, however, is that such comparative assessments of the merits of competing ideas typically depend not on their objective strengths and weakness but rather on their perceived advantages. '[P]erceptions count. The individuals' perception of the attributes of an innovation, not the attributes as classified objectively by experts or change agents, affect its rate of adoption'.[18]

The difficulty is that errors recur in the making of these assessments. Research has shown that the human mind is naturally predisposed to commit certain errors. One prominent example is what the literature describes as availability error where 'decisions [are based] on the most available information and not on all the evidence'.[19] This error is compounded by the unreliable way in which we frequently obtain such information. 'Information may be available because it is widely publicized, recent, dramatic, or emotional'.[20] Similarly:

> [W]e often assign excessive weight to confirmatory data at the expense of contradictory data. This usually involves two mechanisms: first, we often quote anecdotal cases that support our beliefs and ignore those that don't, and, second, we exercise "optional stopping" or "satisfying" in the pursuit of data when the early data supports our convictions, but continue the search for more data when early indicators do not support our predictions.[21]

One infamous recent example of how advertising can take advantage of such tendencies was the Swift Boat Veterans for Truth advertising campaign that took place during the 2004 American Presidential election. Studies of the marketing strategy adopted by those behind this campaign show that their advertising had a deliberately controversial character. This was intended to ensure that the ads received wide coverage and made a greater degree of impact on individuals. The

---

18   Rogers (n14) 223.

19   O. Mahmoud, 'The operation was successful but the patient died: Why research on innovation is successful yet innovations fail', paper delivered at ESOMAR Consumer Insight Congress, Barcelona, 2002.

20   Ibid.

21   Ibid. See also, T. Gilovich *How We Know What Isn't So* (The Free Press, 1993).

media debate about the truth or falsity of the claims made meant the claims received far more attention than their small advertising spend would have secured alone.

Furthermore, the campaign made a significant effort in advance of the broadcast of the ads to contact and brief conservative media outlets whose antipathy to Kerry made it more likely that they would engage in the form of 'optional stopping' referred to above. The strategy was a conspicuous success.

> While most major news outlets debunked or refuted the claims of the Swift Boat Veterans, and although only a very few of their ranks had ever actually served with Kerry in combat, their message was played and replayed throughout the national media, garnering them far more exposure than their limited budget ever could have allowed. Indeed, this was part of their overall strategy.

Regardless of the accuracy of their claims, or perhaps because of their inflammatory nature, the Swift Boat Veterans were successful in casting doubt on one of the cornerstones of Kerry's campaign: his war record.[22]

Another common error of reasoning is asymmetric evaluation. This is 'one special type of the lack of objectivity involving observing and citing occasions when an event occurred and a specific outcome resulted, and overlooking all other event/ outcome combinations'.[23] We are more likely to recall the high-profile performance of an innovation in an atypical situation than the many mundane occasions when it functioned in a different way. In the legal context, this may manifest itself in a focus on the way in which a principle applied in the notorious 'hard case' rather than in an analysis of how it functions in the majority of less dramatic situations.

The importance of perception in assessing relative advantage, and the frequently flawed nature of that perception, has a number of implications for the diffusion of new ideas. The first is that it underlines the fact that the objective merits of an innovation do not guarantee widespread adoption. As a corollary, it also means that the weakness of an innovation will not necessarily inhibit its diffusion.

In terms of the diffusion of ideas, this raises the specific problem that an idea, once adopted, may be difficult to dislodge. Individuals do not directly experience the effects of ideas on a regular basis. They thus will rarely have the incentive to assess the relative advantage of established orthodoxies. In the absence of a radical malfunctioning of the relevant system, individuals are likely to trust the ideas upon which it was originally established. In this way, trust in current suppliers poses a significant barrier to entry for new innovations.[24] In turn, this confers significant first-mover advantages on those ideas that are initially accepted. Research on the

---

22   J. Kolstad, 'Swift boat veterans for truth: Swift boat veterans for truth campaign' in T. Riggs (ed.), *Encyclopedia of Major Marketing Campaigns Volume 2* (Cengage Gale, 2007).

23   Mahmoud (n19).

24   F. Oberholzer-Gee and V. Canalog, 'The speed of new ideas: Trust, institutions and the diffusion of new products', Harvard Business School Working Paper Series (2007), available at <http://www.hbs.edu/research/pdf/07-063.pdf> accessed 14 January 2010.

diffusion of ideas in other fields suggests that the importance of this should not be underestimated.

> Evidence from the pharmaceutical industry suggests that the first-mover advantage is quite substantial, be it due to reputation effects, slow information diffusion, or simply "capture" of the medical profession.[25]

The research also indicates that these first mover advantages are particularly pronounced where the dominant innovation or idea in question successfully obtains a large market share.

> Pioneers such as Coca-Cola and Kleenex have become prototypical, occupying a unique position in the consumer's mind. Their large market shares tend to persist because perceptions and preferences, once formed, are difficult to alter.[26]

The normatively cohesive character of most state's constitutions means, of course, that the prevailing orthodoxies of that system, once initially accepted, occupy an almost monopolistic position in that order. The orthodox position of established constitutional ideas is supported by their repeated invocation and application. Competing ideas are, by definition, presumptively invalid.

Thus, once an idea-only innovation is generally accepted as advantageous, it makes it very difficult for new ideas to move from innovation to wider adoption. That any assessment of their relative advantages is also likely to be flawed further compounds this difficulty.

From the point of view of the separation of powers theory, its historical pre-eminence has arguably conferred this type of first mover advantage on it when compared against alternative potential models of institutional arrangement. It is telling that we tend to think of the 'separation of powers' in tripartite terms. There is nothing in the neutral branding of the concept as one of separating power to indicate that it should necessarily be organised in this way. If a political scientist or constitutional lawyer was asked to design a separation of powers system from scratch, it is questionable whether he or she would distribute power in this way. After all, if the point of the separation of powers theory is to prevent tyranny and the abuse of government power (as many of its advocates claim), why limit this preventative allocation of power to only three institutions? Why not four or five? And why employ a model that is arguably ineffective and unrealistic? The tripartite model's pedigree and long-standing position in the market means that it dominates and effectively defines how we think about separating institutional

---

25   M. Boldrin, D.K. Levine and T.J. Sargent, 'The economics of ideas and intellectual property' (2005) 102 (4) *Proceedings of the National Academy of Sciences of the United States of America* 1252, 1254.

26   M.B. Lieberman and D.B. Montgomery, 'First-mover advantages' (1988) 9 *Strategic Management Journal* 41, 46.

power. As with the examples of Coca-Cola and Kleenex highlighted above, the first-mover's product (the tripartite model) and the market (separating institutional power) may become so intertwined in the popular consciousness that the market is conceived of in terms of the dominant product. This reinforces the position of the product. Thus, a 'good' idea to which people are attracted (that we should separate power to prevent it from being abused) becomes defined in terms of a 'bad' one (that separation must follow the tripartite model), which strengthens the capacity of the bad idea to diffuse and to retain its dominant position.

The influence of the separation of powers model bears out other aspects of this diffusion analysis. The theory's association with celebrated figures of the past such as Madison, Montesquieu and Locke, as well as its citation in landmark cases of constitutional jurisprudence,[27] encourages an asymmetric evaluation of it as an influential and effective theory. We (with the possible exception of specialists in these matters) are more likely to recall these celebrated examples where the separation of powers theory was relied upon to restrain high-profile examples of potential government abuses than the more mundane but common scenario in which its imprecise and indeterminate character complicates arcane or technical issues of administrative law.[28] The absence of any significant impetus for undertaking a reassessment of it, together with the difficulties that any new innovations would face in the conduct of that assessment, further copper-fastens its perceived position as a central principle of constitutional thought.

Complexity

Another key driver in the diffusion of a new idea is the extent to which it is regarded as complex to use or understand. 'New ideas that are simpler to understand are adopted more rapidly than innovations that require the adopter to develop new skills and understandings'.[29] Silvester's research into the impact which complexity has on the success of technological product launches is telling:

> The human mind's inability to assimilate technology is the dark secret of the tech industry [...] The consumer simply doesn't use most of what technologically advanced companies build into their products.[30]

For Silvester, the key to a successful technological product – even one aimed at a young audience – is simplicity. 'Simple devices and software that do one thing,

---

27   See, for example, *Youngstown Sheet & Tube Co. v Sawyer* 343 US 579 (1952); *Buckley v A.G.* (1950) IR 64.

28   See, for example, *CFTC v Schor* 478 US 833 (1986); *O'Brien v Bord na Mona* (1983) IR 277.

29   Rogers (n14) 16.

30   S. Silvester, 'The emperor's new clothes: Technology is useless if consumers can't use it' (2007) 36 *Market Leader* 20, 21.

not several, can have an electrifying effect on consumer mentality, clearing minds, and changing the way consumers think'.

The importance of simplicity applies not only to the product itself, but also to the way in which it is named, branded and positioned.

> [A] brand name can help make the innovation visible because it provides a label for the "news". As a result, it is likely that it will be easier to achieve higher recall and recognition scores around the innovation. It is easier to remember a brand name than the details of a new offering or a branded feature or service. In fact, one of the characteristics of a good brand name is that it is easy to recall.[31]

Again, the migration of the separation of powers bears out the analysis of the diffusion research. The tripartite model arguably provides a textbook example of how combining a selling point which is easy to understand with clear and simple branding can have a very positive impact on the diffusion of an idea. One of the chief strengths of the tripartite theory is its inherent simplicity. The neat model of three institutions exercising three distinct functions is easy to explain and to appreciate. Even the theory's title (or 'branding') is simple, suggesting instantly and clearly what it is that the theory aims to achieve. Of course, this simplicity is also one of the primary reasons why the theory is functionally inadequate. However, while the model's lack of complexity and detail may undermine its utility as a useful instrument of institutional organisation, it is arguably one of the primary reasons why it has migrated so successfully.

Compatibility

The extent to which an innovation is compatible with previous practice can also influence the success and scope of its diffusion.

> Compatibility of an innovation with a preceding idea can speed up or retard its rate of adoption. Old ideas are the main mental tools that individuals utilize to assess new ideas and give them meaning. Individuals cannot deal with an innovation except on the basis of the familiar.[32]

This argument has significant implications for our understanding of the way in which ideas spread. In particular, it provides useful insights about the process by which ideas both diffuse and are adopted.

From the point of view of diffusion, this means that the adaptability of an innovation can have a critical impact on its likely success. In the absence of objective analyses of relative advantage, we are more likely to favour innovations which tally with – or are capable of being understood to tally with – the information

---

31   D. Aaker, 'Innovation: Brand it or lose it' (2008) 41 *Market Leader* 20, 22.
32   Rogers (n14) 243.

and ideas which we already have. For this reason, vagueness or imprecision can be a valuable attribute for anyone seeking to promote a new innovation. '[A]n innovation diffuses more rapidly when it can be re-invented [by its users] and [...] its adoption is more likely to be sustained'.[33] The more user-adaptable an innovation is, the more likely it is to be successful. Studies indicate that this was something of which President Obama's electoral advisors took advantage when, having correctly forecast that 'change' was likely to be a prominent theme in the primary and election campaigns, they devoted much of their early efforts to defining what was a vague and malleable idea of change 'in ways that played directly into Barack Obama's message and his personal strengths'.[34]

In addition, this analysis suggests that an idea which involves little or no innovation is more likely to be adopted than one that genuinely involves a departure from previous practice. The more compatible an idea is with the norms which it purports to improve upon or replace, the more likely it is to secure general adoption within that particular system.

From the point of view of the adoption of new ideas, this argument also suggests that the process of diffusion may be more illusory than it first appears. The importance of compatibility implies not only that a more compatible idea is more likely to diffuse successfully but also that the idea may itself be amended as it is adopted into a system. In other words, an idea which initially exists in a particular form outside the system may be made more compatible with pre-existing norms by the users who ultimately incorporate it into that system. In many cases, the users in question will be unaware that such changes have even occurred. It is because they understand an idea to be compatible with their prior views that they are willing to adopt it. Whether that understanding of the original idea is as its creators or earlier users intended may have little influence on its adoption or subsequent employment.

While terminology such as 'diffusion' or (in particular) 'transplants', may appear to underplay the influence of the recipient on the end result of the process, the critical influence of the adopter has been widely recognised by those engaged in diffusion research. A study on the diffusion of democracy, for example provides a number of findings which – by virtue of that work's concern with the diffusion of ideas rather than products – are particularly relevant to this piece.

One preliminary point to note is that democracy is a particularly adaptable idea. As the study observes at the outset 'the meaning of the term [democracy] may become so malleable that it is difficult to ascertain how widely differing conceptions and aspects of democracy may be reconciled'.[35] The analysis outlined above suggests that this means both that democracy is an idea which is more likely

---

33   Ibid. 17.

34   Benenson Strategy (Oxford University Press), Harstad Research, David Binder Research, Brilliant Corners, Case Study: Obama for President, ARF Ogilvy Awards (2009), available at <http://www.thearf.org/assets/ogilvy-09> accessed 14 January 2010.

35   J. O'Loughlin, M.D. Ward, C.L. Lofdahl, et al., 'The diffusion of democracy, 1946–1994' (1998) 88 (4) *Annals of the Association of American Geographers* 545, 547.

to diffuse successfully and that the end result of that diffusion will differ from place to place.

This was borne out by the researchers' findings. In particular, the study suggested that the diffusion of democracy could not be understood as a consistent or linear process in which the idea of democracy was transplanted from one system into another. The adoption by different states of democratic government was, on the contrary, a more complex phenomenon which was heavily influenced by local circumstances and could not be understood in unitary terms.

> [W]e have shown how the ebb and flow of democracy is regionally variable. Like Starr (1991), we conclude that analyzing regime change will benefit from a 'domain-specific' position. We caution against assuming that "universal laws" govern the growth of democracy. It remains important to recognize that the process is apparently affected by regional and local contextual elements that remain important.[36]

In ostensibly adopting an innovation (whether so perceived by themselves or by those outside to the system), users seem likely to, in fact, develop their own localised or contextual idea. This in turn raises the possibility that the version of the idea ultimately adopted may depart from or even contradict the original innovation, reflecting, as it does, not the idea that is superficially being diffused but rather the particular's system's pre-existing ideas. In such a situation, all that diffuses is, at most, a garbled version of the original idea. This can mean that, even where an idea is objectively advantageous in its own terms, it may be transplanted in a misconceived and less advantageous form.

Once again, elements of such experiences can be seen in the adoption and diffusion of the separation of powers. Magill has described how the separation of powers doctrine represented an attempt to unify two pre-existing institutional ideas – the mixed and balanced theories of government.[37] That the theory was compatible with these familiar conceptions of government must have aided its migration. This was so despite the fact that the 'marriage of the two ideas is a troubled one',[38] which contributes, to a significant degree, to the indeterminate character of the theory.

Similarly, the successful migration of the separation of powers also demonstrates how imprecision can be a significant advantage in the diffusion of an idea. One of the primary criticisms of the separation of powers is that it is inherently indeterminate. It is 'an institutional vision in search of an ideal'.[39] Yet this imprecision has been one of the reasons why it has been adopted and

---

36 Ibid. 568.

37 E. Magill, 'The real separation in separation of powers law' (2000) 86 *Virginia Law Review* 1127.

38 Ibid. 1166.

39 Carolan (n5) 44.

embraced by so many different groups. Munro has noted how the theory's 'open texture, which enabled people to see in it what they liked, and take from it what they wanted, was no disadvantage to its reception or employment'.[40]

In turn, this has meant that the separation of powers has not been uniformly replicated in different systems. The concept's design and its implications for the way in which government operates differ from jurisdiction to jurisdiction.[41] Indeed, it is arguable that the adaptability of the model has led, in some situations, to it being applied in a manner which significantly departs from the purpose of the separation of powers as it was originally understood (to the extent that such an understanding can be said to exist, of course). Brown has criticised how the American courts have rarely considered the liberty of the individual in their treatment of the separation of powers,[42] while the Irish Supreme Court has invoked it to justify its refusal to enforce an individual's constitutionally-protected right to education against the other organs of government.[43] In both these context, the separation of powers has acted as a vehicle for the unacknowledged enforcement of alternative ideas with which it was compatible.[44]

Paths of Diffusion

Thus, it would appear important for comparative constitutional scholars to approach any analysis of an ostensibly popular idea with some degree of caution. Diffusion studies indicate that neither ubiquity nor acclaim can necessarily be regarded as a proxy for the quality or comparative influence of a particular theory. As the previous section suggested, the successful diffusion of a theory may be based not on its inherent advantages but rather on the fact that it has certain characteristics – imprecision, historical or reputational pedigree, adaptability, and so on – which make it a suitable candidate for diffusion. Furthermore, such imprecision or adaptability may mean that the idea becomes much altered in its migration from one jurisdiction to another. It is apparent that the propagation of constitutional ideas involves far more than the simple citation or adoption of foreign authorities by a domestic court. Ideas do not travel alone. On the contrary,

---

40   C. Munro, *Studies in Constitutional Law* (2nd edn, Butterworths, 1999) 302.

41   See, for example, H. Punder, 'Democratic legitimation of delegated legislation – A comparative view on the American, British and German law' (2009) 58 *International and Comparative Law Quarterly* 353.

42   R. Brown, 'Separated powers and ordered liberty' (1990) 139 *University of Pennsylvania Law Review* 1513.

43   *TD v Minister for Education* (2001) 4 IR 259.

44   A useful discussion of a similar phenomenon is contained in Hasebe's account of how French doctrines have influence the development of Japanese constitutional jurisprudence in Y. Hasebe, 'Constitutional borrowing and political theory' (2003) 1 *International Journal of Constitutional Law* 224.

the mechanisms by which they diffuse are complex, multi-faceted and contingent on a variety of shifting considerations. This section considers in brief the implications of these mechanisms for the study of comparative constitutional law.

The comparative exercise involves, at its most basic, the retrieval and relative evaluation of information from different legal systems. Gerber has pointed out that developments in globalisation and information technology have made the retrieval of information a less taxing undertaking than was formerly the case. This has inevitably altered the focus of comparative scholarship from a 'traditional [...] vie[w of] information as a product rather than a tool [and ...] as an end in itself'[45] to one premised instead on the analysis of the information obtained.

> Where the knower has ready access to copious amounts of information, the problem is no longer obtaining enough "information", but rather having the capacity to use the information effectively. The emphasis shifts from the process of getting information to the process of transforming it into useful knowledge – that is, structuring and interpreting information so as to provide answers to the questions posed or problems presented.[46]

If the value of comparative scholarship today lies primarily in the evaluation of information, this means, in turn, that it is necessary for comparative scholars to have regard to the cognitive processes involved in such evaluation. In particular, comparative scholars must be prepared to assess critically the limitations or risks associated with the evaluative exercise. The previous section highlighted the extent to which the presence of particular characteristics may increase the possibility that an idea will successfully diffuse. The value of these characteristics derives from the way in which they feed into certain cognitive biases, some of which were identified above. The remainder of this section considers these processes in a more comprehensive manner in order to assess their implications for the future of comparative scholarship.

From an academic perspective, confirmatory bias is the cognitive tendency which arguably has the most potential severely to undermine the value of comparative research. The social sciences have long accepted that individuals have a tendency to seek out information which tends to confirm the hypothesis under consideration. Importantly, studies have suggested that this may occur regardless of the individual's own views about the hypothesis. Rather, the mere fact that an individual has been asked to consider a particular proposition makes it more likely that they will identify and rely on information which supports that proposition.[47] This poses obvious difficulties for comparative research. As Gerber has noted, the landscape of comparative law has been profoundly altered by the advent of

---

45   D.J. Gerber, 'Globalisation and legal knowledge: Implications for comparative law' (2000–2001) 75 *Tulane Law Review* 949, 960.

46   Ibid. 954.

47   See, for example, Gilovich (n21) 33.

electronic databases containing extensive information about other legal systems. This means that the main challenge for a researcher is to filter that information in order to extract the most relevant or informative material for the particular project being pursued. However, the phenomenon of confirmatory bias means that there is an inherent risk that the information which the researcher will seek out, identify and extract is that which tends to confirm whatever hypothesis they intend to test. The risk is that this would introduce an element of circularity into the research undertaken which would fundamentally undermine its value.

This risk is compounded by the faulty way in which individuals generally tend to incorporate data into their reasoning. It is cognitively commonplace for beliefs to be extrapolated from incomplete or unrepresentative data. In many situations, judgements or beliefs are based on the data which is available to an individual, rather than on the data which would most directly prove or disprove the hypothesis in question. This is not necessarily because of any deficiency in the individual's research. It may simply be that the relevant data is impossible to ascertain. For example, a legal or institutional analysis which focuses on decisions of the courts carries with it the risk that the evaluation is distorted by a reliance on the sort of disputes which are more likely to give rise to litigation (whether because of the character of the claim, or the stakes for the parties involved). Because the courts, by definition, never see non-litigated disputes, they are never captured by judicial decisions or data. Nonetheless, there is an identified human tendency to base decisions on the data to hand without methodically scrutinising the causal relationship between the information in question and the judgment derived therefrom.

Similarly, we are also predisposed to place more emphasis on high-profile examples which may not necessarily be representative. This was canvassed above in relation to the separation of powers. Is it possible that one of the reasons that the separation of powers is regarded as a valuable principle of liberal democracy is because it has been deployed in a small number of dramatic cases to restrain the most egregious executive or legislative tyrannies? Are we predisposed to look to these cases rather than the arguably more representative but less dramatic instances in which courts have been asked to assess the more mundane issue of whether an administrative function is executive, legislative, judicial or some quasi-combination of these three?

This, in turn, highlights the potential relationship for beliefs based on incomplete or unrepresentative data to become a self-fulfilling prophecy. Merton has pointed, in this regard, to rumours of a financial institution's insolvency as an example of a judgment based on incomplete or incorrect data which may nonetheless become true by virtue of its existence.[48] Similarly, there may be circularity between the occurrence of a high-profile phenomenon and the belief in its value. To return to the separations of powers example, there would logically appear to be a likely correlation between its enforcement by the judiciary and the unrepresentative

---

48   R.K. Merton, 'The self-fulfilling prophecy' (1948) 8 *Antioch Review* 193.

character of the case in which that occurs. Regardless of its myriad imperfections and imprecisions, it seems reasonable to speculate that courts are most likely to be willing to invoke the doctrine when faced with particularly severe examples of legislative or executive over-reach. Yet these are also the situations most likely to attract the attention of the public (and, indeed, arguably of constitutional scholars). Thus the data we are most likely to rely upon in assessing the value and merit of the theory is based on those relatively unrepresentative situations when the application of the principle was relatively free of the uncertainty and ambiguity that so often affects its usage in other everyday contexts.

In addition, it is possible that there may be specific biases and risks associated with the diffusion of legal theories or ideas. The formal and hierarchical nature of the legal process lends itself to an unduly limited and simplistic conception of diffusion. From a formal legal perspective, an idea migrates from one jurisdiction to another at the moment it is incorporated into a domestic legal text or decision. This ostensibly singular account of the moment of migration obscures, however, the dynamic and multi-faceted process that has led to that point. In particular, it may serve to conceal the role which various parties and thought processes have played in bringing that idea into the domestic context. As discussed in the previous section, it may also disguise the changes the idea has undergone in the course of its 'translation' into the domestic order.[49]

This reflects the enormous difficulties involved in comparing legal theories. A legal norm does not enjoy an independent existence. It develops and is operated within the confines of a particular social and institutional structure, with its own culture and pattern of power distribution. This is particularly true of constitutional concepts which often echo normatively significant aspects of national culture or ideology. Domestic audiences understand legal norms or values not as free-standing principles but as elements of a structure based on shared assumptions or intuitions. This constrains the extent to which an external observer with limited exposure to the residual logic of the system can accurately process and interpret specific elements of it. In the legal context, this difficulty is exacerbated by the fact that that external observer is likely to bring with him or her a separate set of assumptions or intuitions based on their own experience or expertise, which will, in turn, shape the way in which the observer processes the 'information' obtained. That there may frequently be a superficial similarity between the ideas being assessed only serves further to complicate the process. As Francois Venter has remarked:

> What emerges from a comparison of constitutional material, even where the constitutional roots of the jurisdictions concerned are deeply intertwined, is the fact that in many instances the lyrics sung by constitutional lawyers are the same but the tunes vary, not only due to cultural variety but also in terms of meaning

---

49   See, more generally, S. Sarcevic, *New Approach to Legal Translation* (Kluwer, 1997).

and effect. Humanity is too far removed from a state of similitude to allow for the existence of truly universal constitutional law.[50]

Nor, it should be remembered, is the process of migration or translation typically accomplished by a single observer acting alone. Despite the formal focus of law on a single moment of reception, the reality is that the diffusion of a legal or constitutional idea may be influenced by a variety of individuals or organisations, each of whom may introduce their own institutional influences into the process. International organisations involved in constitutional or legal reform, transnational networks of judges and international associations of comparative legal academics are all examples of epistemic communities through which ideas may be diffused but which may also be susceptible to certain forms of cognitive or normative bias. Is it conceivable, for example, that academics with an established interest in comparative law are more likely to see value in the act of migration than might necessarily be justified?

Conclusion

These issues raise a number of challenges for the practices and conception of comparative constitutional law. Diffusion research may have significant implications for our understanding of the aims and objectives of comparative constitutional law, and of the way in which it ought to be pursued.

For example, it tends to undermine the view of those who envisage comparative law as an engine of universalist convergence.[51] Diffusion research suggests, not simply that true convergence is unlikely to occur, but also that any convergence that does occur will not bring about an enlightened 'international unity of law and legal science'[52] but may instead involve the bare aggregation of simplistic and superficially similar notions. The research indicates that the 'best' constitutional innovations will not necessarily be the same as those that migrate or transplant successfully. Our analytical limitations mean that we may be unable, in the first instance, to distinguish between the objectively or rationally advantageous theory and the one which we are more inclined, for various reasons, to *perceive* as advantageous. Even if experts are able to engage in such an objective assessment of competing constitutional theories, the research still suggests that the ideas that are more likely to diffuse are those that are easier to understand, and those that appear to approximate most closely to existing concepts.

---

50   F. Venter, *Global Features of Constitutional Law* (Wolf, 2010) 49.

51   See, for example, the discussion of the functions and aims of comparative law in K. Zweigert and H. Kotz, *An Introduction to Comparative Law* (trans. Tony Weir, 3rd edn, Clarendon, 1998) 13–31.

52   Ibid. 15.

A gloomy reading of the diffusion research calls into question the purpose of constitutional transplants at all. Given the complexity of constitutional governance, it seems reasonable to question whether transplanting a constitutional concept from one system to another will bring any significant benefit to the recipient state. If the simple ideas are those that transplant successfully, will they be of any real value to the recipient system's constitutional jurisprudence? Certainly, it can be argued that the simplicity of the separation of powers has meant that it has had little operational utility in its various constitutional incarnations, serving instead to mislead more than it guides.

Furthermore, given the apparent tendency for an idea to diffuse successfully when it is compatible with pre-existing values, the question arises as to whether true migration or transplants ever actually occur? If an individual or system is predisposed to favour the least different idea, can transplants have any real impact? This is particularly so given the accompanying tendency for diffusion to occur where the ideas in question are simple and adaptable. If transplants will take only where they are too simple to offer detailed solutions and too similar to involve any significant change, why undertake the operation at all? The analysis in earlier sections of the diffusion literature suggests that constitutional transplants may involve no more than a cosmopolitan re-branding of ideas already latent in domestic legal or political culture. On this analysis, the constitutional transplant is, at worst, a label or slogan borrowed from one constitutional context for use in another and, at best, a means of prompting the system to examine or re-examine domestic issues that, for whatever reason, remain unresolved.

It is clear that, even on this more optimistic analysis, the migration of the idea does not operate as a true transplant in the sense for which Watson, for example, contended.[53] In fact, the overview of the diffusion scholarship provided above suggests there may be a genuine question as to whether such transplants may simply be too difficult to undertake. Constitutional concepts may be so bound up in the political, historical and cultural context in which they develop that they are too complicated to ever truly be successfully transplanted. The donor system's idea is not grafted, fully-formed, onto that of the donee. A 'transplant' involves not a transfer of ideas but (at best) an evolution in the legal norms of the 'recipient' order. Critically, the 'recipient' system retains control of the pace, content and implications of this evolution. Diffusion research suggests that very little of substance passes between the two. Thus to speak of constitutional transplants seems misleading and misconceived.

Of course, the deficiencies of the transplant metaphor do not necessarily deprive the practice it purports to portray of its intrinsic merit. It would take the findings of the diffusion research much too far to claim that the examination of external constitutional innovations by a domestic legal system is inevitably a futile, or even harmful, endeavour.

---

53 A. Watson, *An Approach to Comparative Law* (Scottish Academic Press, 1974). See also A. Watson, 'Legal transplants and law reform' (1976) 92 *Law Quarterly Review* 79.

What the research does suggest, however, is that there is a need to retain a realistic appreciation of what that process involves. In conducting such comparative analysis, it is important to resist the temptation to place too much faith in what the research indicates will most likely be an inadequate, unsophisticated or misguided understanding of the idea at issue. We must remember how little we understand the toolkit that comparative constitutional study provides for us, and exercise our consequent judgements with appropriate caution.

Furthermore, it must be remembered that the exercise in question plays out in, and is almost entirely determined by, domestic legal culture. As Legrand has argued, it is likely that the idea in question will be 'understood differently by the host culture and [...] invested with a culture-specific meaning at variance with the earlier one'.[54] It is also likely that the impulse for a system's consideration of an external constitutional idea will be based not on the inherent validity of that notion, but rather on the way in which it speaks to questions of politics, power or law that already exist in that jurisdiction – or, more cynically, to the interests of influential groups within the domestic order.[55] This suggests that it is necessary to ensure that proposals that are put forward on the basis of constitutional practices in other systems are subjected to duly rigorous assessment. In particular, it is necessary to temper any enthusiasm for the wholesale adoption of comparative constitutional innovations by recalling that the idea in question is unlikely to be used or understood in the same way in either system.[56] Citation of comparative practice should not take the place of rigorous scrutiny of what is actually being proposed – because there would appear to be a real risk that it is different in character and potentially deficient in detail.

These are the difficulties diffusion research poses for the practice and project of comparative research. However, the diffusion research may also provide valuable guidance for the future development of comparative law. The formal and hierarchical structures of law may pose particular challenges in understanding and assessing how migration or transplants *actually* occur but there is no reason to suppose that these are insurmountable difficulties. After all, the cognitive biases identified above are not limited to legal researchers alone. Thus there may be lessons to be learned from the way in which other disciplines have sought to

---

54   P. Legrand, 'What legal transplants?' in D. Neelken and J. Feest (eds), *Adapting Legal Cultures* (Hart, 2001) 55–69. For useful discussion of related issues concerning the use of foreign materials in national courts, see S. Choudhry (ed.), *The Migration of Constitutional Ideas* (Cambridge University Press, 2006).

55   See, for example, the discussion of how domestic politics can shape constitutional design in L. Epstein and J. Knight, 'Constitutional borrowing and nonborrowing' (2003) 1 *International Journal of Constitutional Law* 196.

56   In this regard, see Rosenkrantz' criticism of the effects and legitimacy of the Argentinian courts' practice of adopting American constitutional doctrines without any significant consideration of domestic legal instruments. See C.F. Rosenkrantz, 'Against borrowings and other nonauthoritative uses of foreign law' (2003) 1 *International Journal of Constitutional Law* 269.

deal with these biases. In particular, it would appear reasonable to suggest that comparative law may derive considerable benefit from the adoption of a more rigorously scientific approach to its research methodologies.

One of the core principles of scientific practice in many areas is that the researcher must undertake repeated tests in order to validate a particular hypothesis. This is done to ensure that the research is based on an adequate range of relevant data points. Similarly, scientific practice frequently requires that the research provide a precise and a priori definition of the objective and scope of the research being undertaken. This will involve defining in advance the hypothesis to be investigated, what would constitute successful validation of that hypothesis, and the criteria to be used in defining such success. The main aim of this is to minimise the impact of the confirmatory biases previously discussed.

In many ways, such practices are alien to at least some traditional notions of legal study. After all, one of the chief skills of the practising lawyer is to develop a persuasive argument, based on relevant data, which is favourable to his or her client – in short, the confirmatory bias writ large. For the reasons outlined above, however, a more scientific approach to comparative law seems apposite. This will require the development of new methodological skills which emphasis repetition and causal validation, of more objective forms of data extraction and processing, and of a shared language and approach for determining the scope and output of comparative research. It is only by expanding the comparative skillset in this way that scholars will be able to fully assess the way in which legal ideas spread, and the patterns of institutional influence and power distribution that shape that process.

Index